The Lessons of Lebanon

The Lessons of Lebanon
the economics of war and development

SAMIR MAKDISI

I.B. TAURIS
LONDON · NEW YORK

Published in 2004 by I.B. Tauris & Co. Ltd
6 Salem Road, London W2 4BU
175 Fifth Avenue, New York NY 10010
www.ibtauris.com

In the United States of America and in Canada distributed by Palgrave
Macmillan, a division of St Martin's Press, 175 Fifth Avenue, New York
NY 10010

Library of Modern Middle East Studies 38

ISBN 1 85043 398 4 hb
EAN 978 1 85043 398 9

A full CIP record for this book is available from the British Library
A full CIP record for this book is available from the Library of Congress
Library of Congress catalog card: available

Set in Monotype Dante by Ewan Smith, London
Printed and bound in Great Britain by MPG Books, Bodmin

Contents

Figures

Tables

Acknowledgements

In writing this book I have benefited from conversations with friends and colleagues about Lebanese economic policy and developmental issues, political problems and social issues; from the numerous conferences in which I have participated at home and abroad dealing with issues of development and the Arab region; and from students in my graduate classes, many of whom seemed anxious about the future of Lebanon and their role in its development.

A number of colleagues and friends read parts of the draft as it was being prepared, and offered many insights from which I benefited greatly. To them I wish to express my sincere appreciation. They include Albert Dagher, Ibrahim el Badawi, Yousef el Khalil, Hadi Esfahani, Marwan Hamade, Said Hitti, Simon Neaime, Michel Samaha and Ghazi Sirhan.

I should like to thank the following economics graduate students at the American University of Beirut who patiently provided research assistance: Amer Khaddage, Hilda Maachalian and Fadi Mahmood. I should also like to thank Soumaya Gebara, who was unfailing in providing needed secretarial assistance.

From conversations about Lebanon, the Third World and globalization with my three scholar sons, Saree, Ussama and Karim, I gained many valuable insights. I am, as usual, particularly indebted to my wife, Jean, for her invaluable comments on content and style, as well as her unflinching support throughout this project.

Finally I am grateful to the Consultation and Research Institute in Beirut for providing me with data that were either unpublished or not yet due for publication, and to Rafi Kenderjian at the Ministry of Finance, who always stood ready to provide requested data.

I, of course, remain responsible for any errors or other failings that may have crept into these pages undetected.

To: Saree, Ussama and Karim, whose
faith that intellectuals and scholars should
always speak up for a just and better world
has always impressed me.

Introduction

§ THE course and quality of the national development of countries that have achieved independence from Western colonial rule since the Second World War have been profoundly affected by several interlocking factors. Of these, three stand out – namely, the nature of their domestic political institutions, as reflected in the quality of governance; their geopolitical position; and the traumatic civil wars that have gripped many countries in Asia, Africa and Latin America; since 1945, over 200 intra-state conflicts have occurred.

Certainly the role of domestic institutions in development has been given increasing prominence in academic literature. Cross-country analyses indicate that high-quality institutional performance (usually associated with a low degree of corruption, the rule of law, an independent judiciary, and a certain degree of security of property and contract rights) contributes positively to long-term growth and the quality of economic and social development.[1] Conversely, low-quality institutional performance has been shown to be detrimental to growth.

The development of these institutions, however, is a profoundly political question. In the literature on political economy, special attention is paid to the interaction between the general public, special interest groups and the policy body (policy-makers, administrators and political parties). A common theme is the struggle to gain control of larger rents that are defined as including not only economic rents but also the consolidation of political and religious dominance – processes that have direct consequences in the evolution of domestic economic and social institutions.

What ultimately decides the type of economic and developmental policies to be followed? Who stands to benefit? The role of institutions in this regard is considered crucial in determining the outcome of development, i.e. the degree of efficiency in the use of resources let alone the distribution of the available surplus.[2] The type of political representation, the degree of commitment to efficient policies and the extent of successful coordination in minimizing the waste of resources are regarded as key elements of institutional behaviour which influence economic performance.[3] Hence empirical work has attempted to identify the effects of alternative political systems and institutions on economic performance and/or income distribution by examining their influence on the key features of institutional behaviour mentioned above. This work has included an examination of the impact of unequal access to power, and whether or not institutional constraints on the use of power by ruling groups or on the misuse of budgetary resources exist, particularly when narrow interest groups are in control. In the same vein, cross-country analyses of the interaction between democracy/political freedom and political stability on the one hand, and growth and fiscal performance on the other, have been undertaken. One common view that emerges is that investment, and, by extension, growth, is adversely affected by lack of political freedom and by political unrest. However, there is not necessarily agreement on how alternative political regimes and institutions influence economic performance or the major economic policies that underlie it.[4]

Alongside the analyses of political economy, there is a growing body of work on the economics of civil wars, also based on cross-country studies, with the underlying assumption that such conflicts are typically between the state and a rebel organization.[5] The factors that govern the incidence and duration of civil war, as well as the required post-conflict policies for a successful recovery effort, have been examined. Several analyses have focused on the respective roles of economic 'greed' versus political and/or socio-economic 'grievance' as causes of civil conflict, while others have, in addition, examined the role of external intervention. Thus, the role of primary commodity exports, natural resource wealth, ethnic and social fractionalization, and geography, among other factors, have been investigated to determine their significance (if any) in inciting civil wars. The factors that explain the duration of these wars (e.g. external interventions, ethnic fractionalization, control of economic resources) have been similarly studied. Geopolitical factors have also been seen to have a hand in both promoting national conflicts and influencing their resolution.[6] Of course, as each country has its own national traditions, geopolitical position, history and particular political systems and institutions, cross-country analyses can at best provide an overall analytic framework and guidance. The special circumstances of each country ultimately identify the causes of civil conflict, its duration, and the required post-conflict policies. Individual country experiences may or may not (in whole or in part) corroborate the general conclusions of models based on cross-country studies which, however, can only stand to benefit from detailed case studies of the many countries that have experienced the trauma of civil wars.

The case of Lebanon is a supreme illustration of the interlocking influences of domestic political institutions, civil war and geopolitics on national economic development. The persistently sectarian nature and behaviour of its political institutions, accompanied by the relatively poor quality of its governance; the Arab–Israeli conflict that began in 1948 and is yet to be settled; the major civil war that began in 1975 and lasted sixteen years – all these together define the context in which the achievements and failures of Lebanese development have to be assessed. They also explain the nature of the major national issues that Lebanon has faced since independence, and in large measure continues to face in the post-conflict era, but now with the added dimension of globalization. As such, an in-depth understanding of the course and quality of Lebanon's development will contribute to the discourse on political economy in developing economies in a fast-integrating world.

The development of Lebanon since independence in 1943[7] may be divided into three distinct phases. The first stretches from independence up to 1975, when the civil war began. (This phase includes a civil conflict that took place in 1958 and lasted a few months.) The second is the civil war itself (1975–90). The war officially ended with an accord of national reconciliation, negotiated under Arab auspices in Taif, Saudi Arabia, in October 1989, and thus known as the Taif Accord, which was adopted by the Lebanese parliament in November of the same year.[8] The fighting did not end completely, however, until almost a year later. The third phase is that from the end of the civil war to the present. Each of these stages will be examined in detail in the following chapters.

The political system that emerged after independence was based on a formula for power-sharing among the many officially recognized religious communities in the affairs of government and public sector institutions which, for want of a better term, I shall call 'constrained democracy', regardless of whether the emerging state model tended to be 'neo-patrimonial', 'developmental' or a hybrid of various models. My choice of the term 'constrained democracy' is based on the fact that under the sectarian formula the political rights of citizens differ from one sect to another.[9] 'Sectarian democracy' may possibly serve as an alternate term to 'constrained democracy'. Irrespective of the term we adopt, the main point revolves around the unequal political rights enjoyed by the various religious communities.

Other writers describe the Lebanese political system as a 'consociational democracy', in that it is based on agreed mutual political concessions among the various religious communities.

Whatever description one adopts, the three principal religious communities – Maronite Christians, Sunni and Shia Muslims; or perhaps one should say their respective business and political classes – stood to gain most in terms of political power and influence, with clear advantages being initially accorded to the Maronite community. Among other privileges, the Maronite president enjoyed executive authority, assisted by cabinet members whom the president appointed and from whom he designated a prime minister. In practice, though, the latter shared in executive authority to a greater degree than specified in the constitution. With the approval of the Council of Ministers the president had the prerogative of dissolving parliament before expiration of its mandate. Furthermore, under the unwritten national accord, in parliament the Christian community enjoyed a six-to-five majority.

The basic nature of the political system did not change after the civil war, as the Taif Accord amounted to a readjustment in the formula for power-sharing among the three major communities (in favour of the Muslim communities), and not to the elimination of the political structure along sectarian lines. Sectarianism has had a profoundly detrimental influence on governance and the quality of development, and, I argue, has rendered the political system potentially unstable.[10] Yet the dynamics of maintaining a balance of political rights among the various sects arguably helped produce a relatively liberal political regime that promoted a good measure of freedom at the political, cultural and religious levels, and allowed a relatively free press to flourish.[11]

The liberal political system, in turn, allowed for a liberal economic system, and business-friendly governments permitted a traditionally enterprising (mercantile) private sector to take advantage of emerging domestic and regional opportunities, particularly before 1975. Despite major political and military developments, and the civil war notwithstanding, the essential features of the national economy have remained unchanged, notably the key role played by the private sector,[12] and the openness to the outside world of the foreign exchange system. In contrast with the political regime, the economic regime has been less influenced by sectarian considerations. The behaviour of the private sector has been dictated, as one would expect, by the ideology of free enterprise, with the formulation of economic policy becoming progressively more active only after the outbreak of the civil war. If, however, the private sector was less affected by sectarianism than the public sector, one cannot but recognize that the sectarian power-sharing system also influenced control of economic resources and rent among the merchant/industrial/financial class of the various religious communities.

The relationship between Lebanon's investment climate and its political development before and after the civil war is noteworthy. Before 1975, this climate was not adversely affected to any great extent by the ongoing Arab–Israeli conflict and its domestic ramifications. The in-flow of capital continued throughout this period, investment levels being maintained at relatively high levels. Somehow, domestic economic expansion and the political impact of the regional conflict managed to coexist.[13] This coexistence between conflict and growth was shattered by the outbreak of the civil war. After the war ended, the picture changed in that the in-flow of capital and the pattern of investment became much more sensitive to regional and domestic political developments.

Another difference between the periods preceding and following the civil war is the much greater influence that economic policy came to exert in the post-war years, albeit in the context of persistently weak institutional performance. This influence, as I will demonstrate later, has had far-reaching negative consequences on economic performance and, more importantly, on the quality of development.

There is wide agreement on the fact that sectarianism has become ingrained in Lebanese political culture and behaviour, and that it has exerted a powerful and disruptive influence on institutional performance. There is, however, less agreement when it comes to its impact on domestic political stability and the 'democratic' attributes of the political system. Whatever the case, the elimination of sectarianism will not on its own lead to better institutional performance. After all, other countries where sectarianism does not exist have also suffered from low-quality performance in terms of their domestic institutions. Albeit a major one, sectarianism is but one issue among others that need to be addressed in the wider context of governance in Lebanon.

While poor institutional performance or governance may be a common feature of many developing economies, its effect in the Lebanese context must be assessed against the predominance of the private sector in the national economy, keeping in mind that the respective interests of the private and public sectors are not necessarily independent of one another. In Lebanon the dividing line between private and public interest, though it can be technically identified, has often been blurred, so that the conduct of certain aspects of economic policy, especially after the war, has tended to accommodate the business and other interests of those in power, while being made to appear as though it is serving the national economic interest.

With this caveat, the Lebanese private sector, unlike that of most other developing countries, has played the major role in economic development. As a result of its dominance, and notwithstanding the blurring of the distinction between public and private interest, the poor quality of institutional performance could not significantly hinder aggregate economic growth in the pre-war period. With the increasing influence of governmental policy after the war, the negative effects of poor institutional performance became more pronounced, being especially manifested in the government's inability to control persistent budgetary deficits and a rapidly growing public debt that exceeded 180 per cent of estimated GDP at the end of 2002, with consequent adverse economic effects.[14] Throughout, the quality of development has suffered as a result of poor governance: clearly this has not been a major concern of the national authorities.[15]

The regional conflict that began in 1948 with the creation of the state of Israel and the first of several Arab–Israeli wars has yet to be settled. It has had a profound and multi-faceted influence on Lebanon's development. A major consequence was the in-flow of Palestinian refugees into Lebanon, especially in 1948, and then later in 1967 following the June war and the occupation by Israel of the West Bank and Gaza. A large number of Palestinians became naturalized Lebanese citizens, and, despite an official ban on granting work permits to (non-naturalized) Palestinian refugees, a good number were able to find employment in the informal sector. With time, and especially after the expulsion of the Palestinian Liberation Organization (PLO) from Jordan in 1970, Lebanon became the major base for the Palestinian struggle against Israel and for the creation of a Palestinian state. In the process, the regional conflict weighed heavily on Lebanon's domestic political scene as the PLO's political/military stance clashed with that of the Lebanese state. This led to turbulent Lebanese–Palestinian political relationships, often resulting in armed clashes.

Together, the regional conflict, with its attendant multiple external interventions, and sectarianism (i.e. religious as opposed to ethno-linguistic fractionalization) were the primary causes of the civil war. Their mutual interaction, irrespective of the relative importance of each in this context, finally led to the explosion of violence in 1975. The sectarian factor was mainly rooted in the political grievances of the two major Muslim communities which, over time, increasingly voiced their dissatisfaction with the prevailing system of power-sharing, which favoured the Maronites, and demanded a readjustment that would render the system more equitable. (This demand was eventually embodied in the Taif Accord.) The PLO exploited this sectarian dissatisfaction to bolster its position in Lebanon. It supported Lebanese parties opposed to Maronite hegemony in return for their support in its confrontation with the Lebanese state.

Economic factors (e.g. uneven development among the various regions and socio-economic inequities) played only a supporting role in the onset of the conflict. Once the war began, however, economic greed, associated with the economic/financial benefits accruing to the warring parties and their leadership, became one of two key factors sustaining it. The other was persistent and multiple external interventions throughout the conflict which took various forms, including financial and military assistance, as well as direct military involvement.[16] The war was devastating in terms of loss of human lives and material destruction, but the national economy survived thanks in large measure to the resilience of the formal private sector and an expanding informal economy.

A striking feature of the Lebanese civil war is that it was not strictly between the Lebanese state and a well-defined rebel group. Rather it pitted a coalition of Palestinian and Lebanese groups against a coalition of Lebanese parties that supported the state, which seemed to play a dual role in the conflict. While the Lebanese army clashed with an armed opposition, for most of the duration of the war the government included members who were sympathetic to both sides of the conflict. Even as the state grew progressively weaker, vestiges of public sector institutions continued to function in various parts of the divided country.

More than thirteen years after the end of the conflict, Lebanon has yet to resolve its underlying causes with a view to creating a firm basis for long-term sustained growth. The response to this challenge will determine the nature and quality of Lebanon's future development and society, and, by extension, the future of its coming generations. The civil war is over, but the question remains as to whether the post-conflict recovery policies that have been put in place deal appropriately with the causes as well as the consequences of the war.

A major aim of this book is to critically examine Lebanon's economic development during the second half of the twentieth century and the first few years of the twenty-first in the context of the evolving political/military environment. It documents and assesses the principal phases of development with special emphasis on the civil war and the period since. The factors underlying the successes and flaws of Lebanon's developmental record are investigated, and the major requisite conditions for sustainable development in a rapidly integrating world are identified.

This study of the Lebanese experience will hopefully contribute to the discourse on political economy in developing countries, as well as that on globalization, by highlighting four major themes: the impact of political sectarianism on national development; the resiliency of the private sector in the context of a politically unstable political situation – the civil war representing an extreme case of instability; the economic consequences of a stable sectarian system that neither political fragmentation nor a civil war could undermine; and finally, the role of developing economies in a rapidly integrating world.

Accordingly, some basic sets of questions will be addressed.

The first set focuses on the period from 1950 to 1975. What were its major achievements and weaknesses? How did pre-1975 developments prepare the stage for the outbreak of the civil war? What lessons can be drawn from this experience?[17]

The second set of questions pertains to the political economy of the civil war. What factors accounted for its outbreak and long duration? What was the impact of the war on the national economy and society, and what constraints did it impose on economic performance? What was the relationship between the political and economic factors? What was the impact of the war on the macroeconomic situation and socio-economic conditions? What were the responses of both the private and public sectors? How effective were these responses and what were their consequences? What role did the informal sector play?

The third set of questions relates to the evolution of the national economy since the civil war ended. What trends have emerged? How do they differ from the pre-war trends? What has been the impact of the new political order on socio-economic performance? Have the political and economic policies of the post-conflict era properly addressed the conditions that led to the outbreak of the war? What cost has been incurred on the national level for the resilience of the private sector in the context of a weak institutional performance? Has the private sector further increased its traditionally strong hold over the state since the end of the civil war, and has its role in the national economy essentially changed? To what extent have post-war governments succeeded in restoring a healthy economy and in establishing the basis for a lasting national reconciliation? This question takes on added significance when considered in the context of globalization and the new economic and political realities, both regional and global, than it has created.

A fourth set of questions addresses the future. What direction will national developments take from here on? What major challenges lie ahead in the context of globalization? What are the necessary conditions for reducing, if not totally eliminating, the risk of national conflict in the future? Put differently, what are the conditions for viable long-term reform?

The fifth set of questions focuses on the Lebanese case in a global context. What lessons can we derive from it as regards other small open economies in a fast integrating world? How does the Lebanese experience shed light on the relationship between domestic political institutions and national development, and how does it add to the discourse on globalization?

The answers to all these questions cut across fields beyond economics (history, culture, education, etc.), which lie outside the scope of this study. Even within the field of economics itself there are major areas to be considered beyond those that I have chosen to tackle. This book concentrates on the macroeconomic dimension of Lebanon's development while focusing on the quality of that development in the context of the changing political/military environments.

It is organized in five chapters as follows.

Chapter 1 assesses economic developments – both quantitative and qualitative – in the period before 1975 within the political framework. It identifies the areas of success and describes the failures that eventually led to the civil war.

Chapter 2 analyses developments in the war period, 1975–90, beginning with an assessment of the causes underlying the civil war and the factors accounting for its duration. It then moves on to examine the impact of the war on the national economy; economic resiliency in the face of military action and political fragmentation; and the responses of the public and private sectors, as well as the role of civil society in the era of militia power. It concludes with some general reflections on the war period.

Chapters 3 and 4 assess the post-war period, 1990–2002, in detail. The first focuses on growth and macroeconomic developments in the context of the new political environment. It analyses the quantitative aspects of growth, the evolving financial/monetary/banking situation, the reconstruction programmes, and the economic policies that have been put in place to cope with emerging macroeconomic imbalances. Chapter 4 concentrates on the labour market and the quality of development, i.e. governance and major socio-economic issues. It concludes with a note on the aspirations as opposed to the reality of the post-war period.

Chapter 5 offers concluding remarks on the successes and flaws of Lebanon's development over the second half of the twentieth century and the conditions that should be met to assure, in the future, a viable political system and sustainable development. It then goes on to examine the relevance of the Lebanese experience to other developing countries in a global context, touching on issues of civil war, political economy and globalization.

A number of specific subjects that are taken up in the book and are of great significance to Lebanon and other countries that witnessed civil wars need to be further researched in depth. They include the relationship between sectarianism and development, the political and fiscal decision-making process, the underlying economic and political causes of the civil war and violence (in particular the role of religious fractionalization), and the impact of the political set-up on the quality of development. If this book manages to inspire further work in these areas it will have achieved one of its objectives.

Sources

These may be grouped into five categories: (i) research work and results based on field investigations and/or collection of primary data, some of which is unpublished; (ii) national official data and reports on Lebanon, published and unpublished; (iii) reports of international and regional organizations; (iv) reports of private research organizations and consulting firms; and (v) other published economic/financial work on Lebanon.

On various occasions during the period under investigation I have been involved with Lebanese economic and financial policies, either in an advisory capacity or as member of various official committees. In 1992 I served as Minister of Economy and Trade in the Lebanese government. While the knowledge gained from such experiences cannot be quantified, it is clearly highly significant because of the light it throws on the inner working of policy formulation and implementation, as well as on some of the various issues that confronted policy-makers during the period under study.

The period preceding the civil war: relative economic stability, growth, socio-economic gaps and underlying political instability

§ NOTWITHSTANDING occasional domestic political conflicts – sometimes escalating into military confrontations – associated with both internal and external factors, and the persistence of underlying elements of political instability, Lebanon experienced an impressive rate of growth in the pre-war period, accompanied, on the whole, by relative financial stability. The qualitative, socio-economic, aspects of development were less successful. What were the major manifestations of economic growth and what factors accounted for the relatively rapid rate of development and relative financial stability? What were the major characteristics and shortcomings of the developing socio-economic situation and did that play a role in the outbreak of the civil war? What were the major features of the prevailing political environment and what was its impact on economic performance? How can we portray the major features of pre-1975 development? These are the questions that this chapter will address.

1 The political environment

Despite its sectarian nature, the pre-civil-war Lebanese political system exhibited features that are normally identified with modern Western political systems, such as freedom of expression, a variety of political parties and groupings (many of which were rooted in religious communities), openness to the outside world and support of the private sector, along with 'historical' political traditions associated with familialism, sectarianism and clientism. The latter features dominated the governmental power structure. To that extent, the political system was sectarian/familial/clientist in nature. Nevertheless, this juxtaposition of two contrasting sets of political characteristics permitted the emergence of a political order that, to a great extent, was liberal. Perhaps it would be preferable to coin a more apt term, 'quasi-liberal'. We may even speak of 'Lebanese political liberalism' to differentiate it from other forms of liberalism identified with contemporary Western societies. Essentially,

Lebanese liberalism was characterized by the fact that, in the context of the applicable sectarian formula, relatively free parliamentary elections were held, freedom of expression was allowed, presidents and cabinets changed, and political parties and other political groupings (both sectarian and non-sectarian) competed with each other. Political and intellectual dissidents from other Arab countries took refuge in Lebanon. The Lebanese press reflected a wide spectrum of political persuasions from extreme right to extreme left.[1]

While the Lebanese political system continued to function, as the years passed it showed signs of increasing strains.[2] Because elements of potential political instability were not properly addressed, they gained momentum over time. These included political calls to readjust the formula for power-sharing between Christians and Muslims; uneven development among the various regions with wide disparities in income distribution; and rural migration to the urban centres, accompanied by unchecked and rapid growth of the poor suburbs that surrounded the major cities, Beirut in particular. Despite attempts at administrative reforms, most notably those undertaken during President Chehab's term in office (1958–64), public administration was ponderous and generally inefficient.[3] The Chehabi reforms, intended to modernize the public sector and render it more efficient, took three main forms. The first was the preparation of a comprehensive study of Lebanon's future developmental needs (see below). The second was the creation of new administrative bodies such as the Civil Service Council,[4] while the third was the attempt to redress social and regional inequities. A social security law was introduced in April 1963 and greater attention than before was paid to the developmental needs of the regions. In the long run, however, the impact of these reforms on the performance of the public sector was limited. Steps were taken to put in place the necessary administrative apparatus, but the entrenched political establishment and the nature of the country's governance proved to be major obstacles in the face of serious reform.[5]

Over and above all these purely domestic factors, Lebanon witnessed the rising military power of resident Palestinian organizations, particularly after the 1967 Arab–Israeli war. While their activity was ostensibly directed at keeping the Palestinian cause alive and continuing the struggle to reclaim Palestine, their presence in Lebanon became intricately and inevitably linked to Lebanese domestic political affairs. In consequence, the domestic and regional political agendas could hardly be separated.[6] The prevailing weaknesses of the political system were exploited to enhance the status of the Palestinian organizations. Alliances were forged with disenchanted Lebanese sectarian and non-sectarian political parties and groups. For the latter, such an alliance was a means not only of serving the overall Arab cause, as was often declared, but also to pressure the Lebanese authorities into bringing about political reforms. The nature of the reform desired differed from one political group to another. Leftist and non-Establishment groups wished to introduce fundamental changes to render the system less sectarian,[7] while traditional Muslim groups aimed at readjusting the sectarian formula to ensure a more equitable distribution of power-sharing between the Christian and Muslim communities.

Political scientists and other observers of the Lebanese political scene have extensively analysed the pre-1975 political system.[8] Some have argued that the flaws in this system – sometimes cast in terms of 'loads' over-straining 'capabilities' of survival, or the inability to 'modernize' (the model of Western democracies being the point of reference) – rendered the Lebanese political set-up potentially explosive. Others have argued that the ability of Lebanon to develop before 1975 and to cope with emerging crisis situations demonstrated the adaptability of the system, despite its sectarian nature, and that consequently the abolition of sectarianism would undermine its democratic nature. And what led to the breakdown of the system, which began in 1975? Was it the inherent political and/or socio-economic domestic flaws in the system? Was it the presence of armed Palestinian organizations and intervention by neighbouring countries? Was the sectarian system, or a specific combination of interacting internal and external factors, responsible? If the Palestinian variable had been neutralized, would we have witnessed a peaceful evolution of the political system similar to what was finally accomplished in the Taif Accord?

The answers to the questions posed above are considered in detail in Chapter 2, which argues that mutually reinforcing external factors (the regional conflict) and internal factors (religious fractionalization) together led to the breakdown of the Lebanese political system.[9] Retrospective analyses of the causes of the Lebanese war are certainly of value. Even in the absence of agreement as to the principal causes, they help shed light on the circumstances leading to the conflict and the reasons for its long duration. Hence, for those who wish to learn from historical experience, they are instructive in charting future national development. In this respect what is crucial is to identify the post-conflict policies that need to be implemented to ensure a long-lasting resolution of its basic causes. This matter will be taken up in Chapter 5.

Whatever the judgement on the nature of the Lebanese political system before 1975, the liberal environment that prevailed was certainly conducive to the sustenance of economic liberalism. This, it should be remembered, was in stark contrast with the then prevailing systems in most countries of the region, which exhibited state domination of the economic field. Lebanese economic liberalism was manifested in two principal forms: (i) a truly open economy based on a liberal trade and payments regime, with no restrictions whatsoever on current payments or capital transfers, supported by a flexible exchange rate, and (ii) limiting the economic role of government to supporting the private sector. The government was active in building the country's infrastructure and, at the same time, endeavoured to maintain financial stability in the conscious or unconscious belief that this was a prerequisite for private sector initiatives. Direct economic intervention by the government was limited to a few specified areas, such as public utilities and tobacco marketing. Regulatory mechanisms were put in place in respect of some economic activities, such as rent, the prices of certain basic foodstuffs, tobacco production, and transportation fees.[10] It should be observed that economic policy targets were not explicitly formulated by the authorities, but a reading of their economic acts or stance helps formulate what might be termed the implicit targets of the pre-1975 period noted above (see section IID).

Political liberalism in the pre-war period was sustained, in my opinion, by a number of interacting factors. Though the Maronites constituted the single most influential religious community, the delicate sectarian balance, which had to be preserved, implied that no one single political, religious or politico-religious group (including the army) could impose its hegemony or ideology. In addition to religious freedom, free expression and association were, it seems, the logical outcome of the inability of any single group to dominate the others. Hence, the parliamentary system worked, no matter how imperfectly, and Lebanese institutions – educational, social, political, as well as the press – developed under conditions of relative freedom. Domestic political conflicts, whether of a sectarian nature or not, did not disrupt Lebanon's brand of political liberalism; indeed, it may be argued that such liberalism was needed for the survival of political parties, organizations and groups of different persuasions. On the other hand, the delicate sectarian balance also led to the emergence of a weak state (but not necessarily weak presidents, who enjoyed substantial powers in the running of the government and the dispensing of favours) and, in consequence, the inability to implement substantive administrative reforms. In practice, the prevailing political set-up tended to foster corruption, nepotism, clientism, and laxity in upholding the public interest when it came to conflict with private interests.[11]

With the above in mind, we now turn to a brief review of the quantitative and qualitative performance of the pre-war Lebanese economy.[12]

2 Economic performance: quantitative aspects

The Lebanese economy experienced substantial expansion in the pre-war period: generally high rates of growth were accompanied by relative financial stability. In this respect, Lebanese economic development was the model that many other countries would have liked to emulate. It should be remembered that in the 1950s, 1960s and 1970s, the economies of numerous developing countries suffered from high rates of inflation, sluggish rates of growth and varying forms of exchange restrictions and controls. In contrast, the Lebanese economy, which was and remains open, managed to expand under conditions of both relative price and exchange rate stability. An enterprising private sector was supported by a governmental economic stance that was conducive to its expansion. This was reinforced by generally relative, although at times precarious, political stability at home[13] (in contrast with occasional major political and military upheavals in the region) and by a prevailing local environment that helped attract foreign enterprises and capital to Lebanon.

In what follows, we trace the general trends that characterized the Lebanese economy in the pre-1975 phase.

2.1 Rapid growth and relative financial stability

There is no consistent series of national income estimates for the whole pre-war period. Official estimates span the years 1966–73. For earlier years, there are non-official estimates, going back to 1950, though a consistent series is available only for the period 1950–58.[14]

Available estimates indicate a relatively rapid rate of growth in the period 1950–73. In the 1950s the average annual rate, in real terms, was about 7.5 per cent. From the mid-1960s to 1973, the average annual rate declined to 6.0–6.6 per cent. While no estimates for the intervening years appear to be available, existing indicators point to a similarly rapid rate of growth.

At the sectoral level, the most notable development was the declining share of agriculture, which in 1974 was estimated at about 9 per cent of total GDP (down from 12 per cent in 1964). By comparison, the industrial sector expanded substantially, accounting for about 17 per cent of GDP for the same year (up from 13 per cent in 1964). New industries were established, for instance paper, chemical and metal industries, in response to growing demand both locally and in the region as a whole, which comprised important outlets for industrial exports. Their value increased rapidly: from LL50 million ($13.7 million) in 1952 to LL1.5 billion ($652 million) in 1974, constituting the bulk of total exports. In addition to the growing markets in the region, a number of factors contributed to this tremendous expansion, including tax incentives granted by the government, aggressive marketing on the part of industrialists and a relatively stable exchange rate which seems to have encouraged, or at least did not discourage, Lebanese exports.[15] It should be remembered that this was a period when many countries of the region lagged behind Lebanon in the industrial and services sectors and did not possess the entrepreneurial and marketing know-how of its industrial/merchant class. Other growth sectors in the 1950s were communications and finance, and in the 1960s administration and non-financial services. The services sector (transportation and communication, financial and other services) accounted for 22 per cent of GDP in 1974 (20 per cent in 1964). Overall, however, the trade sector continued to dominate with a share of a little over 30 per cent (32 per cent in 1964). The share of public administration ranged from 7.0 to 8.7 per cent of total GDP.

Rapid growth was accompanied by relative financial stability. The manifestations of this stability were: (i) a low inflation rate and (ii) a relatively stable exchange rate.[16] The two tendencies reinforced one another.

As measured by the whole price index, the inflation rate averaged about 2–3 per cent annually up to 1971, but tended to accelerate in the subsequent three years, averaging about 8 per cent per annum. Admittedly the existing price indices were not reliable and the actual rise in the general price level may have been somewhat greater than recorded, though it would have remained moderate. The factors that helped maintain relative stability were the rapid expansion in domestic liabilities (money and quasi-money, akin to national savings) in relation to the expansion in domestic credit (associated with spending), along with an open economy and a relatively stable exchange rate. The rapid expansion in domestic liabilities of the banking system, and especially in quasi-money, is explained on the demand side by (a) the relatively rapid growth in national income and (b) the tendency after 1963 for interest rates, particularly on balances held in foreign currencies, to rise, reflecting the general rise in Eurodollar rates; this rise had a positive impact on national savings. On the supply side, the openness of the national economy, along with the prevailing favourable political environment, tended to attract foreign capital into Lebanon and enhance confidence in the Lebanese pound; and the rapid development of the banking system helped siphon real savings into monetary outlets such as savings deposits.

On the other hand, domestic credit expansion was influenced by the generally conservative policies of the commercial banks, the Intra Bank crisis of 1966 notwithstanding.[17] With certain exceptions, the commercial banks maintained large cash reserves and directed most of their operations to ventures that were normally of short duration and did not carry a substantial risk. Further, a large portion of investment expenditure was financed by the retained earnings of individual investors or family-owned enterprises, in direct competition with bank credit operations. Equally important was the conservative budgetary policy of the government. More often than not, public sector budgetary operations tended to generate surpluses. Whenever deficits arose, they were of relatively small magnitude. Thus governmental operations did not generate inflationary pressures as was the case in many other countries and was to be experienced in Lebanon in later years. If anything, budgetary policy tended to be deflationary.

The exchange rate movements before 1975 were generally characterized by the absence of large short-term fluctuations. Long-term movements were gradual, and the pound was relatively stable. This was accompanied by almost continuous balance of payments surpluses and occasional Central Bank intervention on the exchange market to dampen the appreciation of the pound. The result was that the Central Bank accumulated over this period sizeable foreign exchange reserves (excluding gold), which at the end of 1974 amounted to 54 per cent of estimated imports for that year.[18] Regression analysis for the period 1950–70 shows that the effect of the exchange rate on the price level was substantial. It would appear that the relative stability in the exchange rate contributed significantly to the relative stability of the domestic price level. In contrast, after 1971 the influence of the exchange rate variable on the price level was much less. Other factors such as domestic credit were more influential.[19]

2.2 Human resources, the labour market and employment

Before 1975, Lebanese educational standards were recognized as probably the most advanced in the Arab region, although, over time, the educational gap between Lebanon and the rest of the Arab countries narrowed. Schools and universities in Lebanon attracted a good number of students from the region,[20] just as Lebanon's hospitals and other healthcare facilities attracted patients. Owing to the unavailability of the necessary data, no empirical studies have been carried out to quantify the role of education in pre-war economic development. Nevertheless, the major impact of human capital formation on the process of growth has come to be widely recognized in economic literature.[21]

Many indicators reflect Lebanon's relatively advanced standing in the 1950s, 1960s and early 1970s. Four will be cited by way of illustration, namely: (a) literacy rates, (b) school enrolment ratios, (c) university enrolment, and (d) number of professionals in certain categories.[22]

Available data on adult literacy rates (i.e. for the population over fifteen years of age) for five Arab countries in the region (Lebanon, Iraq, Jordan, Kuwait and Syria) reveal that in the late 1950s to the early 1960s these rates ranged from 47 per cent for Kuwait to 15 per cent for Iraq. This compares with about 60 per cent for Lebanon. In subsequent years, rapid progress was made in reducing the levels of illiteracy, but Lebanon continued to lead with a literacy rate of about 70 per cent. For the other Arab countries, literacy rates ranged from 30 per cent (Iraq) to 49 per cent (Kuwait).

Similarly, in the first half of the 1950s (adjusted) school enrolment ratios for the first and second levels combined ranged from 4 per cent for Saudi Arabia to 27 per cent for Jordan, compared with 47 per cent for Lebanon. By the early 1970s, the gap between Lebanon and the other Arab countries had been reduced. Available data indicate that by 1974 gross enrolment ratios for the first and second level combined (bearing in mind that the data for the earlier and later periods are not strictly comparable) ranged from 55 per cent for Jordan to 74 per cent for Kuwait, compared with 76 per cent for Lebanon. For third-level education, Lebanon also remained ahead. Comparable data for 1970 show a range from 2.19 per cent for Jordan to 8.88 per cent for Syria, compared with 23.5 per cent for Lebanon.

Total student enrolment in 1970, measured as number of students per 100,000 of population, ranged from 197 for Jordan, 363 for Kuwait and 862 for Syria to 1,728 for Lebanon. In the early 1970s, the number of professionals per capita (teachers, scientists, doctors, engineers, artists, etc.) was higher in

Lebanon than in other Arab countries. Available data for 1971, for example, show that the number of physicians in Lebanon was 8.4 per 10,000, compared with 4.6 in Jordan, 3.5 in Iraq and 2.5 in Syria. Also, the number of teachers per 100 people was 5.6 for Lebanon compared with 4.2 for Iraq, 3.5 for Syria and 3.4 for Jordan. A good number of Lebanese university students continued their higher education abroad with a large proportion of them returning home upon completion of their studies. In 1974, over 6,000 Lebanese students (including postgraduates) were studying abroad, comprising roughly 11 per cent of the higher-level student population in the country. On the other hand, Lebanon's vocational training lagged behind, and was not significantly ahead of some of the other Arab countries, if indeed it was at all.[23]

What the above data illustrate is that as far as educational standards were concerned, Lebanon was in a comparatively comfortable position. This, in turn, influenced the quality of the Lebanese workforce, which in 1970 was estimated at about 27 per cent of the population. A good proportion of this workforce was well educated. For the same year, about 20 per cent had completed 'complementary' or higher levels of education (4.3 per cent were university and 6.3 per cent high-school graduates), and another 15 per cent had completed elementary education (35 per cent did not complete it). The non-educated workforce comprised about 30 per cent of the total.[24] The occupational distribution of the workforce showed 9 per cent being in the teaching and other professions; 25 per cent in the trade and services sectors (over one half of those in the trade sector owned their own business); 20 per cent in the agricultural sector (a little over one half being agricultural workers); 11 per cent in administration; with the remaining 35 per cent being non-agricultural workers, many of whom were self-employed (tailors, drivers, etc.).

With a generally expanding economy, the rate of unemployment seems to have been relatively low, officially estimated at 3.1 per cent of the workforce in 1970, excluding seasonal unemployment and those seeking work for the first time. If these two categories were added, the rate of unemployment would rise to about 8 per cent.[25] However, other sources estimate that the level of unemployment was significantly higher than that.[26] Whatever the case, several factors influenced the level of unemployment and more generally the evolving demand and supply side of the labour market. They include emigration, the in-flow of non-Lebanese workers into the country, internal migration, the real wage level, the educational system, and the size and legal form of enterprises.

Unfortunately, there are no studies dealing with the years before 1975 which systematically analyse the impact of the above factors on the labour market. Some fragmented data are available, however. For example, it is estimated that up to 1975 about one fifth of the resident population had moved internally.[27] The main factor behind internal migration was economic. People sought work opportunities available in urban centres that enjoyed higher standards of living than rural areas. Emigration lessened the available supply of those seeking employment, particularly in activities requiring skilled or professional expertise. One source points out that at least two-thirds of the engineers and one third of the doctors who graduated in Lebanon in the 1960s emigrated to North America.[28] Another, citing US immigration data, indicates that in 1976 (admittedly a war year) about 46 per cent of Lebanese emigrating to the USA belonged to the professional and managerial categories.[29] On the other hand, the in-flow of foreign manpower – generally associated with unskilled labour – expanded the supply of this category of labour. Further, it has been pointed out that industrial enterprises tended to recruit young (i.e. aged under twenty) workers because the Labour Law of 1948 allowed employers to pay them less than the minimum legal wage.[30]

What can be said is that there emerged various degrees of imbalance between the supply and demand associated with different categories of manpower. This tendency was reinforced by the lack of symmetry between the specializations gained at university level and the requirements of an expanding economy. In the market for unskilled labour, the 'excess' labour supply tended to hold back any significant increase in the level of real wages. In the markets for skilled and semi-skilled manpower, the outcome with respect to the level of real remuneration tended to vary. For certain professional categories (e.g. physicians, engineers and highly skilled managers) 'excess' demand emerged which pushed their average level of real remuneration upwards. Indeed, this imbalance became more pronounced in later years.

It should be noted that the labour movement was not sufficiently strong to act as a substantial pressure group feared by employers or the government. The movement remained divided until 1970, when the various labour unions were brought together under the umbrella of the General Labour Union (GLU). Even after unity was achieved on 1 May of that year, leftist and rightist unions continued to clash over both the GLU's tactics and its policies for achieving economic and social goals.[31] The disunity of the labour unions should not, however, lead us to the conclusion that they did not attempt to improve the lot of the workers, or to address shortcomings in social legislation and benefits. Numerous labour strikes were carried out, particularly in the first half of the 1970s, and some gains were achieved, for example in expanding the coverage of social security. With mounting inflation after 1971, labour protests against the rising cost of living led the government to decree a wage increase of 5 per cent in August 1973. Further, with growing political divisions in the country, especially after 1969, political and socio-economic goals were often linked in an attempt to pressurize the government to acceding to the combined demands of opposition political groups and the labour unions. Overall, however, the bargaining power of the labour movement did not match that of the employers, who were usually supported by the government.

2.3 Macroeconomic policy stance

Public economic policy was not well defined during the period under consideration. There was no policy framework to guide the national authorities, who either were not aware of, or did not recognize, the concept of economic policy coordination. Nevertheless, a reading of budgetary statements, especially after 1962, and the actual policies adopted over an extended period of time reveals the following major characteristics of the official economic policy stance of successive governments.

(i) The authorities maintained an open economy in conjunction with a flexible exchange rate policy. The Lebanese economy interacted freely with the world economy. Balance of payments adjustments were resolved through exchange rate movements with occasional Central Bank intervention on the foreign exchange market when deemed necessary. It was observed earlier that this intervention was usually intended to counter the tendency for the Lebanese pound to appreciate.

(ii) Although the Central Bank was established at the beginning of 1964, up to 1967 monetary policy was generally absent, with little supervision over banking activities apparent. The bank's monetary regulations were designed to limit its credit operations, including a ceiling on governmental borrowing. The law that created the bank provided it with powers to influence monetary developments but did not spell out all the tools at its disposal, save for its power to impose minimum reserve requirements up to 25 per cent on demand deposits and up to 15 per cent on time deposits.

(iii) Following the Intra Bank crisis of 1966, the authorities were compelled to take several measures designed to ensure sound banking practices. These included measures to meet possible additional liquidity requirements, to weed out weak banks, and to ensure more effective control of banking operations. Under Law no. 28-67, enacted on 9 May 1967, a Higher Banking Council was created which was empowered, among other things, to take over unsound banks. Under the same law a Banking Control Commission was established. It was given the authority to control and supervise banks. In practice, it concerned itself with scrutinizing bank investments in the light of existing resources and ensuring that banks adhered to existing regulations. Towards the end of 1967 a Deposit Insurance Fund was established.

(iv) There was limited use of monetary instruments to control directly the flow of commercial bank credit up to 1973, when major amendments to the Law on Money and Credit were enacted (decree no. 5038 of 2 March 1973 and implementing decree no. 6102 of 5 November 1973).[32] The basic aim of these amendments was to enable the Central Bank to have greater flexibility in its monetary policy, to establish a more effective monetary management, and to help develop the financial market. The emergence of inflationary pressures beginning in the early 1970s, combined with a substantial appreciation in the value of the pound, led to Central Bank policy becoming more active. However, measures designed to counter both trends were not put into effect until mid-1974. These measures exhibited various internal inconsistencies, and their impact was not effective because their desired effect on credit flows was submerged by the increasingly adverse influences associated with the outbreak of the civil war. Although the economic and financial measures adopted in the first half of the 1970s could have constituted the beginning of a well-defined and active economic policy, the outbreak of the civil war disrupted this trend.[33]

(v) A conservative fiscal policy was followed, though the budget was nominally regarded as an important tool in attaining policy objectives. Policy formulation, as reflected in national budgets, while possibly indicative of the economic thinking of the authorities at the time, could not be considered as having been a serious endeavour.

In 1972, the authorities announced a Six Year Development Plan (1972–77). It was one step in the direction of portraying a better-defined official economic and developmental policy stance. It stated the objectives of the authorities more clearly than before, but did not evaluate the consistency of these objectives, and discussed only partially and inadequately the means by which they were to be achieved. In any case, no effective implementation of the plan took place. It was overtaken by the outbreak of civil war in 1975.[34]

2.4 Factors underlying growth

The rapid economic expansion of the pre-1975 period can be briefly explained by a number of interacting factors which may be summarized under the following headings: financial stability, an open economy, an enterprising private sector, helpful regional circumstances, a supportive internal environment, and non-obtrusive labour market conditions.

To begin with, the maintenance of relative price and exchange rate stability was certainly conducive to Lebanon's economic growth. A stable financial environment has long been recognized in the literature as a major contributor to – not to say a prerequisite for – sustained economic growth. Lebanon was successful in maintaining relative financial stability partly as a result of the conservative economic policies followed by successive governments, while the open economy permitted the private sector to interact freely with the outside world and encouraged the in-flow of capital. This helped generate balance of payments surpluses and strengthened the Lebanese pound. As noted above, a stable pound contributed, in turn, to domestic price stability.

The conditions of financial and exchange rate stability induced the enterprising private sector to invest and expand, taking full advantage of emerging regional and domestic opportunities.[35] At the regional level, major political upheavals and uncertainties rendered Lebanon, with its open economy, attractive not only for investment purposes but as a place of refuge for capital from countries that maintained exchange controls.[36] The relatively developed

Beirut money market (in comparison with other markets in the region) and expanding banking system acted as a conduit for Arab capital. The attractiveness of Lebanon was further enhanced by the government's economic stance, which was supportive of private initiative.

As for labour market conditions, it is true that vocational training lagged behind the requirements of industrial expansion, and that certain categories of domestic professional skills were in relatively short supply. However, the economy was open and heavily dependent on the trade and services sectors, and the country's manpower was in good measure relatively educated and skilled. Where needed, resort to foreign expertise was not uncommon. Furthermore, the non-inflationary environment that prevailed at least until 1971, along with the openness of the economy to outgoing Lebanese and incoming foreign labour, rendered wage issues less important than would otherwise have been the case. No wage policy existed: the government did not intervene in the setting of nominal wages.[37] All these factors helped ensure that any emerging imbalances in the labour market did not pose serious constraints to the expanding private sector.

It is interesting to observe that the political conflicts that Lebanon witnessed before 1975, alongside the existence of potential elements of political instability, did not seem to affect the country's economic position negatively. The attitude of the private sector seems to have been based on a separation between domestic developments and economic initiatives. This separation was rooted in the belief that major political actors – whether pro- or anti-government – did not differ significantly in their attitude towards the economic system. Calls for political and economic reform (e.g. greater equality) notwithstanding, they all supported the prevailing economic system and the major role accorded to the private sector. Despite their advocacy of some form of planning, the mild 'socialism' of certain political parties was not construed as undermining the system; indeed, it was supposed to support it.[38] The more radical leftist parties were not considered sufficiently strong to be able to assume the reins of power. Lebanon's liberal economic system has throughout successfully coexisted with domestic political conflicts, including the sixteen years of civil war, albeit in the latter case at tremendous human, social and economic cost (see Chapter 2). Hence, throughout the pre-1975 period, capital was flowing in and the private sector was expanding. It is true that some of the inward flows were associated with, or were in support of, the political activity of Palestinian and Lebanese political organizations, but this was not a major factor in the rapid expansion of economic activity. Rather, it is the convergence of the above-cited factors which helps explain Lebanon's generally rapid economic growth before 1975.

3 Socio-economic developments: qualitative gaps

Impressive as the quantitative aspects of Lebanon's economic growth were, the socio-economic aspect of development lagged behind. The manifestations of this lag were multi-faceted, but can be grouped under two broad headings: (i) striking unevenness of development between the various regions of the country, and (ii) limited progress in narrowing the gap, in real terms, between high-income and low-income groups. In making the claim that socio-economic development lagged behind economic, I have two considerations in mind. First, from a socio-economic point of view, it would have been desirable to further reduce the existing disparities in development between the various regions and to narrow the gap between the rich and low-income groups (noted below). Second, appropriate corrective policy measures should and could have been applied to improve the existing situation beyond what was actually achieved.

At the same time, the contention that socio-economic development lagged behind economic should not obscure the fact that Lebanon did witness in the period before 1975 social advancement at various levels. As already observed, this was most notable in the field of education, which distinguished Lebanon from most of its neighbours and, indeed, from most other developing countries. Similarly, in the field of health, hospital beds increased from 6,300 in 1959 to 9,149 in 1971, the number of resident medical doctors from 1,262 to 2,000 respectively, and the number of pharmacies from 165 to 274 respectively.[39] These increases were a little ahead of population growth. Further, there was awareness of the need for labour legislation as far back as 1946, when the Labour Code was promulgated.[40] It regulated conditions of employment, including that of women and children, as well as labour organizations, arbitration boards, industrial unions and employment offices. Admittedly, the code pertained only to wage earners in trade and industry and excluded rural workers, domestic helpers and civil servants. It was not until 1965 that social security legislation was adopted for the first time and a code pertaining to employer–employee relationships established by the government.

With the above in mind, let us briefly examine the question of income distribution. Unfortunately, except for a 1966 household survey, which covers Beirut only, there are no official statistical surveys for the period before 1975 pertaining to this subject. Instead we have to rely principally on a few ad hoc private and semi-official enquiries that were carried out beginning in the 1950s, along with a number of other studies of the socio-economic situation.

Writing in 1955, Elias Ghanage observed, on the basis of available rough statistical enquiries carried out in 1953, that about 78 per cent of the active Lebanese population belonged to the working class, which accounted for only 20 per cent of national income. The middle class comprised 20 per cent of the population, and the rich the remaining 2 per cent.[41] Together, the middle and upper classes accounted for 80 per cent of national income. Later, in the early 1960s, at the request of the government, IRFED[42] prepared its study on the needs of and possibilities for development in Lebanon. One of its preliminary surveys indicated that the proportion of the population that earned levels of income above the general average was only 18 per cent (in comparison with 35–40 per cent for Denmark, Italy and the USA but 8 per cent for Colombia). It was estimated that about one half of the population could then be classified either as poor (41 per cent) or very poor, i.e. destitute (9 per cent). Together, the poor and very poor accounted for about 18 per cent of national income. By comparison, it was roughly calculated that the richest 4 per cent accounted for about one third of national income, and the upper 18 per cent for about 60 per cent. The middle class (32 per cent of the population) accounted for 22 per cent of income.

Subsequent enquiries, carried out in the mid-1960s and early 1970s respectively, point to the fact that at least half the population could still be classified as poor or very poor. The 1966 official household survey (based on random sampling) referred to above reveals that over 50 per cent of those covered in the sample belonged to groups whose annual expenditure would classify them below the middle class. The latter comprised about 27 per cent and the well-to-do and rich the remaining 23 per cent. The poor classes accounted for about 29 per cent of expenditure, the middle class 33 per cent, the well-to-do 8 per cent, and the very rich the remaining 30 per cent.[43] Had a sample survey been carried out for all Lebanon, the results would probably have shown a notably more uneven distribution. A later statistical study, conducted in the mid-1970s, indicates that for 1973–74 roughly 54 per cent of the population corresponded to the IRFED classification of poor and very poor. The middle class comprised about 25 per cent, the well-to-do and very rich the remaining 21 per cent.[44] Estimates of income distribution corresponding to the above categories were not made.

On the basis of the above studies, it can be cautiously concluded that during the period up to 1975, (i) the percentage of the very limited income groups (poor and very poor) in the total population may have declined from the early 1950s to the early 1960s but thereafter remained the same until the early 1970s at roughly one half of the population, or a little over, but accounted for a larger share of income than in the early 1960s; (ii) the position of the middle class improved and came to account for an increasing proportion, anywhere from one fourth to one third, of national income; and (iii) there continued to exist a very rich class whose composition has changed over time. The IRFED report has ascribed a relatively sizeable proportion of national income to this class, and the 1966 household survey for Beirut indicates that it continued to account for a substantial but declining proportion of income. We have to bear in mind, however, that a sample survey for the whole country may have produced different and more skewed results. Some writers point to social changes during this period, which were partly manifested in an increasing concentration of economic/financial power in the hands of a small class.[45]

Certain observers of the Lebanese scene, however, have argued in connection with their assessment of the causes of the Lebanese crisis that Lebanon's noted pre-1974 inequality in income distribution compared favourably with that of many other countries, including some Western countries. Lebanon was among the group of states with moderate income inequality. Indeed, one writer cautions that the IRFED results were biased in that they exaggerated the situation of the poor and limited income groups as well as the small very rich class.[46] The earnings of the top 20 per cent of the population, it was pointed out, were not out of step with those of a sample of countries, which included the Netherlands, Tunisia, Mexico and West Germany.[47] Some claim that the socio-economic factors hardly played a role in the outbreak of the 1975 crisis, which was mainly caused by adverse regional political developments.[48]

In the absence of reliable official statistical surveys, disagreements as to the degree of inequity in income distribution may arise (irrespective of its political implications). However, what is equally important to consider is that this inequity was more pronounced in certain regions of the country than in others. For example, the position of the middle class was much more important in Beirut and the mountain region than in areas such as the south, the Beqa' and the Akkar regions, where large landholdings and class distinctions were prominent.[49] This, in turn, gave a sectarian colouring to the question of inequity in income distribution associated in particular with the Shia community, which had a major or predominant presence in these regions. Indeed, in 1974 the then religious leader of the Shiite community, Imam Musa al Sadr, launched a political movement, Amal, with the objective of enhancing the political and economic position of the Shia community in the Lebanese sectarian set-up, as well as to act as a countervailing force to the growing influence of Palestinian organizations in southern Lebanon. Amal presented itself as a 'movement of the dispossessed'. Its appeal was to a large extent based on the lagging socio-economic conditions of the Shia community in comparison with other communities in Lebanon.[50] Amal was to develop, especially after 1982, as one of the major warring factions in the Lebanese civil war.

The available evidence indicates that corrective policy measures were called for to address problems other than the unequal distribution of income. The social conditions of a sizeable portion of the population were extremely inadequate, and were exacerbated by migration from rural areas to urban centres, which consequently became surrounded with belts of poverty.[51] Studies confirm the unequal socio-economic development of the various regions of the country. One study of village life in the central Beqa' valley carried out in the mid-1950s, for instance, indicates that schooling for men averaged 2.6 years and for women 0.6 years. In Beirut, on the other hand, schooling for male heads of family averaged 6.1 years and for women heads of family 3.9 years.[52] According to official statistics, in 1948 the ratio of doctors to population in Beirut was 8.3 per 10,000, which was 10.7 times its ratio in southern and northern Lebanon respectively. While some progress in reducing certain socio-economic gaps between Beirut and the regions was made over the years, these gaps remained large. By 1970, for example, the ratio of doctors to population in Beirut was reduced to 5.6 times its ratio in northern Lebanon, but remained roughly the same for southern Lebanon.[53] As for health facilities, those available in the regions were generally very poor and extremely limited in comparison with Beirut.

Again the IRFED report provides a general picture of comparative regional developments. Regions which – at least until the early 1960s – witnessed good rates of growth were those primarily of central Lebanon, i.e. Beirut and its suburbs and the central mountains, but also the district of Koura in the north and the town of Zahleh in the central Beqa'. By contrast, the regions that witnessed poor rates of growth were those in northern, southern and eastern Lebanon.[54] Within some of these regions, there were also substantial differences in standards of living. The contrast, however, was particularly obvious between Beirut and the major cities, on the one hand, and the rural areas on the other.

One needs to trace and measure socio-economic developments over the pre-war period as a whole. The major source of data for the latter part of the period is the major statistical enquiry conducted by the Central Bureau of Statistics (CBS) in 1970.[55] The basis for this enquiry differs from that of the IRFED mission. This limits the validity of strict comparisons of the results of the two enquiries, particularly when the objective of the comparison is to determine the degree to which the gaps noted in the IRFED mission tended to narrow or widen. Nevertheless, the CBS enquiry, along with other sources, in particular the 1971 Annual Report on Health Statistics prepared by the Ministry of Health (the last report to be prepared prior to the civil war), provides a good picture of the prevailing socio-economic situation in the early 1970s. The following illustrations will suffice.[56]

In terms of education, male residents with a baccalaureate or higher degree in the age bracket over twenty-five comprised 24.1 per cent of the total for Beirut, 9.4 per cent for its suburbs, 9.4 per cent for other cities, and 4.6 per cent for rural areas. For women residents the percentages are much lower: they vary from 1 per cent in the rural areas to 12.5 per cent in Beirut. Illiteracy rates for Beirut residents ranged from 10.6 per cent for the age bracket ten to fourteen to 45.5 per cent for the age bracket sixty-five to sixty-nine. For the other regions, the corresponding illiteracy rates varied from 11.1 per cent to 78.5 per cent respectively for the same age brackets. This indicates a notable drop in the illiteracy rate between the generations, and the increased demand for schooling was very evident. Furthermore, the relatively developed transportation network enabled many of those living in rural areas to attend schools and universities in Beirut. However, the level of educational instruction varied substantially between institutions located in Beirut and those in other regions.

As to housing, the continuous migration from the rural areas to the cities, especially Beirut, in addition to the in-flow of non-Lebanese workers, led to housing congestion in Beirut and the suburbs. The housing shortage was estimated at about 20 per cent for Beirut and 14 per cent for the suburbs compared with 12 per cent for the other cities and 8 per cent for rural areas. Levels of household facilities differed substantially, though. For example, during this period 83 per cent of all apartments in Beirut had bathrooms compared with 52 per cent for northern Lebanon, 46 per cent for southern Lebanon and 43 per cent for the Beqa' region in the north-eastern part of the country.[57]

In the health sector, two phenomena are noteworthy: the first was the heavy concentration of medical and health facilities and personnel in Beirut, with much lower health standards in the other regions. The second was that a relatively large number of families did not benefit adequately from available health facilities either because of their limited financial means or on account of the inadequacy of existing social security coverage. According to Ministry of Health statistics in the early 1970s, 65 per cent of all doctors resided in Beirut, which accounted for only 27 per cent of the total population. This proportion rises to over 80 per cent if the neighbouring mountain regions are included: together, they accounted for roughly half the population. In contrast, 5.5 per cent of physicians provided care for southern Lebanon, with 18 per cent of the population, and only 3 per cent for the Beqa', with 13 per cent of the population. Hospital beds in Beirut and Mt Lebanon (i.e. the regions surrounding Beirut) comprised 84 per cent of the total compared with 6 per cent for southern Lebanon and less than 2 per cent for the Beqa'.

It might be argued that because Lebanon is a small country with a relatively well developed road network, these disparities did not necessarily impinge – or should not have impinged – as adversely on the health welfare of the rural population as might be the case in much larger countries with comparable or lower health standards. Whatever the merits of such an argument, we have to bear in mind that a large proportion of the rural population could not avail itself financially of existing care facilities in Beirut and other cities. Indeed, the state should have taken advantage of the relatively favourable transport situation to establish adequate health facilities in the regions. Admittedly, moves in this direction were made: for example, a few hospitals, with limited bed capacity, were established. Overall progress, however, was minor.[58] In addition, a social security system was not put in place until 1963. Initially coverage was confined to specified categories of employees and restricted to end-of-service benefits and family allowances. Healthcare insurance was not provided until the early 1970s, when the social security system was opened to categories of employees not previously included.[59]

The disparities in Lebanon's socio-economic development in the pre-1975 period were certainly not unique. As has been pointed out by certain observers, other developing countries had fared less adequately in this regard. For our present purposes, however, how Lebanon compared with other developing countries before 1975 is not the issue at hand. Rather, as mentioned above, it is the fact that, given the country's socio-economic situation, corrective policy measures were called for. Had these measures been taken and appropriately implemented, they would have contributed to a relatively more stable socio-economic environment and a more equitable social system. These are desirable ends in themselves, irrespective of their presumed impact on Lebanon's political development. A policy leading to a more effective reduction in income and regional socio-economic disparities may not have prevented the outbreak of the civil war in 1975, but it would have contributed to the strengthening of inter-communal relationships, particularly given that existing socio-economic inequities had an important sectarian dimension.[60]

If it is true that the real causes of the civil war were political and not socio-economic in nature, it is equally true that socio-economic elements played a supporting role in its onset.

4 A summary overview of development until 1975

The broad model of Lebanon's development until 1975 may be abstracted into a set of characteristics, four of them economic in nature, and three non-economic, i.e. political, educational and social respectively. The non-economic characteristics constitute the socio-political framework within which economic initiatives were undertaken and, hence, substantially influenced the country's economic development.

Politically, the prevalence of a liberal environment was conducive to economic expansion, despite frequent and serious domestic disturbances. The role of the state was viewed by the political and business leadership as being basically confined to supporting private sector initiatives. In education, the relatively high level of schooling attained by Lebanon provided needed manpower skills. On the social front, the relatively liberal environment which, along with an open economy, facilitated interaction with the outside rendered Lebanon attractive for foreign business interested in the area.

As far as the economy was concerned, the characteristics were:[61] first, a high rate of growth in the 1950s tending to drop in the 1960s, and a quantitative expansion accompanied generally by relative financial stability; second, a generally successful external economic stance taken by the national authorities, which maintained a liberal exchange system and a relatively stable exchange rate; third, the lack of effective public economic direction because of the absence of overall economic policy targets and coordination (although it might be possible to argue that this lack was an implicit policy objective);

and fourth, despite the progress made, the fact that the qualitative nature of development was less than adequate: the authorities did not pay sufficient attention to the socio-economic aspect of development. The major shortcomings of development were in this domain.

Even at the macroeconomic level, however, a number of corrective policy measures were called for despite Lebanon's generally impressive quantitative record.[62] A lack of understanding of the workings and purposes of policy coordination implied the absence of a well-defined economic policy. The latter began to manifest itself only in the early 1970s under the impact of inflationary pressures and an appreciating Lebanese pound due to capital in-flows. Policy coordination could have acted as a guide for policy action aimed at coping with and steadying the rate of economic expansion or enhancing the level of savings, and more generally taking advantage of emerging opportunities. Cases in point are more expansionary monetary policy after 1963 to shore up the rate of growth along with a more adequate supervision of banking operations; influencing the flow of domestic credit to enhance employment opportunities; the development of the financial market; implementing policies that would have lessened the flow of internal migration towards the cities, and so on. The flexible exchange rate policy, accompanied by relative financial and exchange rate stability, provided opportunities for a more active policy which the authorities were either unaware of or chose not to seize.

Overall, the corrective macroeconomic measures that were called for before 1975 served more to steady the course of development and lay the foundations for policy coordination than to correct basic maladjustments in the domestic economy.

5 Lebanon on the threshold of civil war

It is generally agreed that 13 April 1975 is the date that marks the beginning of the civil war. That day, armed clashes between members of the Kataeb Party on the one hand and members of Palestinian organizations on the other took place in the Beirut suburb of Ayn al-Rammaneh.

Irrespective of the particular circumstances that led to this clash,[63] what matters is that the clouds of an impending widespread armed conflict between Christian political parties and Palestinian organizations had been gathering for some years, particularly after the expulsion of the PLO from Jordan in 1970. With this expulsion, southern Lebanon became the only sanctuary for PLO operations against Israel. The Cairo Agreement of 1969 was supposed to have provided the understanding that governed these operations but it failed to contain rising political and military tensions between the two sides.

The increasingly strained relationships between the two sides took various forms, and became intricately linked with purely domestic political issues. Throughout this period, Israeli raids against Palestinian strongholds and southern villages became a common occurrence. Fuelled by mutual mistrust and opposing objectives, periodic armed clashes took place between the Palestinians and the Lebanese army or its allies among the Christian parties.

To the Palestinians and their supporters among the various local political groups, armed struggle against Israel took precedence over everything else. In addition the Lebanese parties allied with the PLO saw in the alliance a means to alter the domestic balance of power in their favour. They wished to establish a less sectarian political system, or at the very least readjust the sectarian formula whereby what they regarded as Maronite hegemony gave way to a more equitable sharing of sectarian power. Many Lebanese, on the other hand, particularly the traditional Christian parties, regarded national sovereignty as being violated, and the delicate balance that underlay the political set-up as being placed in jeopardy. Lebanon, it was further argued, was shouldering the burden of the Arab–Israeli conflict alone, as all the other countries neighbouring Israel had sealed their borders, and therefore suffered none of the Israeli attacks, or the ensuing strain on their political systems.

Both sides took to arming themselves in preparation for what was perceived to be the inevitable clash. Domestic political tensions mounted, cabinets changed and unrest increased. These developments could not be separated from the issues pertaining to the Arab–Israeli conflict. Radicalism on both sides grew more extreme. All efforts, domestic and Arab, aimed at reconciling existing differences failed to produce more than temporary reprieves. This was the prevailing atmosphere prior to the clash of Ayn al-Rammaneh which ignited the civil war.[64]

CHAPTER 2

The war period, 1975–90: resilience versus fragmentation

1 Introduction: the phases of the civil war[1]

The civil war period may be divided into three principal phases. Although not strictly distinct, they can be differentiated on the basis of the specific developments that characterized each of them.

The first phase covered the period from 1975 to 1977, comprising two years of war followed by a year of relative peace. The protagonists were, as we have seen, the traditional Christian parties allied with the government on the one hand and, on the other, the PLO and a supporting coalition of Lebanese political parties which together became known as the National and Islamic Forces.[2] Beirut was divided: the PLO/Lebanese coalition had effective control of West Beirut, while the Lebanese army and traditional Christian parties were in control of East Beirut. This period witnessed ferocious battles between the Kataeb party and Palestinian armed organizations in the out-skirts of Beirut where refugee camps were to be found, and ended with the Kataeb establishing control over these camps and the forced eviction of their residents. In parallel, Christian towns south of Beirut, notably Damour, were sacked by Palestinian and allied Lebanese militias. Atrocities were committed by both sides in the conflict; thousands of people died or were injured, and thousands more were displaced.

In April 1976, Syrian forces entered Lebanon in support of the government and its political allies, and clashed with the opposing PLO/Lebanese coalition. The objective of the intervention was to contain the expanding military, and by extension political, dominance of the PLO and their Lebanese allies. During the summer, the six-year term of President Suleiman Frangieh ended, and a new president, Elias Sarkis, was elected by parliament. In October 1976 an Arab summit meeting took place in Riyadh which called for a ceasefire to be supervised and enforced by an Arab Deterrent Force (ADF) comprising troops from Syria, Sudan, Saudi Arabia and Yemen. In practice, the bulk of the ADF, which totalled 30,000 men, was made up of Syrian forces (27,000) that were already in Lebanon. The other Arab troops arrived in November, and with their arrival Beirut was reunified.

With the outbreak of the war, economic and social conditions began to deteriorate, but the level of the Lebanese pound, while depreciating in 1976/7, remained close to that prevailing in the early 1970s without significant Central Bank intervention.[3] The extent of variation in the exchange rate remained limited.[4]

Following the declaration of the ceasefire, the process of reconstruction planning was initiated by the government (see below, pp. 65–8), and hopes grew that the end of the civil war was indeed in sight. These hopes were dashed when a clash between Lebanese and Syrian army units took place outside Beirut in February 1978. The conflict resumed, and quickly spread to other parts of Lebanon.

The second phase of the war covers the period 1978–82, and ended, both politically and militarily, with the Israeli invasion of Lebanon on 6 June 1982. This is a period that witnessed an escalation in the fighting between the protagonists in Beirut and elsewhere in the country. Both Israeli and Syrian troops became involved in factional fighting. In March 1978 a major Israeli incursion into Lebanon took place which ended with Israel's occupation of a large strip in the south, the establishment of a proxy militia (the South Lebanon Army) and the deployment of UN troops on the Lebanese/Israeli border. In 1980 Syria concentrated troops in the Beqa' valley and clashed with Phalange militia entrenched in the city of Zahleh near the Beirut–Damascus highway. The alliances had shifted, with Syria now on the side of the PLO and its allies.

A significant development took place in July 1980 when Bashir Gemayal, then leader of the Kataeb militia, succeeded in uniting by force all Christian militias in one organization named the Lebanese Forces. The country became effectively divided into regions that were militarily controlled either by Syria, the Lebanese army and Lebanese Forces, or by the PLO and the Lebanese parties allied with it. Beirut was again divided.

During this period, the pound tended to depreciate somewhat, but its volatility remained limited. During 1981 the exchange rate averaged LL4.1 per US dollar. In the following section we refer to the in-flow of political money in support of the warring militias; this was one factor that helped prevent a dramatic depreciation of the pound following the outbreak of the war until 1982. Socio-economic conditions, however, continued to deteriorate.

The third phase of the war, June 1982–October 1990, witnessed the climax of outside intervention, beginning with the Israeli invasion of June 1982 and concluding with the Taif Accord of October 1989. Shortly after entering Lebanon, Israeli forces reached the outskirts of West Beirut, and then laid siege to it for many weeks. Fighting took place not only between the PLO and their Lebanese allies on the one hand and the Israeli army and the Lebanese Forces on the other, but also between the Syrian and Israeli armies in the Beqa' valley. The Lebanese Forces decided not to participate in ground attacks on West Beirut. Eventually the USA brokered a ceasefire under the terms of which the PLO forces were to withdraw from Lebanon, Syrian troops were to withdraw from West Beirut, and Israel would stop its devastating assault on Beirut.

Israel now attempted to impose a friendly government in Lebanon. Bashir Gemayal was elected president by parliament, only to be assassinated on 14 September 1982, before taking office. This was followed by the entry of Israeli troops into West Beirut, during which brief occupation the infamous massacres in the Palestinian refugee camps of Sabra and Chatila took place. Parliament met again on 22 September and elected Bashir's older brother, Amin Gemayal, as president. In the meantime, the United States, Britain, France and Italy agreed to send troops to Lebanon, ostensibly on a peace-keeping mission and to protect the refugee camps in the greater Beirut area following the withdrawal of the PLO.

Aside from the massive costs in human lives and limbs, and the displacement of thousands of people, the Israeli invasion brought in its wake economic havoc. Estimates of damage to physical property alone exceeded $2 billion.[5]

In April 1983, the United States embassy in Beirut was blown up, and in October of the same year both the American and the French army barracks in Beirut were attacked and suffered very high casualties. Soon afterwards, the remaining Western forces withdrew, their mission terminated without accomplishing its main objectives.

The government of Amin Gemayal entered into negotiations with Israel for a peace treaty that, among other things, called for the withdrawal of Israeli troops from Lebanon. There was strong opposition to this treaty on the part of Syria, as well as political groups and militias allied with it: these now fought against the parties that supported the president. The opposition was founded on the grounds that the treaty would take Lebanon into the Israeli orbit and undermine Syrian–Lebanese relationships and the Arab struggle for Palestinian rights. While the treaty was approved by parliament on 17 May 1983 (and thus became known as the May 17 agreement), it was not signed by the president and hence never came into force.[6]

This phase of the war witnessed vicious fighting, particularly in the summer of 1983 in the Shouf mountains east and south-east of Beirut between the Progressive Socialist Party (Druze dominated) and the Lebanese Forces. The fighting followed the sudden withdrawal of Israeli troops from the region: some observers contend that this move was intended to ignite the conflict between the two parties. The end result was a mass exodus of Christian communities from the region, the destruction of many Druze and Christian towns, and the killing of hundreds of civilians.

Meanwhile, from the time of the withdrawal of the PLO in September 1982 greater Beirut had again come under the control of the government and the army. On 6 February 1984, however, the army was forced to withdraw from

West Beirut, which again came under the control of militias and political organizations opposed to the government, in particular Amal and the Progressive Socialist Party. The strife between East and West Beirut was reignited, although it was not always confined to the protagonists. Intra-militia fighting frequently took place in both sectors of the city, but especially in the more heterogeneous West Beirut. After the Israeli invasion Hezbollah, supported by Iranian funding, began to grow in stature in the southern suburbs of Beirut and in Shia-dominated regions of the country. During this period it frequently clashed with Amal in West Beirut for political control of the Shia community. Clashes also occurred between the Progressive Socialist Party and Amal, while the smaller Sunni militia, the Mourabitoon, was subdued and its leadership driven out of the country. Indeed, intra-militia fighting occurred throughout the war, not only in Beirut but in other parts of the country as well.

At the request of the authorities in West Beirut, Syrian forces re-entered this part of the city in February 1987 to maintain order and prevent the continuation of the murderous and thoroughly destructive intra-militia clashes. When the six-year term of President Amin Gemayal was about to end in September 1988, and no agreement had been arrived at as to his successor, he appointed the then General of the Army, Michel Aoun, as president of an interim Council of Ministers, which was composed of the six members of the army command. Although the constitution stipulates that in such circumstances an interim prime minister be appointed, Gemayel's action was unilateral and met with opposition. The three Muslim members of the appointed council refused to serve, and the existing government, headed by Salim al Hoss, refused to acknowledge the legitimacy of Aoun's government. Thus there came to be two competing governments in Lebanon. This situation ultimately led to ferocious fighting between Lebanese and Syrian army units, and later between the Lebanese army led by General Aoun and the Lebanese Forces militia.

In principle, the civil war ended when, with Arab and international encouragement and backing, the Lebanese parliament met in October 1989 in Taif, Saudi Arabia, to discuss and ratify modifications to the constitution, which were eventually embodied in the Taif Accord (formally known as the Document of National Understanding). On 5 November 1989, parliament met in a small town in northern Lebanon and elected Rene Mouawad as President of the Republic. He was assassinated on 22 November, and two days later Elias Hrawi was elected president.

In the meantime, the government of General Aoun refused to recognize the legitimacy either of parliament or of the Taif Accord, which had been preceded by fighting on a major scale between his forces and the parties opposed to him and supported by Syria. Later, more fighting took place between pro-Taif Maronite forces (most notably the Lebanese Forces) and that part of the army still under Aoun's command. Finally, with tacit US approval, in October 1990, a joint Syrian–Lebanese military action forced Aoun out of the presidential palace. He took refuge in the French embassy, and was later allowed to leave the country, thus paving the way for the unification not only of the Lebanese government and public administration, but also of Beirut.

President Hrawi served a full six years, his term ending on 24 November 1995, but it was extended for an additional three years until November 1998, when General Emile Lahhoud was elected President of the Republic.

The Syrian troops that had originally entered Lebanon in 1976, the second year of the civil war, have continued to be deployed in Lebanon to this day, in principle to help the Lebanese armed forces maintain law and order and withstand Israeli pressures. After its invasion of 1982 and subsequent withdrawal from most of the territory it had held, Israel continued to occupy a strip of southern Lebanon, which it ran with the help of its surrogate militia, the South Lebanon Army (SLA). Armed resistance to Israeli occupation mounted throughout the period of occupation. Finally, in May 2000, Israeli troops were forced to withdraw. The SLA was disbanded, and many of its members were arrested and placed on trial.

Given the intensified war conditions, it is not surprising that the period from 1982 to 1990 witnessed rapidly deteriorating economic and social conditions accompanied by a worsening of the financial situation and accelerating emigration. The nominal and real value of the Lebanese pound declined rapidly, and there were increasing budgetary deficits and mounting inflation. The heavy human and economic toll mounted as the war raged.

Estimates put the loss of human lives during the war period at over 144,000 (5 per cent of the then resident population). This figure does not include the death toll resulting from Israeli aerial attacks on Palestinian refugee camps, fighting among Palestinian armed groups, or armed clashes between Amal and Fateh in and around the camps. In addition, it is estimated that over 184,000 people were injured, over 13,000 maimed, and over 17,000 disappeared (mostly kidnapped and killed).[7]

The national economy suffered huge losses, which will be discussed below. However, although severely battered and fragmented, it was able to survive, albeit at a very heavy cost. The state was greatly weakened, at times appearing to wither away, and the militias reigned in their respective domains, but civil society did not totally crumble, and on more than one level continued to resist the adverse influences of political fragmentation and militia power.[8] The private sector, faced with tremendously adverse circumstances, proved to be resilient in many ways. Even the weak public sector, as indicated in the section below, attempted to respond to the evolving economic situation, at times with some success.

In the context of the military and political turbulence, four major features of the war period are worth highlighting.

The first is that the forced eviction of Palestinian refugees from the camps in the eastern districts of suburban Beirut in the years before 1982 led to the creation of a central zone (including Beirut) that was effectively under the control of the Lebanese authorities, in contrast with their nominal control elsewhere in the country. In the wake of the Israeli invasion, and following the short-lived attempt by the Lebanese Forces to expand to new areas in the mountain districts, the civil war settled down to an equilibrium of zones largely but not totally formed along sectarian lines.

The second is that throughout the civil war the national monetary authorities remained effective, especially prior to 1984. This was in contrast with other governmental institutions, whose role greatly diminished as they came under the influence of the various militias.

The third is that despite the weakening of the state, especially in the fiscal domain, creative and at times effective attempts at coordinating economic policies were considered and put into effect.

The fourth is the resiliency of the private sector throughout the war period. Thanks in large measure to this resiliency, the domestic economy was able to survive the tremendous battering it received.

This chapter will assess the performance of the Lebanese economy under the military and political conditions of the civil war. It will address the following questions: What was the impact of the war on the national economy? Despite the blows it received, how was it able to escape total breakdown? How did the private and public sectors respond? What role did civil society play in the face of militia power? What in the end was the economic, political and social outcome of the war? What are some of the lessons of the civil war? However, before we address these questions it is important to try to understand the underlying causes of the civil war and the factors that accounted for its long duration. This, in turn, will help us assess the nature of the issues that ought to be addressed in the post-conflict era and to evaluate the appropriateness of the policies that have been put into effect.

Accordingly, we begin by considering the causes and duration of the civil war, and then move on to examine the political/military context in which economic development took place. This is followed by a detailed evaluation of the impact of the war on the national economy and the respective roles of the private and public sectors under conditions of military and political conflict. A brief survey of the social impact of the war follows. The chapter concludes with some reflections on the war period and a very brief comment on the Taif Accord.

2 On the causes and duration of the civil war: economic versus non-economic factors[9]

The Lebanese civil war lasted sixteen years, a relatively long time, and certainly much longer than the average duration of the civil wars that have taken place since the end of the Second World War. One source puts this average for the period 1945–99 at about 8.5 years; another puts it at nine to ten years for the period 1960–92 (which saw twenty-seven civil wars).[10] In both the Introduction and Chapter 1, I attributed the outbreak of the war to domestic and regional political factors. What about economic factors, and specifically the prevailing economic/social inequality? What factors accounted for its long duration? In examining these issues it would be useful to begin by referring to major preliminary findings of the emerging economic literature on civil wars, which until recently had focused on African wars, and then assess the Lebanese case in the light of these findings.[11]

A basic question concerning the underlying causes of civil war which the economic literature has addressed is whether they are attributable to economic greed or to some form of grievance linked to political and/or economic injustice, as might have been argued in previously published economic and political research, or to a combination of the two. Certain recent economic studies on civil wars have claimed that in the popular mind such wars are largely ascribed to grievances (political, economic or ethnic), partly because rebel groups and governments alike resort to the rhetoric of grievance to garner support. In reality, there is little correlation between oppression (as measured by various indices) and the incidence of war.[12] Based on cross-country studies, the hypothesis of economic greed (loot-seeking) rather than grievance has been advanced as the major cause of civil war (especially in Africa). With greed as a primary motive, factors that tend to raise the risk of rebellion against the state include dependence on primary commodity exports, i.e. the availability of a taxable and lootable economic base, low average incomes, slow growth and a large diaspora. Further, the degree of risk of conflict rises with ethnolinguistic dominance, i.e. where the largest single ethnic group comprises between 45 and 90 per cent of the population. In contrast, this risk becomes lower in ethnically or religiously diverse societies. Thus, societies that are more fractionalized into ethno-linguistic groups are less prone to civil war than highly homogeneous societies.[13]

Some studies have minimized the role that ethnic differences play in civil conflict. It is often the case, they maintain, that ethnicity – and the importance attached to it – is shaped by conflict rather than the other way around.[14] Other studies, however, have concluded that ethnicity does indeed play a central role in certain conflicts. Some indices of religious polarization that prove to be insignificant when all civil wars are considered have a positive and significant relevance in the case of civil wars in which ethnicity plays a fundamental role.[15]

The role of natural resources in civil conflict has been the focus of several investigations. Diamonds in Sierra Leone, timber in Cambodia and cocaine in Colombia are cited as examples of natural resources that can be readily exploited by the winning side and which hence act as a major incentive for a civil war motivated by economic greed. However, very high levels of natural resource wealth imply that central governments can acquire important financial resources; in turn, this permits them to maintain strong armies that can quell a rebellious movement. In other words, the incidence of war is likely to have a non-monotonic relationship with the level of natural resources, whereby after a certain threshold the efforts of the rebels to gain victory become increasingly more futile.[16] Other investigations into the link between natural resources and civil wars, however, point out that it is more complex than has been suggested. One study, for example, contends that the correlation between resource dependence and civil war gives weak support to the greed hypothesis mentioned above, and that this dependence is, in any case, related to both the causes and the duration of civil wars.[17] Another study differentiates between renewable and non-renewable resources. It concludes that the incidence of civil war is not related to the availability of natural resources when defined to include both types of resources. However, the higher the per capita availability of sub-soil (non-renewable) assets (e.g. mineral wealth), the greater the incidence of conflict, whereas the abundance of renewable resources is not an important factor.[18]

Once a civil war begins, the factors that explain its duration are not necessarily the same as those that explain its cause. Collier and Hoeffler argue that societies with moderate ethnic fractionalization (i.e. two or three ethnic groups) tend to suffer prolonged wars. Societies that are homogeneous or highly fractionalized tend to experience short wars. The reason, it is contended, is that it is easier for the government to divide the rebel organization in the latter type of society than in the former.

Another factor that accounts for the length of civil wars is that war economies become lucrative sources of income and wealth, thereby providing strong incentives to prolong the conflict. Diasporas can also play a role in prolonging the duration of war to the extent that they constitute a significant source of funding for rebel movements, particularly if they keep in close contact with their home country and tend to wish to preserve their cultural heritage. Other factors that may affect the duration of civil wars include the level of male secondary school enrolment and the presence or absence of wars in neighbouring countries.[19]

Further preliminary research, also based on cross-country studies, has drawn attention to the role of external intervention as a cause of both the onset and/or the duration of civil wars. This intervention, it is pointed out, is less likely in ethnic wars or in regions that are democratic or where the state has a strong military. However, for a given level of ethnic polarization, external intervention will prolong the duration of the war. This implies that with such intervention longer civil wars can be sustained even in diverse, as opposed to ethnically dominated, societies.[20] Finally certain studies have stressed the need to study the interaction between greed and grievance in that both elements play a role in contemporary conflicts.[21]

Clearly, the objective of cross-country studies is to help shed light on commonalities that underlie the incidence and duration of civil wars, although a broad consensus on these matters, in particular on the links between the factors underlying both the outbreak and the duration of war, is yet to emerge. Helpful as these studies may be, the special circumstances of individual countries that have experienced domestic conflicts may differ considerably, as will the diagnosis of their causes and duration, and, therefore, the required post-conflict policies. In the final analysis, broad theses on civil conflicts can only be based on thoroughly investigated individual case studies

In the case of Lebanon, as pointed out in Chapter 1, the primary causes of the civil war were political grievance arising from unequal power-sharing among the three major religious communities (religious fractionalization or the sectarian factor), in conjunction with the political/military stance of the PLO which clashed with the interests of the state. Irrespective of the relative importance of each factor in causing the outbreak of war, the mutual interaction of the sectarian and Palestinian factors (which had been building up before 1975) finally led to the explosion of 1975. The PLO supported Lebanese parties (comprising the so-called Islamic and Nationalist Forces) that opposed Maronite political hegemony and demanded a change in the political set-up in favour of more equitable power-sharing. In return these parties supported PLO operations against Israel launched from Lebanon. In this alliance, the Palestinian side was militarily stronger than the Lebanese parties.

As the Lebanese population is basically both ethnically and linguistically homogeneous,[22] this factor clearly had no bearing on either the causes or the duration of the civil war. As for religious fractionalization, it can be looked at in two ways: that is, the population can be divided either into (i) the eighteen officially recognized religious communities, with an acknowledged dominance of the Maronite, Shia and Sunni communities, estimated at anywhere between 70 and 80 per cent of the total;[23] or (ii) a broad division between the Christian and Muslim communities which at the time of the outbreak of the civil war was in the region of 45–55 per cent respectively.[24] In the years before 1975 calls for more equitable sectarian power-sharing centred basically on increasing the political power of the Muslim community as a whole *vis-à-vis* the Maronite community. While increased participation for the Shia community in the formula for power-sharing was recognized, this was not to become explicit until the Taif Accord was agreed.[25]

With the above in mind, it may be tentatively postulated that Lebanon's religious division in the years preceding the war was akin to ethnic divisions in other countries that witnessed civil wars where the largest single group comprised over 45 per cent of the population. To that extent, and assuming the validity of the role of ethnicity in civil wars referred to above, religious fractionalization in Lebanon was conducive to the onset of the civil war. However, this postulate needs to be examined in the light of two issues before a final conclusion can be arrived at. The first is whether religious and ethnic fractionalization can be considered as substitutes for one another in terms of their influence as potential causes of civil wars. The second involves external intervention: in the Lebanese case, as in other countries that witnessed external interventions, the question is how important would religious fractionalization, on its own, have been as a cause of the civil war and/or its long duration in the absence of such interventions? This question needs to be fully investigated before a definitive answer can be given. We cannot address it here. As mentioned above, we propose to consider the sectarian and external elements as being jointly responsible for the onset of the conflict without at this stage being able to identify their respective influences separately.

Of course, implicit in the demand for redressing power-sharing among the main religious communities is a corresponding change in their relative share and involvement in public administration, and more generally the public sector. However, in the absence of fundamental reforms in public institutions, this would not necessarily imply a change in the nature of the Lebanese state or in national political behaviour.[26] At the same time, this should not obscure the fact that some of the actors involved in the conflict, both individuals and political groups, were motivated by non-sectarian ideologies and genuinely embraced a secular viewpoint. To them, the conflict was either a means to shift the sectarian order towards a more secular and equitable system, or an event that provided an opportunity to do so. As it turned out, however, this shift was not to materialize. If anything, the sectarian nature of political behaviour became more accentuated in the post-war era.

At the time the conflict began, Lebanon was enjoying one of the highest per capita income levels in the region, and among developing countries generally.[27] As we saw in Chapter 1, the national economy had been expanding at a relatively fast rate. Further, abundance of natural resource wealth (either renewable or non-renewable) and a readily lootable tax base were not important features of the Lebanese economy. Still, if these factors tend to downplay the role of economic causes in the outbreak of the civil conflict, economic and/or social factors played a supporting role in helping create a crisis situation.[28] The unevenness of development in Lebanon's regions before 1975 gave rise to a socio-sectarian division which, given the appropriate circumstances, could be exploited to support violent political change via the unleashing of sectarian conflicts. In the early 1970s rising inflationary pressures accentuated the explosive potential of these divisions. On the other hand, a vigorously expanding national economy that provided growing work opportunities had a tempering influence in that it tended to lessen the danger of a conflict based on mainly socio-economic factors that could be exploited along sectarian lines. Furthermore, given the limited role played by purely leftist parties and the workers' movement, class conflicts or the economic grievances of the underprivileged *vis-à-vis* the privileged groups were not an important element in inciting the civil war. Indeed, as it turned out, the underprivileged, on both sides of the sectarian/political divide, fought one another while various warlords (most of whom fought the war under 'national' slogans) exploited sectarian feelings to sustain their efforts in waging combat to achieve their own political/sectarian and economic ambitions.[29]

However, once the civil war broke out, greed, associated with the economic/financial benefits accruing to the warring parties and their leadership, increasingly became a major factor in sustaining it. The militias sought to enhance their economic/financial position by various means, including confiscation of private property and the imposition of taxes in the regions under their control. They became involved in the cultivation and trading of drugs, in contraband, in looting and in outright thievery. In 1975–76, the port of Beirut and the downtown district were pillaged; and bank robberies and fraudulent banking practices took place.

The militias stood to gain a great deal financially from the ongoing war.[30] There are no reliable and systematic data on the financial resources accruing to the militias during the civil conflict. Scattered estimates, however, are available (see Table 2.1). One source estimates that over the war period the militias were able to amass from the above-mentioned activities a total of $15 billion, quite apart from outside financial assistance.[31] A comparable estimate of $14.5 billion (for the aggregate turnover of the so-called black or informal economy) was published in the daily *Annahar*.[32] One study mentions that on the eve of the Israeli invasion in 1982, the PLO budget was close to that of the Lebanese state, and at the time of the PLO departure that year its investments (fixed and liquid) were estimated at about $1.5 billion.[33] Given also the external financial assistance provided by intervening outside powers, the major militias had sufficient resources at their disposal to finance their military and civilian operations, permitting, indeed inducing, them to sustain the long-lasting and profitable armed conflict. Along the way, the various militia leaderships and their henchmen accumulated substantial personal wealth. Estimates of the direct costs of the war vary. For a single day's fighting one source puts the cost at anywhere between $150,000 and $500,000.[34] Another source puts the cost of warfare at about $150 million to $1.5 billion a year.[35] Assuming an annual average of $800 million, this implies a total of a little less than $13 billion for the whole war period.

External interventions were also a key element in sustaining the war. They were manifested in several forms: provision of arms and substantial financing of the warring parties, as well as direct multiple military interventions on the part of Syria and Israel in support of one group or another, and at one point by Western powers in the form of a peacekeeping mission that failed to achieve its objectives. G. Corm estimates that foreign financial assistance to warring parties totalled twice the amount they raised locally, i.e. about $30 billion, if not more.[36] Some estimates put Libyan financial assistance to the PLO and their Lebanese allies at about $50 million a month, at least prior to 1982, which adds up to a total of $4.8 billion during the period 1975–82. For the whole war period, *Annahar* estimates the total of political money and military resources at about $10 billion.[37] Another source quotes an estimate of $300 million for the annual in-flow of political money prior to 1982, and a total of $2.7 billion.[38]

As the direct intervention of Syrian and Israeli troops in the war served opposing objectives, a modus vivendi was established which contributed to the prolongation of the war as long as the Lebanese parties concerned could not independently arrive at national reconciliation. Despite several attempts, this was not to materialize, and the 1989 Taif Accord was finally agreed upon only with outside pressure. But, as noted earlier, hostilities did not cease until a year later with the ousting of General Aoun from power in October 1990. The threatened Iraqi invasion of Kuwait, which actually took place in August 1990, intensified the interest of outside powers (both Arab and Western) in ending the civil war before the US-led campaign in the Gulf at the beginning of 1991.

The role of the Lebanese and Palestinian diasporas in the civil war is not readily quantifiable. The warring parties certainly attempted to secure assistance from their respective communities abroad. This support took the form of political lobbying and/or propaganda, as well as financial assistance. No estimates of the in-flow of financial resources are available, but it is known, for example, that Palestinians working in Kuwait were subject to a tax on their earnings earmarked for the PLO. I would conjecture that the impact of the Lebanese and Palestinian diasporas on the civil war was probably minor. Active support for the warring militias among the diaspora was in all likelihood confined to small groups.

The Lebanese case differs in a number of other respects from other civil war cases. The protagonists were not simply the state and a well-defined rebel group, as recent literature on civil wars postulates. As mentioned above, several parties to the conflict at one point or another fought among themselves. In practice, while the state took sides against the Palestinians and their Lebanese allies, the composition of the government continued to reflect the sectarian formula for power-sharing, and to include members who were sympathetic to the side opposing the government. Equally, to the extent that they were allowed to do so, governmental institutions continued to function in various parts of the country, and paid the wages of their employees irrespective of their political loyalties and the areas in which they served. Furthermore, external intervention at times shifted support from one side to another: for instance, the initial direct Syrian intervention in the early stages of the war was in support of traditional Maronite parties, but later shifted to the opposing groups. Israel, although initially acting only in support of traditional Christian parties that opposed the Palestinians, played one side of the conflict against the other and created a surrogate army in the south that included both Christians and Muslims.

Whatever the reasons behind the prolongation of the war may have been, the Taif Accord can be regarded only as an interim imposed arrangement for the settlement of the Lebanese crisis. In the long run, the stability of Lebanon will require a more fundamental political agreement than is provided for under this accord (see Chapter 5).

3 The political/military environment and the constraints on national economic performance: a summary view[39]

The conflict's impact on the Lebanese economy must be viewed in the context of three general observations concerning the economic system.

The first is that despite the political and military upheavals and the tremendous socio-economic changes that took place, the economic system remained essentially unchanged. It continued (and continues) to be characterized by a dominant private sector and a free foreign exchange market. The government came to assume a more active role in formulating economic policy, and budgetary operations, characterized by growing deficits, had an increasing impact on the national economy. This latter development, however, did not reflect a policy decision, but rather the government's inability to control the fiscal situation. Nevertheless, the continuous growth in budget deficits forced the authorities to take policy measures in an attempt to deal with the deteriorating fiscal situation.

The second general observation concerns the major political/military groups. They did not appear to differ substantially in their economic ideology. All of them seemed to accept the essentials of the existing system although their respective views of the role that should be played by the public sector may have differed.[40] Political platforms often made general calls for corrective action within the system, without necessarily challenging its basic characteristics. Such calls were not new and had been heard since the early days of independence, especially from intellectuals and academicians. Proposed reforms were intended to render the economic system more efficient and equitable, and to improve its performance through better management. The major obstacle to reform was (and, in large measure, remained at least until 2002) the inability of the ruling political body to move in this direction. Evolving conditions during the war period rendered the economic system less efficient and less equitable. Intermittent attempts were made to introduce socio-economic reforms and set up the institutional framework required for this purpose, but they were overtaken by the unsettled political/military situation in the country.

The third point pertains to the direct involvement of outside forces in the Lebanese conflict. Their presence did not lead to any interference in the workings of the economic system or economic policy decisions. This permitted the Lebanese authorities to try to cope with emerging economic difficulties without additional constraints on economic management being imposed from outside.

Bearing these three observations in mind, how has the political/military conflict affected Lebanon's economic performance? The answer may be summarized as follows.

First, the government lost control over public revenues, especially customs revenue, as a result of its inability to control existing ports, which came under the sway of political/military groups. The loss of customs revenue accruing to the government represented a major loss of budgetary revenue. In 1973–74 customs revenues comprised about one third of total budgetary revenues. In 1983–85 they accounted for about one quarter and in 1987–89 for 3 per cent of a much lower total, in real terms.

The government lost other revenues as well, including income taxes, which generally only salaried persons did not evade, and electricity fees, which the thousands of households that had illegally diverted electricity lines for private use did not pay, a phenomenon that continued in the post-civil-war period. Essentially, Lebanese budgetary policy became asymmetrical, and a new de facto fiscal law emerged: the government should spend but could not collect taxes, or at least the major portion of tax revenue due to it. This asymmetry between expenditure and revenues created a lopsided budget that affected the economy adversely and undermined the attempted reconstruction.

Second, the unsettled situation prevented the authorities from effectively carrying out their planned reconstruction programmes, and hindered the implementation of economic policies. Thus only very limited public restoration to damaged infrastructure and other real assets, such as factories, houses, schools, and so on, could be undertaken. The country's productive capacity was accordingly severely curtailed. The private sector, on the other hand, in many instances coped positively and courageously under adverse conditions. At various times a number of damaged factories were rebuilt while companies moved to safer areas. Nevertheless, the prevailing situation dampened private initiatives for reconstruction and caused many companies to close down or seek footholds outside the country (see below, pp. 61–4).

Third, the failure to resolve the conflict led, particularly from 1985 on, to the emergence of highly pessimistic expectations about the future. While prior to 1982 the country was politically fragmented, there was a general sense among various groups that reconciliation was still possible. The pessimism of the post-1982 period, combined with shrinking work opportunities, had, among other things, accelerated the emigration of skilled workers and professionals and the transfer of financial assets abroad (see 'The labour market: effects of the conflict', below).

Fourth, as the conflict greatly enfeebled central government, particularly in view of the political fragmentation that the country was to witness, its ability to carry out its functions was, in turn, substantially weakened. The erosion of central authority placed important additional constraints on the economic policy performance of the national authorities. One area where a semblance of national economic policy did remain is in the monetary arena: there was still a monetary authority (the Bank of Lebanon) capable of giving directives to the national banking system and, in principle, of devising a monetary policy. Generally, however, decisions concerning major economic and social issues could no longer be readily taken by central government, or could be taken only after protracted delays. Even then, their proper implementation was not assured.

In brief, the economic effects of the conflict were dealt with in the context of an unchanged open economic system. The policy measures that were undertaken were highly constrained by the prevailing political/military circumstances. As it turned out, at the external level the burden of economic adjustment was borne by a rapidly depreciating national currency. Its depreciation, in turn, led to increasing domestic inflationary pressures. Internally, the burden of adjustment was borne, among other factors, by the eroding purchasing power of fixed incomes, lower standards of living for the average citizen and increased emigration in search of employment opportunities elsewhere. These external and internal factors tended to reinforce one another (see below, section 4).

4 Economic and financial performance: impact of the war and the national response

As observed, the conflict passed through several stages. Open warfare raged periodically, engulfing various parts of the country at one time or another, with Beirut being the main centre of military action. The political aspects of the conflict manifested themselves almost continuously with brief periods of respite. The impact of the war on the national economy thus varied from one phase of the war to another, influenced by the prevailing intensity of the military/political conflict, its geographic location, the major actors involved, and the evolving private sector expectations concerning future prospects. Overall, the conflict manifested itself in various forms. Major economic manifestations included forgone production, inflationary pressures, budget deficits, depreciation of the national currency, private capital transfers abroad, closure or emigration of companies, manpower emigration, income and asset redistribution, market disruptions, de facto economic decentralization, and substantially reduced provision of governmental services. In what follows we shall first discuss the macroeconomic and financial performance of the national economy (section 4.1), and then consider the responses of the private and public sectors to the evolving situation (section 4.2). Social issues associated with the war are taken up in section 4.3.

Two preliminary observations are in order. The first is that a quantification of the economic impact of the war is severely constrained by data limitations, particularly as concerns the real sectors of the economy as well as asset and income distribution. Furthermore, for certain areas where data are available, their reliability may be questioned, as in the case of the constructed price indices. Banking data, as would be expected, are much more reliable, although even here the degree of disclosure of details was not necessarily up to recognized international standards.

The second observation is that while the record up to 1990 shows general economic deterioration encompassing periodic phases of relative revival, financial developments up to and including 1983 – as manifested in exchange rate movements, balance of payments developments and the rate of inflation – hardly reflected the impact of eight years of intermittent wars and continuous political conflicts. Overall, the pound tended to depreciate, but exchange rate fluctuations remained relatively limited. While inflationary pressures intensified, the average annual rate of inflation for the period remained in the range of 13–18 per cent. The financial picture worsened dramatically in 1984, a somewhat delayed consequence of the Israeli invasion that further aggravated the political/military conflict.

4.1 Economic performance
Destruction of production capacity, forgone production and the rate of growth

The amount of production forgone, as a result of the civil war, may be calculated as the cumulative loss of output over the war period, 1975–90, measured as the value of deviations of real Lebanese GDP from trend real GDP which it is assumed would have been attained in the absence of the war. One study that attempted this calculation postulates three trend growth

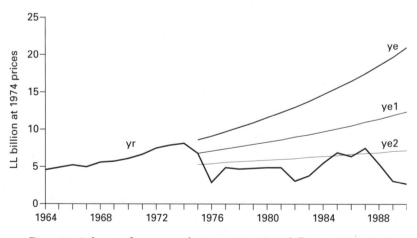

Figure 2.1 Lebanon: forgone production, 1975–90 (LL billion at 1974 prices)
Source: Based on data in Table 2.2

rates: 6, 4 and 2 per cent respectively. [41] The first is based on the actual aver-age annual rate of growth experienced in the pre-war period, 1964–74. The other two are arbitrarily postulated on the assumption of less robust growth trends. [42]

Figure 2.1 and Table 2.2 indicate the amount of forgone production for the period 1975–90 on the basis of the three postulated assumptions for the growth trend in the absence of the war.

Using the 6 per cent assumption, forgone cumulative production is esti-mated at LL144 billion at 1974 prices (equivalent to about $63 billion at the 1974 average exchange rate). The 4 per cent assumption yields forgone output of LL71 billion ($31 billion) and the 2 per cent assumption LL21 billion ($9 billion). Were we to adopt the middle 4 per cent rate of growth assumption, the actual level of real GDP in 1990 would stand at about one fifth of the estimated trend level. Were the lower rate of 2 per cent assumed, the actual real GDP for 1990 would stand at about one third of the trend level.

It should be borne in mind, of course, that over the whole war period real GDP varied considerably from one year to another. On the basis of the available indicators (which may reflect a large degree of error) GDP declined during 1975–76, recovered somewhat in 1977, following the initial two-year war, and grew slowly until 1981 but fell substantially in 1982, at the time of the Israeli invasion. For the 1983–90 period, changes in real GDP did not maintain a consistent trend. After rising in 1987–88, GDP fell back substan-tially in the subsequent two years that witnessed the war of 'liberation' and the military conflict between the army and the Lebanese forces in East Beirut and its suburbs. [43] Estimates of real per capita GDP indicate that its 1990 level was about one third of its 1974 level. [44]

No annual GDP estimates are available to indicate the structural evolution of the economy over the war period; instead we have to rely on a compari-son of available GDP estimates for the pre-war year of 1973 with that for the years 1988–90 (see Table 2.2). This comparison indicates that while the structure of the national economy did not undergo fundamental changes, a few notable sectoral developments occurred.

The most significant development concerned the contribution of non-finan-cial services to national income, which fell from about 27 per cent in 1973 to 17.5 per cent in 1988. This was partly compensated by the rise in the share of financial services from 4 per cent to 8 per cent respectively. Overall the share of the services sector fell from about 31 per cent in 1973 to 25.5 per cent. The share of the trade sector declined a little from 32 per cent to 28 per cent. Thus the trade and services orientation of the economy continued to be dominant, although the share of these sectors fell from about two-thirds in 1973 to about 54 per cent in 1998. Other noteworthy sectoral changes relate to the contributions of construction, manufacturing and administration. The share of construction rose from over 4 per cent to 10 per cent, and that of manufacturing from 14 per cent to 20.5 per cent. The share of administration fell from about 9 per cent to over 5 per cent.

The decline in the share of non-financial services may be attributable to several factors, including the fall in the share of rent as a result of rapid inflation as well as the decline in the tourist industry; the declining level of real income may have also caused a decline in expenditure on services. The fall in the share of public administration was due to the constraints that the war imposed on the public sector. Many governmental services were severely disrupted and partially replaced by private sector initiatives, although the bureaucracy remained basically unchanged. Rapid inflation led to a decline in real wages despite annual cost of living adjustments.

On the other hand, the rise in the contribution of manufacturing was due in part, at least since 1983, to the depreciation of the pound, which encouraged industrial exports. Furthermore, the military conflict led to politico-geographic decentralization. This may have helped partially shield industry from the havoc of war, which not only tended to flare up intermittently but was also confined, on the whole, to particular geographic areas.[45] The increase in the share of construction may be explained by the proliferation of construction activity – both authorized and unauthorized – in the various regions of the country, and especially in areas then considered relatively safe.

Extrapolations made for 1989 and 1990 reveal the impact of the war conditions that prevailed in those two years in the larger Beirut area. Most notably we observe a drop in the share of manufacturing to 14 per cent and the rise in the share of administration to over 15 per cent. Manufacturing suffered as the intra-Maronite conflict of 1990 took place in the eastern suburbs of Beirut with their relatively heavy industrial concentration.[46]

The labour market: effects of the conflict[47]

The civil war affected the evolution of the Lebanese labour market in several important ways. Five factors will be noted: (a) accelerated emigration; (b) forced internal migration; (c) emerging economic imbalances (i.e. generally the deteriorating economic and financial situation); (d) wage policy; and (e) the role of the labour unions.

Historically, Lebanon has been an exporter of manpower, the waves of emigration varying in intensity from one period to another. Not surprisingly, the civil war period witnessed extensive emigration of Lebanese residents. Estimates vary from 500,000 to about 895,000.[48] Obviously the war conditions and their attendant casualties and atrocities constituted the most significant factor in inducing emigration. In addition, however, the search for work opportunities abroad was an important and related factor, particularly in the second half of the 1970s when the oil boom attracted many workers, technicians and professionals to the Gulf region. The emigrants, some of whom returned to Lebanon after 1990, included a good proportion of skilled or semi-skilled workers, professionals or those with a university education. For the period 1975–94, it is estimated that the latter category constituted about 25 per cent of the total.[49] Accelerated emigration tended to check the rising level of unemployment engendered by the ongoing civil war and the related drop in economic activity. Available estimates of open unemployment for the period 1987–92 have ranged from 10 to 35 per cent.[50] By comparison, the estimated rate of unemployment in 1970 was a little over 8 per cent.

Whatever the actual rate towards the end of the civil war period, the employment or unemployment effect of emigration was not evenly distributed among various occupational groups. To illustrate, a large portion of emigrants, especially to the Gulf region, were initially semi-skilled workers in addition to professionals and businessmen. Subsequently, highly skilled workers and technicians tended to emigrate. The emigration of skilled workers and technicians led to shortages on the local market for various skills and a consequent rise in their level of remuneration. Furthermore, most emigrants were from the younger age group, which implied a lower rate of entry into the labour market than would otherwise have been the case. Also, the global economic activity rate of the emigrants is estimated to have been higher than that of the resident population. This in turn meant a deceleration in the rate of growth in the supply of manpower resources.

Other factors that checked the rise in the rate of unemployment included the prolongation by the authorities of the required years of schooling, the emergence of parallel or informal economic activities, expanding public sector employment despite or perhaps due to the war conditions, and the rise in the rate of global activity (the ratio of the workforce to the population).[51] Bearing this in mind, the estimated rate of unemployment of 10 per cent arrived at in a 1987 study might not be unreasonable.[52]

It is worth noting that before 1975 emigration was counterbalanced by in-flows of foreign manpower into Lebanon, comprising basically non-skilled workers. Available studies indicate that in the early 1970s non-Lebanese workers, including those registered with the Ministry of Labour and Social Affairs as well as those not registered, constituted about one fifth of the total labour force. They were mostly Palestinians or Syrians working in the construction sector and in agricultural activities of a seasonal nature. With the outbreak of the civil war, although the in-flow did not stop, the overall number of registered non-Lebanese workers declined, only to rise again after the settlement of the conflict.[53] Presumably, the same pattern applied to non-registered workers.

Prior to 1975 internal migration, principally towards the capital and other cities, was primarily induced by the search for work opportunities.[54] With the outbreak of the conflict, internal migration was primarily a result of the forceful removal of residents from one region to another. One study estimates that during the period 1975–87 the number of people forced to leave their place of residence as a result of acts of hostility was about 625,000.[55] By 1990, this figure, according to the Ministry of Refugees, had risen to about 810,000, including temporarily displaced persons, as a result of the 1989–90 conflict. Forced internal migration and the emergence of quasi-independent regions under the influence of the different militias at war with one another resulted in the fragmentation of the national labour market. This disruption of the normal flow of labour within the country led to the emergence of local labour markets that, in turn, adversely affected economic activity, especially agriculture, in those regions. Indeed, as would be expected, the rate of economic activity of those forcefully evicted declined in comparison with the national average. One symptom of this phenomenon was the relatively higher rate of unemployment among the displaced, which acted as a further inducement to emigration.

The deterioration in the economic situation, manifested in the drop of real national income accompanied by the disruption of economic activities and the emergence of substantial inflationary pressures (see the section on financial performance below), led to a general fall in the rate of growth in the demand for labour, at least until the mid-1980s. Subsequently, as noted below, the decline in the real wage induced substitution of labour for capital. Emigration in search of employment opportunities abroad did not arrest the drop in real wages that encouraged wage earners to seek multiple jobs in compensation for the decline in family earned income.

The government's wage policy relied on the periodic adjustment of nominal wages to compensate for price inflation. Agreement was usually reached after protracted negotiations with both the General Syndicate of Labour and

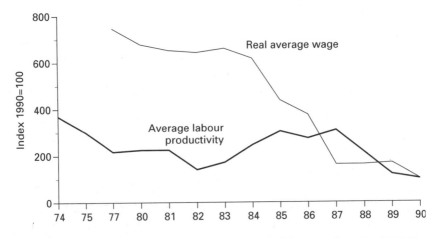

Figure 2.2 Lebanon: indices of real wages and average labour productivity, 1975–90 (1990 = 100) *Source*: Based on data in Table 2.4

the Association of Employees. Wage adjustments, however, failed, especially after the mid-1980s, to catch up with the inflation rate, leading to a fall in real wages.[56] It is reported that the index of the average real wage fell from 747 for 1977 to 100 for 1990 (the base year), representing a factor of decline of about 7.5 times[57] (see Figure 2.2 and Table 2.4).

The drop in real wages negatively influenced the rate of supply of skilled labour, which sought employment outside Lebanon. However, the declining real wages did not have the same effect as far as generally unskilled workers were concerned. Instead, the latter resorted to multiple jobs. For the same reason family members who previously had not worked sought employment, under the prevailing circumstances, in order to raise the level of family earnings. Consequently the supply of unskilled labour tended to increase instead of decrease as a result of the drop in real wages.[58] Furthermore, when inflation began to accelerate after 1983 and the level of real wages declined, there was an increasing demand for unskilled labour. Also, a process of substitution of labour for capital took place, induced not only by the fall in real wages but also by the lack of capital renovation and investment as a result of the war. The demand for skilled labour was not significantly affected by the changes in real wages.

The influence of the labour unions on the labour market manifested itself in three ways. The first is their annually negotiated wage adjustments, the second their success in preventing mass lay-offs of labour and third the ability of sectoral labour unions to achieve (through separate collective agreements with the employers) more favourable terms for their own membership than those negotiated by the General Syndicate of Labour. The effect on the labour market was to create rigidities in both the supply and demand sides of labour. Employers could not readily lay off workers when output declined and profit margins shrank. The negotiated collective agreements also raised the average cost of labour beyond what it would have been in their absence. However, while recruitment of new labour was constrained in so far as old workers could not be laid off, the collective agreements protected labour from arbitrary lay-offs and an unregulated wage policy.

In brief, the interacting influences of the above factors on the labour market during the civil war may be summarized as follows. On the supply side, the war fragmented the national market in favour of regional (but still connected) markets; national labour supply and demand were, in turn, fragmented into 'regional' labour supply and demand. Economic deterioration dampened the general demand for unskilled labour, especially up to the mid-1980s. On the other hand, the emerging 'regional markets' induced demand for various categories of skilled labour. The decline in the supply of unskilled workers through emigration or recruitment by the militias was partly counterbalanced by the in-flow of non-Lebanese labour. Thus shortages emerged primarily in the market for skilled rather than unskilled labour. The sharp drop in real wages encouraged the substitution of labour for capital and induced workers to seek multiple jobs. It also encouraged skilled workers and professionals to seek employment outside Lebanon. The overall picture that emerged was one of excess demand for skilled workers, which raised their level of remuneration in real terms, and excess supply of unskilled workers, which tended to reduce their remuneration in real terms. Overall, available estimates show that the labour force declined during 1975–80 and then rose slowly through 1990 at an annual average of less than 2 per cent. Also, on the basis of available estimates, labour productivity declined from 1974 to 1982, and then rose to 1985 only to decline again to 1990. Overall the index of labour productivity declined from 370 for 1974 to 100 for 1990 (base year) – see Figure 2.2 and Table 2.4. In securing minimum wage adjustments and preventing mass lay-offs, the labour unions managed to introduce some rigidity into both the supply of and demand for labour. On the other hand, they offered partial protection to workers in a deteriorating economic situation.

4.2 Financial performance
The macro-financial environment

Inflationary pressures started to build up prior to the outbreak of the civil war: during the period 1972–74, the annual inflation rate averaged about 8 per cent (see Chapter 1).

The outbreak of the war did not initially lead to rapidly mounting inflation or currency depreciation, as was to happen in later years. Indeed, from 1975 to 1982, inflationary pressures were moderate. Available estimates indicate annual rates of 8–13 per cent. The nominal exchange rate of the pound depreciated gradually over this period with relatively limited fluctuations in its trend. Except for 1976, the balance of payments recorded overall surpluses to 1982. In the aftermath of the Israeli invasion and the consequent intensification of the political/military conflict, the financial situation began to deteriorate dramatically to 1987. A modest improvement experienced in the first half of 1988 was soon disrupted by the political deadlock that resulted from the inability of parliament to elect a new president of the republic, and the consequent military clashes which ended with the departure of General Aoun in October 1990.

1975–82/3: resisting monetary collapse Lebanon's financial performance during this period, while suffering from a number of drawbacks, was superior to its economic performance. Except for 1976, the Lebanese balance of payments was in overall surplus.[59] Helping to sustain this surplus, despite growing trade deficits, were emigrant remittances, especially from the Gulf region, and the capital in-flows to support Palestinian and Lebanese militias referred to in section 2 above. The in-flow of emigrant remittances has been estimated as rising from about $300 million in 1975 to $2,000 million in 1982.[60] Whereas the foreign financing of the war in Lebanon had a positive impact on the Lebanese pound during this period, the conflict itself was the cause of the outflow of civilian capital and the departure of both Lebanese and non-Lebanese enterprises from Lebanon.

Further, the purposes of financing should be considered. Emigrant remittances and other in-flows in support of civilian causes contributed to the sustenance of domestic economic activity. In contrast, the financing of the war led to the destruction of the national economy and its physical assets. Similarly, the notion that Palestinian and Lebanese politico-military organizations provided employment in civilian and non-civilian pursuits and hence supported the national economy is one that cannot be given credence. This presumably positive economic aspect of their presence does not begin to compare with the negative economic aspect of the conflict in which they were engaged, resulting in tremendous human losses and havoc in the national economy.

Although the fluctuations of the pound – measured in terms of the US dollar – tended to increase, on the whole its movements were moderate. Volatility (measured as the ratio of the monthly difference between the minimum and maximum rate quotations to the monthly average exchange rate) was generally less than 4 per cent up to and including 1981 (see Table 2.8a). Following the Israeli invasion of June 1982, rate volatility increased, reaching 14 per cent in September of that year and tending to decline later on. The Bank of Lebanon intervened on the foreign exchange market to smooth out fluctuations and maintain orderly market conditions. At times, the bank's intervention was intended to secure foreign exchange to cover public sector foreign obligations. Nevertheless, the net foreign assets of the Central Bank (excluding gold) rose from $1,218 million at the end of 1975 to $2,597 million at the end of 1982,

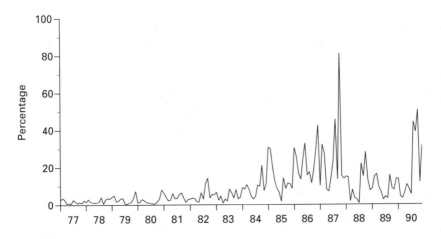

Figure 2.3 Lebanon: exchange rate volatility, 1975–90 (monthly maximum–minimum/average rate) (per cent) *Source*: Based on data in Table 2.8a.

falling to $1,897 million at the end of 1983. Similarly the net foreign assets of the banking system increased from $2,156 million to $4,515 million, falling back to $3,574 million – see Figure 2.4 and Table 2.5.

Despite the balance of payments surpluses, however, the pound, measured in terms of the US dollar, tended to depreciate (except in 1978), notably in the period 1979–82. The rate averaged LL4.7 per US dollar in 1982 and LL4.3 in 1981, compared to LL2.9 in 1976 and LL2.45 in 1975, an annual average depreciation of 7.5 per cent (Table 2.8).[61] This lack of correspondence between balance of payments and exchange rate movements (first noted in the internal reports of the Bureau of Economic Policy Coordination – see below) was largely due to the increasing switching of currencies between resident-held accounts denominated in national and foreign currencies respectively. This movement, then usually from Lebanese pound to foreign currency accounts, is not recorded in balance of payments statistics. Thus, if the total currency balance were considered, i.e. including conversions between resident accounts, the overall foreign currency picture would change. As an illustration, for the period 1979–81 during which the Lebanese pound depreciated (particularly in 1981), while the balance of payments recorded surpluses, the overall currency balance incurred deficits.[62] The phenomena of currency substitution and dollarization assumed increasing importance in later years of the civil war (see below).

Given the government's inability to collect tax revenue, especially customs duties, the fiscal situation came under increasing pressure. The estimated budget deficit increased sharply in 1976 as a result of a substantial decline in revenue collection. Following the temporary cessation of the war at the end of 1976, the fiscal situation improved in 1977, but thereafter the budget came under mounting pressure as a result of revenue shortfalls. The overall deficit increased from 28 per cent of estimated actual expenditure in 1978 to 38 per cent in 1979, 51 per cent in 1980 and 71 per cent in 1982, declining to 63 per cent in 1983, when actual tax receipts (including customs duties) increased substantially in comparison with the previous year – see Table 2.6. One principal means of financing the deficit was (and remains) treasury bills taken up by the commercial banks. Another source was Bank of Lebanon financing. As a result, internal public debt rose rapidly, standing at LL53.1 billion ($9.68 billion) at the end of 1983 (roughly twice the estimated GDP in nominal terms for that year), of which LL15.8 billion ($2.87 billion), or 30 per cent of the total, represented outstanding treasury bills.

The financing of growing budgetary deficits via the issuance of treasury bills amounted, in practice, to the diversion of an increasing share of domestic credit towards the public sector (the crowding-out effect). Net claims on the government increased gradually from a negligible amount at the end of 1975 to about 30 per cent at the end of 1982 and 1983, and were to continue their rise in subsequent years. During 1975–82 credit to the private sector increased annually by about 21 per cent, while total domestic credit increased at an annual rate of about 30 per cent. This compares with an average rate of growth in Lebanese pound denominated deposits of about 24 per cent. It thus appears that pressure on the economy from domestic credit expansion emanated primarily from growing budgetary deficits. All the above rates exceeded the estimated average annual rate of inflation for the period and hence both deposits and credit grew in real terms. The issuance of treasury bills afforded the commercial banks a safe outlet for excess reserves. It was also a profitable outlet since the interest rates these bills carried were relatively remunerative. This was an important development at a time when the prevailing situation imposed constraints on domestic outlets. Indeed, given these constraints and the motivation to reap rapid profits, credit expansion was flawed: some banks engaged in speculative real estate and foreign exchange activities which the Central Bank could not effectively control (see below, p. 62.)

Inflation intensified during the 1975–83 period, partly reflecting international trends. Various internal and external factors contributed to this inflation, including a rapid expansion in domestic expenditure (especially expenditure associated with growing budget deficits), cost increases caused by wartime disruptions, the impact of international inflation, and the depreciation of the Lebanese pound. Although no official estimates of the inflation rate have been made, unofficial estimates exist. According to the cost-of-living index compiled by the General Confederation of Workers in Lebanon, the annual average rate of inflation for the period 1975–77 was about 20 per cent. It fell to a little over 10 per cent in 1978, increased to about 24 per cent in 1982, and stood at 6.6 per cent in 1983. The average annual increase for the whole period was about 18 per cent. According to another index compiled by the Chamber of Commerce and Industry, the annual average rate of inflation was slightly over 14 per cent in 1980, 16 per cent in 1981, below 14 per cent in 1982, and 7 per cent in 1983. In sum, the average annual rate of inflation in the 1980–83 period appears to have ranged from 13 to 18 per cent, but declined significantly in 1983.

1984–90: currency depreciation and inflation The Israeli invasion brought with it heightened political and military turmoil that eventually led to a sharp deterioration in Lebanon's financial performance, and a crisis of confidence in the pound. While available indicators of real GDP point to a rising level in the mid-1980s, any improvement in the real sectors was overshadowed by the sharply deteriorating financial situation.

The underlying causes of the dramatic deterioration vary. The principal ones relate to (i) the continued uncontrolled rapid growth in budget deficits with all their adverse consequences; (ii) waning confidence or rising waves of pessimism regarding the future of Lebanon generated by the ensuing military/political conflict, compounded towards the end of the period by the inability to elect a new president of the republic and the emergence of the two-government situation; and (iii) the inability of the authorities concerned to implement their policy decisions effectively in the context of the evolving political/military situation.

While the imbalance in budgetary operations had already begun with the outbreak of the conflict, its magnitude increased considerably in later years, particularly from 1984, when the estimated ratio of budgetary deficit to public expenditure reached over 80 per cent, climbing to over 90 per cent in 1988 and falling back to about 84 per cent in 1990. Deficit financing was by far the most important source of the expansion of the Lebanese pound component of domestic liquidity. Of total governmental expenditure during 1985–90, wages and salaries are estimated to have accounted for about 25 per cent, domestic interest payments for 20 per cent (they exceeded governmental receipts), petroleum subsidies for 13 per cent, extra budgetary advances (i.e. transfers to municipalities and other public sector bodies) for 19 per cent, and capital expenditures for less than 6 per cent.[63] Continuous reliance on treasury bills and Bank of Lebanon financing raised the outstanding internal public debt to LL1,483 billion at the end of 1990 (of which about LL63 billion constituted outstanding short-term treasury bills), compared to LL22 billion at the end of 1983. However, in dollar equivalents the outstanding debt declined during the same period from $3.96 billion to $1.76 billion. The reason is that the rate of depreciation of the pound exceeded the rate of debt accumulation in pounds. Combined with rising pessimistic expectations, the continued injection of liquidity via budget deficits led to an acceleration in currency substitution (use of the dollar as a means of exchange) and dollarization (use of the dollar as a unit of account and store of value), which, in turn, led to increasing pressure on the pound[64] (see Table 2.7).

The monetary authorities attempted, as explained below, to cope with

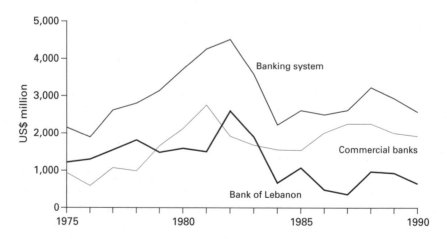

Figure 2.4 Lebanon: net foreign assets of the banking system, 1975–90
Source: Based on data in Table 2.5.

this situation. But in the absence of an appropriate fiscal policy and more generally the inability of the central government to implement the required fiscal action, monetary measures on their own were insufficient, particularly when effective control over commercial bank operations could not always be exercised. The deterioration itself gave rise to further adverse expectations, especially the belief that national reconciliation did not appear attainable prior to the Taif Accord.

The manifestation of the financial imbalance during the period under consideration may be summarized as follows:

First, for the period as a whole, the overall balance of payments was in deficit (of more than 1 billion dollars), with modest surpluses being registered for 1985 and 1987 and a larger surplus for 1988. The net foreign assets of the banking system (excluding gold) declined from the equivalent of $3,575 million at the end of 1983 to $2,496 million at the end of 1986, rising to $3,227 million at the end of 1988 and falling again to $2,569 million at the end of 1990 (see Figure 2.4 and Table 2.5). Contributing to the overall deterioration in balance of payments performance was a substantial reduction in Lebanese workers' remittances from the Gulf region, as well as the declining in-flow of financial support for Palestinian organizations in Lebanon in the aftermath of the departure of the PLO. In addition, as already noted, continued switching of funds from the Lebanese pound to foreign-denominated resident accounts put further pressure on the pound.

Second, this pressure was reflected in rapid exchange rate fluctuations and depreciation of the pound, beginning especially in the last quarter of 1984. Comparing annual averages (LL in terms of the US dollar), the pound depreciated by about 30 per cent in 1984, about 150 per cent in 1985, 134 per

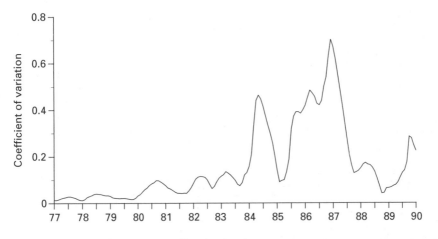

Figure 2.5 Lebanon: co-efficient of exchange rate variation, 1975–90
Source: Based on data in Table 2.8b.

cent in 1986 and 485 per cent in 1987. The rate of depreciation decelerated in the subsequent three years to 82, 21 and 41 per cent respectively. Thus for 1990 the exchange rate averaged about LL702 per US dollar compared to an average of LL6.5 per US dollar for 1984. For the same two years, the index of nominal effective exchange rate (with 1990 as a base year) fell from 14,571 to 100 (see Table 2.5). Equally significant, the depreciation of the pound was often accompanied by rapid fluctuations around its trend: the monthly coefficient of variation rose to a peak of 70 per cent for December 1986–November 1987 (see Table 2.8b). It tended to decrease in the following three years but the pound fluctuations became much more volatile than in the pre-1984 period (Figure 2.5). Estimates for the index of the real effective exchange rate reveal a lower rate of depreciation for the Lebanese pound than that recorded by the index of the nominal effective exchange rate (see Table 2.5).[65] To the extent that the former index is reliable, this indicates that inflation was one factor, among others, which weakened the pound.

Third, growth in Lebanese denominated deposits and in domestic credit lagged in real terms, especially in 1985–87. The fall in the real value of deposits is partly explained by the continuous switch from Lebanese pound to foreign currency denominated deposits, whether held in the Lebanese banking system or transferred abroad (see Figure 2.6 and Table 2.7). The fall in the value of domestic credit is partly explained by the uncertainties of the prevailing situation and the reduction in domestic outlets. Indeed, the issue of non-performing bank debt assumed an increasing importance during this period – bank loans had to be rolled over since debtors could not settle them owing to the war-related losses they had incurred. Some debtors capable of repaying may have refused to do so, taking advantage of the prevailing situation. Official

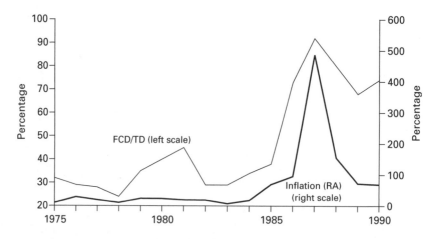

Figure 2.6 Lebanon: inflation rate and ratio of foreign currency deposits to total deposits, 1975–90 *Source*: Based on data in Tables 2.5 and 2.7.

attempts to deal with the situation were made, but in practice it was left to each bank to reach settlement with individual clients (see below).

Fourth, inflation accelerated. Available estimates show that the consumer price index for Beirut (using period averages) rose by 15 per cent in 1984, 54 per cent in 1985, 95 per cent in 1986 and 450 per cent in 1987, falling back to 70–75 per cent in 1989–90 (see Figure 2.6 and Table 2.5). Of the various causes behind the accelerating inflation, two related ones should be highlighted: the rapidly growing budget deficits and the dramatic depreciation of the pound. A depreciating national currency quickly translated itself into consumer price increases. However, the reverse, i.e. an appreciation of the pound, while influencing the rate of inflation, did not seem to apply with equal force.[66] As pointed out earlier, the Lebanese currency came to lose much of its attribute as a store of value. Indeed, beginning in 1987 it became common practice to price imported goods on the basis of the dollar, and in certain instances even require payment in dollars instead of the national currency.

In brief, the national economy during the period 1984–90 was characterized by generally worsening domestic imbalances (the possible modest improvement in GDP in specific years such as 1987/8 due to an improved trade balance in real terms notwithstanding), combined with a rapidly deteriorating external position in the context of an unsettled political situation. The basic elements of a sustained macroeconomic disequilibrium became firmly established with domestic and external imbalances reinforcing one another.

The banking sector

The banking sector has occupied a vital position in the Lebanese economy since the end of the Second World War. By traditional measures of monetization (e.g. ratios of deposit, credit or financial assets to GDP), the national economy is highly monetized even by comparison with the industrial economies, hence the important role in the economy of banking and money markets. Indeed, prior to the civil war Beirut was a regional financial and entrepôt centre. This position was greatly diminished during the war period, and it remains to be seen to what extent, and in what ways, Beirut will be able to regain its importance as a regional financial centre, in competition with other centres in the region which have emerged since 1975. The Beirut capital market, on the other hand, has traditionally been small and limited. Minor steps were taken in the pre-war period to promote financial deepening; during the war period the responsible authorities could not initiate any serious moves in this direction. In the mid-1990s legislative measures were initiated for the purpose of developing the Beirut financial market, in recognition of the important potential role it could play in mobilizing financial resources for various economic and developmental purposes (see below). There is a long way to go in this regard. In terms of capitalization, Beirut ranked as the smallest of the formal Arab emerging markets as of the end of 2002.[67]

Given the importance of the banking sector in the Lebanese economy, it is useful to highlight its evolution and performance during the war period.[68] For this purpose, we shall again consider the two periods 1975–82 and 1983–90 respectively. Banking performance paralleled, more or less, general financial performance. During the first period, despite all the destruction and losses incurred, the Lebanese banking sector managed to adapt to the war situation and expand its activities. In contrast, banking performance during the second period was adversely affected, and a banking crisis eventually emerged with which the authorities had to cope (see below).

The 1975–82 period was characterized by three important developments. The first was the increase in the number of banks from seventy-nine in 1974 to eighty-seven in 1982. This expansion was made possible after the issuance of Legislative Decree no. 77 (27 June 1977), which ended the freeze on the opening of new banks and branches of foreign banks that had been in force for the previous ten years.[69] On the other hand, seven jointly owned Lebanese–foreign banks and one long-term credit bank closed down. The second development was the proliferation of bank branches outside Beirut in response to the destruction of the Beirut commercial district.[70] This development enabled the banks to meet new needs that arose as a result of the destruction of the downtown district and the emergence of new commercial markets and banking centres in regions outside the capital. The third development was that Lebanese banks attempted to compensate for the loss of Beirut's position as a regional financial centre by expanding their activities abroad. They opened branches, subsidiaries and representative offices in over twenty countries to serve the Lebanese business community that had left the country.[71]

What is noteworthy is that over this period banking activity expanded in real terms. The share of deposits denominated in foreign currency (primarily the US dollar) in total deposits remained unchanged over the period as a whole, standing at about 29 per cent at the end of both 1974 and 1982.[72] Equally significant is the fact, noted earlier, that the real rate of growth in deposits outpaced that of credit expansion to the private sector. Although the capital adequacy ratio dropped from 4 per cent at the end of 1974 to 3.5 per cent at the end of 1982, it remained within acceptable international norms.[73] One study indicates that the annual growth rates of selected banking indicators (measured in US dollars) for the period 1974–82, while tending to decline somewhat, compared favourably with the growth rates in the pre-civil-war period, 1964–74.[74]

Several factors contributed to the positive banking performance during this period of intense political/military conflict. Among others were: (i) the gradual movement of the pound and its relatively limited variability despite the prevailing difficult political/economic circumstances; this tended to slow down (though not halt) the conversion of pound denominated deposits into foreign currency denominated deposits; (ii) the pick-up in economic activity, manifested in the rising level of real GDP, after the two-year war up to 1982; (iii) the relocation of business and banking activities to regions considered relatively more safe, offering less disruptive work conditions; and (iv) general expectations on the part of the Lebanese (false, as it eventually turned out) that the conflict would be settled before too long, especially after the end of the two-year war and the beginning of the attempts at reconstruction and the implementation of macroeconomic policies intended to cope with the emerging financial situation. The adverse effects of the conflict on the national economy, including the departure of foreign companies, had not yet deeply influenced national economic resistance to the evolving situation. It is as though the possibility of a national settlement – albeit with the intermediation, if not direct sponsorship, of the major neighbouring Arab countries and the international powers concerned – was still a dominant national view.

The almost continuous deterioration experienced in 1983–90 eventually took its toll on the evolution and performance of the banking sector. Foreign-owned banks decided to leave the country and most representative offices closed down. However, Lebanese banking capital moved in to replace the retreating foreign banks and jointly owned Lebanese–foreign banks.[75] Banking activity suffered. In dollar equivalent terms it registered a substantial retreat. At the end of 1990 total assets (LL8,708 million or $1.03 billion) represented 57 per cent of their 1982 value, their lowest during the civil war period. Similarly, deposits stood at 62 per cent of their 1982 value, domestic credit at 41 per cent and capital at 11 per cent respectively.[76] Total shareholders' equity dropped to 0.68 per cent of total assets at the end of 1990 after attaining an all-time low of 0.24 per cent at the end of 1987. Various ratios that measure the solvency and capital adequacy of the banking system declined substantially in this period.[77] The Banking Control Commission attempted to partially deal with this situation by repeatedly recommending to the Lebanese banks that they add yearly profits to their free reserves. In a circular, no. 435 issued on 26 October 1983, the Central Bank set a new liquidity ratio (defined as capital funds divided by total assets plus engagement by guarantees and endorsement) with a grace period for compliance up to 30 June 1986. But it seems most banks, if not all, could not cope with this requirement. Capital and reserves continued to be denominated in Lebanese pounds against a background of continuous depreciation of the pound. This implied a sharp erosion in the value of assets denominated in pounds, with a corresponding decline in their share of total assets which had declined to a record low of 8 per cent at the end of 1987, rising to 26 per cent at the end of 1990. Under the circumstances, the Bankers Association opposed this measure and submitted proposals for modifying the calculation of the ratio; in practice, despite frequent consultations between the two parties, their opposing views could not be reconciled; in practice the solvency ratio, as defined in circular no. 435, was not enforced.[78] This matter was taken up again in the post-civil-war period.

At the beginning of 1988 the banking sector witnessed a major crisis with the failure of Al Mashreq Bank, the second-largest operating bank in the country, to meet withdrawal demands for deposits. To avert the possible spread of the crisis the Central Bank decided to assume the assets and liabilities of the holding company owned by Al Mashreq, along with other banks and financial institutions, and to arrive at a settlement of the outstanding financial issues created by the Al Mashreq debacle.[79] More generally, by this time the banking climate had sunk to a low ebb and a number of minor banks began to face a crisis situation. External and internal factors were responsible for this situation. Externally, the continuing civil war led to a substantial reduction in the activities of the banking sector, as well as a dramatic depreciation of the pound. In turn this led to increased risks, a freeze on new lending and a rise in costs. Internally, some banks suffered from bad management owing to lack of expertise and/or appropriate ethical conduct. Accordingly, they became exposed to various malpractices: fraud, sometimes outright theft, unjustifiable and excessive positions in foreign exchange holdings, speculation against the pound and/or other infringements of the Code on Money and Credit and Central Bank directives. These practices were facilitated by the lack of competent internal audit in some of these banks, as well as the inability of the Banking Control Commission, particularly in 1988–89, to enforce bank legislation and directives properly.[80] In the meantime, in an effort to salvage the situation, the Central Bank extended liquidity to commercial banks short of cash, initially with shareholders' real estate serving as collateral, with the option of restitution within a two-year period. It is estimated that the bank extended the equivalent of $140 million to five commercial banks that faced liquidity shortages.[81] But as the crisis broadened to reach branches outside Lebanon, and in view of the Central Bank's inability to inject funds indefinitely into the banking sector, a wave of bank failures followed in 1989–90 involving fourteen other (fortunately) small and medium-size banks.[82] The issue of bank reform was addressed shortly after the civil war ended.

4.3 Responses

The private sector

Though weakened by the long civil war, the Lebanese private sector proved to be resilient. In various ways it responded positively to the challenges posed by Lebanon's difficult situation. Some enterprises, particularly foreign ones, moved out of the country in 1975–76, but others continued to operate in Lebanon despite the physical damage or financial losses incurred. Many firms eventually established footholds outside Lebanon while maintaining domestic operations – witness the internationalization of Lebanese banking activities. As observed earlier, the destruction of Beirut's central commercial district led to the proliferation of local or regional business centres. Decentralization of business activity, in turn, encouraged a number of firms to open regional branches, permitting them to cope with fragmented consumer markets created by de facto partition.

Another aspect of the private sector's positive response was the unwillingness of thousands of individuals to remain forcibly idle in the shrinking domestic market. They opted instead to seek work abroad, especially in the Gulf region, which absorbed large numbers of skilled workers and professionals. The Lebanese economy thereby lost their services, but it benefited from their large remittances (especially before 1982), which helped support the balance of payments; work abroad (in many instances akin to temporary emigration) helped restrain the rise in the level of domestic unemployment.

The private sector did not generally abandon the pound prior to 1982, the moderate switching during the period of Lebanese pound resident accounts into foreign currency accounts notwithstanding. There was sufficient confidence in the pound to sustain its relative stability, or, to put it differently, non-collapse. Until then, outstanding deposits in Lebanese pounds had grown in real terms. Currency substitution was not accompanied by massive capital transfers abroad. Indeed, while some of the currency shifts were motivated by precautionary considerations, they were also influenced by purely financial factors, such as the widening, during this period, of the interest rate differential in favour of foreign currencies. A large proportion of the deposits switched into foreign currency denominations were held in the Lebanese banking system and not transferred abroad. Loss of confidence began in the wake of the Israeli invasion and accelerated as of 1984. As already pointed out, the rate of growth in Lebanese pound denominated deposits and in domestic credit fell behind the inflation rate, and concomitantly the rate of switching national currency deposits into foreign currency deposits accelerated with an increasing proportion transferred abroad.[83] The rapid depreciation of the pound beginning in 1984 was at once a cause and a consequence of waning confidence.

On the other hand, the economic resilience of the private sector under prevailing conditions carried with it a substantial social cost. With governmental authority greatly weakened, the proliferation of business activities was unregulated. Sometimes this amounted to de facto expropriation by private groups and individuals of public and private property, which in turn caused further deterioration of existing facilities. Uncontrolled trade flourished, depriving the government of revenue, while unchecked growth in suburban areas widened the belt of poverty around Beirut and other cities. The supremacy of private over public interests (already a strongly established tradition) was further strengthened, with increased adverse social consequences which ordinary citizens had to bear.

In addition to the economic resiliency of private enterprises, the role of various private civil groups and NGOs in attempting – sometimes successfully and sometimes not – to maintain a semblance of social order should not go unremarked. Such groups sprang up in different parts of the country, which progressively came to be divided along sectarian lines imposed by the warring factions. There remained many areas, however, with multi-religious groupings where civic social action was undertaken without regard to religious affiliation in the interests of what was perceived to be the good of the community in the face of militia power. The action of many of these civic groups focused on social issues: e.g. first-aid training, coping with water and wheat shortages, maintaining ambulances to move injured civilians to hospitals, attempting to minimize the threat of occupation of vacated apartments by members of various militias as a result of war conditions, establishing contact with militia leaders to try to solicit their cooperation in maintaining a minimum level of social order and to protest when major breakdowns took place as a result of militia action. It is not uncommon that during periods of civil strife private civic groups go into action to help maintain social order, often in support of the de facto factions in power. In the context of the Lebanese civil war, characterized by religious antagonisms, it is the efforts of civil groups in multi-religious communities towards maintaining a working society which, in particular, should be recognized. Their influence in their respective societies may have been limited – there is perhaps no way one can quantify it. But it was highly significant in terms of the goals they set for themselves and the activities they undertook, in conditions of sectarian strife.[84]

The public sector: policy responses

Social issues apart, the civil war created a two-dimensional policy problem that had to be addressed. The first dimension concerned the external policy stance of the government. There was implicit official unanimity, or near-unanimity, of belief among the responsible authorities (as well as among academicians and policy advisers) that, despite external pressures, the openness of the Lebanese economy, exemplified in a free foreign exchange market and a floating pound, should be maintained. There were no serious calls for the imposition of exchange controls as a policy response to the deteriorating external situation. This policy option, particularly in the post-1982 civil war period, meant (probably unbeknown to most government officials) that the burden of balance of payments adjustment was to be borne by the exchange rate, with all the consequent economic and financial implications noted earlier. Consciously or unconsciously, such a policy was judged to be superior to introducing exchange controls and restrictions as a means of coping with the external situation. Their introduction, it was feared, could only further weaken confidence in the Lebanese economy and, in the longer run, discourage the in-flow of private capital once the conflict was over and the reconstruction effort began. Furthermore, there was a general belief that exchange controls in Lebanon (as was the case in many other countries) could not be effectively implemented. This stance focused attention on the second policy dimension, namely the necessity of relying on fiscal/monetary policies to cope with the problems of reconstruction and emerging financial imbalances.

Accordingly, with the end of the two-year (1975/6) war, the authorities hastened to create the institutional framework that was to guide the reconstruction effort. The Council for Development and Reconstruction (CDR) was established in early 1977, and a year later a ten-year reconstruction plan was in place. Attempts at reconstruction continued throughout the civil war period, although they were greatly constrained by the prevailing situation. At the policy level, it came to be recognized that any measures aimed at minimizing pressure on the national economy and maintaining, as far as possible, a climate of confidence required close coordination between reconstruction, monetary and fiscal policies. For this purpose the Bureau of Economic Policy Coordination was created in November 1979.[85] Policy coordination worked well until 1983, when the bureau ceased functioning as a consequence of the rapidly deteriorating political/military situation. Nevertheless, monetary policy, while greatly constrained by enfeebled fiscal policy and authority, remained active. The monetary authorities tried to cope with the deteriorating financial and external situations and to maintain as sound a banking system as possible.

In addition, the government took measures designed to restore working relationships between various economic interest groups, and attempted to settle issues related to debtor–creditor relationships, particularly the rescheduling of private debt owned to banks.[86] In practice, though, these issues were settled directly between creditors and debtors. In addition, the government took steps to revive industry. For instance, through the CDR, credit was extended on concessionary terms to industrial, tourist and health establishments that had suffered war damage.[87] Also, interest subsidies on bank loans were extended to industrial firms to finance the purchase of new machinery.[88]

In what follows we shall consider the reconstruction policy and efforts undertaken by CDR, the experiment with policy coordination and the role of monetary policy as the principal policy responses of the public sector to the evolving situation.

Council for Development and Reconstruction (CDR): attempted reconstruction With the conclusion of the first two years of civil war (1975–76), which was formally brought about by the Arab summit meeting held in Cairo in October 1976, it appeared that Lebanon was ready to plan seriously for the reconstruction of its economy and future growth.[89] On 31 January 1977 the government issued Decree Law no. 5, which abolished the existing Ministry of Planning and created the CDR. It was charged with the responsibility of preparing a general plan for development and reconstruction; at the same time, it was empowered, among other things, to finance programmes or projects assigned to it by contracting internal and external loans with a governmental guarantee of up to 15 per cent of its total annual budget without recourse to parliament.[90] And with the objective of overcoming Lebanese bureaucratic constraints, the council was exempted from otherwise mandatory supervision by governmental supervisory bodies. The CDR was intended to guide the future economic growth of Lebanon in the wake of the two-year war. Implicit in its creation was the belief that the Lebanese conflict had come to an end. However, by the time the CDR had completed its Reconstruction Project in late 1978, the political situation had again begun to deteriorate and the resumption of hostilities was imminent.

In preparing the Reconstruction Project, the CDR had requested that a number of Lebanese and non-Lebanese experts prepare background papers on various aspects of the Lebanese economy, in collaboration with the professional staff of the CDR. This collaborative work involving Lebanese and foreign professional expertise was carried out with the full conviction on the part of the then CDR leadership that planning for Lebanon's reconstruction and development could only be a national responsibility. While making full use of the collective expertise of outside consulting and/or international organizations, the elaboration of national targets and the means of attaining them were to be a national task. Equally importantly, public interest – as defined by professional expertise not burdened by conflict of interest constraints – was to be the guiding principle of any recovery programmes and their implementation. This may sound like an obvious policy principle that need not be emphasized. In the context of Lebanon's various official attempts at development programmes in the pre- and post-civil-war periods, however, it was not always the principle by which the responsible authorities chose to abide. On the other hand, given the sectarian nature of the Lebanese political system, the council set-up, and at times its operations, were subject to political/sectarian influences, particularly after 1982.

The 1978 Reconstruction Project was prepared with the declared intention of proceeding with the reconstruction process before the full re-establishment of internal peace and security. The private sector was to be relied upon as the primary generator of economic activities. For this purpose, the project called for extending loans to private enterprises to help finance industrial, commercial and agricultural projects. As to public sector projects, priority was given to the housing and infrastructure sectors (ports, airports, telecommunications, the transport network, etc.).[91] The Reconstruction Project was submitted to the Arab summit meeting held in Tunis in October 1979. At this meeting it was decided to grant Lebanon $2 billion, half of which was to be used to help southern Lebanon withstand the impact of frequent Israeli military incursions. In practice, Lebanon received only $417 million of the above amount.

The 1978 Reconstruction Project called for total expenditure (at 1978 prices) of $4,750 million, of which one third consisted of loans to the private sector. Of the public sector projects, the share of the housing sector was 32 per cent and highways another 11 per cent. The CDR attempted to secure external grants and concessional loans and planned that local counterpart funds would comprise about one quarter of total financing. The deteriorating security situation, however, severely constrained reconstruction financing efforts. The CDR had to confine its scope of activities to available foreign and local financing and, further, was obliged to implement projects in areas where it was feasible to reconstruct. As a result, for the period up to and including 1982, actual expenditure of about LL1.8 billion amounted to roughly one quarter of the planned amount, and over 70 per cent of actual expenditure was directed to physical infrastructure projects.[92] Foreign financing covered a little less than 80 per cent of the total. (It should be noted that this was a period in which the Lebanese pound had remained relatively stable.)

Following the June 1982 Israeli invasion, the World Bank, on the basis of its evaluation of past reconstruction efforts, submitted a three-year plan (1983–85) to finance reconstruction projects, to be backed by an international loan of $225 million which the bank undertook to arrange. Partly because of evolving political/military circumstances, this plan was not implemented. In 1983 the CDR prepared an alternative plan for the post-1982 period based on a reassessment of Lebanon's reconstruction needs in the wake of the substantial damage caused by the Israeli invasion and continuing civil war. The basic objective of the new plan did not differ from that of the previous one. A recosting of sectoral projects was undertaken, taking into account the new damage sustained as a result of the ongoing conflict and work that had already been completed as well as changing cost estimates resulting from mounting inflation.[93] It was estimated that simply to restore basic facilities throughout the country to their pre-war standards would require a huge investment of about $25–27 billion (based on the exchange rate prevailing in mid-1982) to be implemented over a period of eight to nine years under circumstances that would permit favourable project implementation.

The years 1983–90 saw an escalation of the civil war and a deterioration in financial and economic conditions, including the rapid depreciation of the Lebanese pound. By necessity CDR had to adopt a pragmatic approach to project implementation. Because foreign financial assistance was not forthcoming, as had been expected, CDR had to rely increasingly on local sources of financing to cover its planned expenditure. In the context of the overall global project that had been prepared, three shorter-term expenditure programmes were drawn up: respectively in 1983, 1984/5 (extending until 1986) and 1987 (not approved by the Council of Ministers, which ceased to convene from the latter part of 1986). All in all, the increasingly deteriorating political/military situation greatly hindered the implementation of planned projects. Consequently, actual expenditure during 1983–88 did not exceed 35 per cent of planned expenditure.[94] The share of foreign financial assistance in total project financing dropped substantially, ranging annually from 13 to 31 per cent in 1983–86.[95] It rose to 53 per cent in 1987 and 92 per cent in 1988, not because of increasing levels of foreign assistance but as a result of the rapidly deteriorating Lebanese pound (which raised the share of the pound counterpart of foreign assistance or alternatively reduced the share of internal funding denominated in US dollars) – along with a reduced level of actual internal expenditure on projects. It is estimated that in 1988 actual expenditure dropped to $25 million, which was about 20 per cent of the annual average for the previous five-year period. The period 1989–90 witnessed the war of 'liberation' and the emergence of the two-government situation.

The 1979 Tunis pledge apart, external funding of reconstruction projects came primarily from Arab development funds. Additionally three protocols were signed with France (1978, 1983 and 1988), and bilateral aid agreements were concluded with other Western countries and the European Community. However, the level of actual foreign aid was much less than expected, which forced the CDR to resort to medium-term commercial loans. For the period 1977–87, the total value of contracted external loans amounted to US$727 million and grants to $171 million, a total of $898 million. The rate of disbursements, however, was only 55 per cent in the case of loans ($400 million) and 41 per cent in the case of grants ($70 million) for an overall rate of utilization of 52 per cent ($470 million).[96]

Policy coordination To my knowledge, the first official attempt at macro-economic coordination in Lebanon was undertaken in 1979 with the setting up of the Bureau of Economic Policy Coordination. As noted above, it functioned effectively for less than four years. Nevertheless, it was a highly useful experiment, which demonstrated the value of serious coordination between fiscal, monetary, exchange rate and developmental policies. As they developed, the tasks of the Bureau were not only to coordinate policies in order to achieve desired shorter and longer term macroeconomic objectives. Under the then prevailing political and military conditions, the officials concerned were anxious to develop policy measures that could be acted upon in a relatively short period of time.[97] An important function served by the bureau was that it brought together, on a regular basis, the officials concerned with macroeconomic policies to exchange opinions on evolving economic and financial conditions at a time when the country was facing tremendously difficult political/military circumstances.

With the above objectives in mind, and in view of the then evolving fiscal developments (i.e. increasing Central Bank financing of governmental operations and increasing inflationary pressures), the bureau set three tasks for itself. The first was to try to contain internally generated inflationary pressures, the second to maintain an orderly foreign exchange market, and the third to coordinate fiscal policy with the reconstruction programme of the CDR.

The objective of controlling inflationary pressures was to be achieved via control of the budget deficit (which was increasing on account of falling revenues due to the impaired ability of the government to collect taxes) while minimizing any possible adverse impact on the reconstruction programme. This implied, among other things, agreement between the fiscal, monetary and developmental authorities on the means of financing the deficit, i.e. issuance of treasury bills (TBs), preferably with longer-term maturity, to the public and commercial banks versus financing from the Central Bank. Resort to external resources was difficult in view of the prevailing political/military situation. The authorities succeeded in reducing the share of Central Bank credit to finance governmental expenditure: at the end of 1979 bank loans made up over 50 per cent of outstanding public debt compared to 40 per cent comprising TBs. By the end of 1982 bank loans stood at only 11 per cent of the total in comparison with 79 per cent for TBs. However, the share of longer-term TBs (maturing after more than one year) fell from 76 per cent of the total at the end of 1979 to 43 per cent at the end of 1983 (including special TBs, which could be held as part of the required reserves). TBs were issued on a regular basis and were taken up mostly by commercial banks. This policy served to soak up excess liquidity in the banking system and thus helped reduce its diversion to undesirable outlets, e.g. speculation on the foreign exchange and real estate markets. However, speculative activities, in violation of the monetary code, could not be completely eliminated. Reliance on treasury bills was intended as a temporary measure to give the government time to cope with the fiscal imbalance. As it turned out, the political situation continued to deteriorate and fiscal deficits to grow, which resulted in mounting internal debt and a growing level of servicing. In parallel, steps taken to support the Lebanese pound and reduce its volatility included the raising of the effective yield on TBs and thereby rates on Lebanese deposits. In turn it was hoped that this would lessen the rate of switching of Lebanese pound denominated to foreign currency (mainly dollar) deposits. The three-month TB rate was raised from an average of over 3 per cent for 1979 to a weighted average of 10 per cent for 1982 and 9.75 per cent for 1983.

At the same time, in its attempt to assess the impact of planned developmental expenditure on the monetary and fiscal situation, the bureau stressed that the regular governmental budget, particularly its chapter 11 (equipment and construction) and chapter 111 (long-term capital expenditure), should be properly coordinated with the CDR development plan. Further, as the governmental budget was not consolidated and budgetary classification did not reflect a clear distinction between current and investment expenditure, an attempt was made in 1980 to consolidate and reclassify the budget into properly defined current and capital expenditure categories.[98] However, no formal decision was taken on the reform of the budget. The bureau's deliberations on the fiscal situation and the means of controlling the budget deficit indicated that the following categories of expenditure were to be given priority: (i) emergency relief measures to care for the injured and provide for people displaced from their houses on account of the ongoing war; (ii) the civil service, which had to be maintained even during periods when the provision of governmental services was drastically curtailed; and (iii) the CDR's reconstruction programme as far as possible and within the constraints of available foreign financing.

Macroeconomic performance showed signs of improvement during the period in which the bureau functioned. The share of Central Bank financing of governmental expenditure was curtailed, the inflation rate decelerated and exchange rate movements were moderate. On the other hand, prevailing political instability and continued military conflict did not permit the CDR to implement reconstruction projects as had been planned. The macroeconomic outcome, of course, was not necessarily a reflection of policy measures taken by the authorities concerned. Other factors beyond their control (e.g. short-term capital movements, the expectations of the private sector) influenced the evolving economic situation. However, irrespective of how effective the policy measures agreed upon were within the framework of the bureau, its work, under difficult political/military circumstances, clearly demonstrated the usefulness of policy coordination. It was a pioneering step in the formulation of Lebanese macroeconomic policy.

Monetary policy While the enfeeblement of the central government greatly constrained fiscal policy, monetary policy remained active throughout the civil war period. As we have seen, the twin problems of inflation and currency depreciation, accompanied by volatility of the exchange rate, emerged, in particular after 1983, as primary policy concerns that needed to be addressed. To contain inflationary pressures, monetary policy aimed at limiting Bank of Lebanon financing of budget deficits in favour of financing them with treasury bills that soaked up part of the existing excess liquidity. And when voluntary subscription of TBs by banks did not accomplish the intended objectives, the authorities resorted to obligatory subscriptions. Along with other measures, the bank also attempted to decelerate, if not halt, the rate of depreciation of the pound and reduce its short-term volatility. Finally, as noted, steps were taken to strengthen the banking system, though bank supervision suffered from a number of deficiencies.

As monetary policy operated within a difficult economic/financial and political context, it could not, on its own, achieve the objectives of monetary and exchange rate stability. But under the circumstances, it should be credited with attempts to decelerate the rate of domestic financial and currency deterioration. It may not be possible to quantify the extent to which monetary policy succeeded in this regard. At the very least, it was active and, on the whole, steered in the right direction.

The Central Bank resorted to traditional tools of monetary control: e.g. reserve requirements, discount rate, credit ceilings, and later obligatory subscription of treasury bills by commercial banks, in addition to intervention on the foreign exchange market. Measures affecting the banking system included, among others, the setting of liquidity and capital adequacy ratios as well as net creditor positions in foreign currency, settlement of problem loans and at times of individual bank crises, providing the banks concerned with the necessary liquidity subject to the fulfilment of specific conditions. The intensity of monetary policy action picked up as the financial situation became increasingly difficult. The first measures were taken over the course of 1979 in response to an accelerating rate of credit expansion and increasing pressures on the pound. The Central Bank introduced in February of that year a 5 per cent reserve requirement, subsequently raised three months later to 15 per cent. Credit ceilings were imposed and the bank discount rate was raised. Subsequently, both were adjusted in response to evolving conditions. Beginning in June 1985 the Bank of Lebanon linked its discount rate to the rate of interest carried by treasury bills. As discussed earlier, up to 1983 the financial situation had not deteriorated greatly, and monetary policy probably helped, among other policy initiatives, in lessening the rate of deterioration, if not maintaining monetary stability. Of course, other factors, over which the government had no control, had a significant impact on the evolution of the financial situation.

Beginning in 1984, monetary measures became more intense in view of accelerating inflation and currency depreciation, and increased currency substitution (from pound to foreign exchange denominated assets) and dollarization, accompanied by widening fiscal deficits. Monetary policy tried to cope with the burgeoning deficit and the pressures on the pound, partly associated with adverse speculation against it. Several measures were promulgated with the aim of lessening the pressures on the pound. They included, among others: (a) effective 22 October 1984, the imposition of a 100 per cent reserve requirement on pound deposits placed in Lebanon by non-resident banks of which 83 per cent had to be kept in a special account at the Central Bank;[99] (b) effective 8 February 1985, a requirement that banks deposit in Lebanese pounds the equivalent of 15 per cent of newly opened letters of credit (LCs) in place of the foreign currency deposit previously required;[100] (c) effective 5 January 1986, a prohibition on resident banks accepting deposits from, extending credit to or opening accounts in Lebanese pounds for non-resident banks;[101] and (d) the raising of reserve requirements to 17 per cent (effective 15 November 1984), 18 per cent (effective 25 March 1985) and 22 per cent (over the period 13–27 March 1986).[102] These measures were accompanied by shortening the period over which the banks had to ensure compliance with the reserve requirements.[103] Subsequently (in the context of other measures taken by the Central Bank – see below) reserve requirements were reduced effective 10 June 1986 to a range of 8–10 per cent but raised again to 13 per cent effective 5 January 1987.[104]

The Central Bank intervened actively on the foreign exchange market. Its intervention had two objectives: (a) to decelerate, whenever possible, the rate of depreciation of the pound, and (b) to finance the foreign exchange requirements of the government. Under prevailing circumstances, bank intervention could, at times, dampen exchange rate volatility and create more orderly market conditions. It could not, however, counter the basic market trend, and had it attempted to do so, this would have been at the cost of depleting its foreign exchange reserves with only a short-lived positive effect on the exchange market. The bank was not facing a cyclical movement in the exchange rate but a falling long-term trend in the value of the pound. Furthermore, the bank had to accommodate the foreign exchange requirements of the government, often by purchases on the foreign exchange market. The required purchases pertained to current payments (e.g., among other items, fuel and wheat imports, both of which were sold at subsidized rates) as well as defence and some capital expenditures.[105] The Bank of Lebanon held substantial amounts of gold reserves (equivalent to $3.554 billion at the end of 1990 or about 40 per cent of imports for that year). But the responsible authorities have always maintained the position that Lebanon's gold stock should not be used for purposes of intervention or other uses. They feared that using this stock (including its conversion into a basket of interest-earning foreign assets) would serve only to further weaken confidence in the national currency and thereby add to the pressures it was facing.

It was observed earlier that in an attempt to absorb excess liquidity and divert part of available bank resources to financing the budgetary deficit (in preference to Central Bank financing), the Central Bank had resorted since the mid-1970s to the issuance of treasury bills (TBs) to commercial banks as well as to the public. Until March 1986, commercial banks voluntarily held the greater proportion of the issued TBs, being attracted to them by their relatively high yield and low risk. However, given growing budgetary deficits and the desire to ensure sufficient bank financing, on 25 March 1986 the Bank issued circular no. 635 which stipulated minimum ratios of TBs to bank deposits ranging from 30 to 70 per cent, depending on the level of outstanding deposits. The Bankers Association opposed this measure, arguing that it was too restrictive and might lead to undesirable consequences. The Central Bank continued with its policy of maintaining minimum ratios of TBs to deposits, however. After a number of changes, they were set effective 5 December 1986 (circular no. 688) at 30 per cent for banks with deposits of less than LL1 billion and 45 per cent for banks with deposits of LL1 billion or more. Effective 19 February 1987 new deposits were made subject to a ratio of 60 per cent, and reserve requirements, as noted, were raised to 13 per cent, effective 5 January 1987.[106]

The Central Bank resorted to other measures in its attempt to reduce governmental reliance on bank credit. Noteworthy is its refusal to transfer to the government account, beginning in 1985, 'profits' related to foreign asset revaluation in Lebanese pounds (foreign exchange revaluation account).[107] The bank (among others) correctly argued that such 'profits' represented accounting and not real profits, and hence had the same inflationary impact as any direct lending by the bank. Despite strong governmental pressures to have such 'profits' transferred to its account (legally, the government was on firm ground), the Central Bank stood by its decision. This policy stand was particularly important since the rapid depreciation of the pound beginning in 1984 gave rise to substantial revaluation 'profits'.[108] Had they been transferred to the government account, they would have represented an important, but an uncontrolled, source of liquidity upon which the government could automatically draw.[109]

While reliance on treasury bills was definitely preferable to direct Bank of Lebanon financing, growing budget deficits limited the effectiveness of monetary policy. Excess liquidity drained from the banking system was reinjected via growing budget deficits. The bank correctly attempted to limit commercial bank speculation on the foreign exchange market with the aim of reducing the pressure on the pound. Nevertheless, apart from any speculative, short-term influences, fundamental market forces were at work to weaken the national currency. In the context of continued political turmoil, huge budget deficits and waning confidence, the prescribed monetary measures could have only a limited impact, particularly since they were taken in the absence of an overall policy framework, and especially in the absence of an effective fiscal policy.

4.4 Social issues

The social impact of the Lebanese war was multi-faceted, but four major social consequences must be emphasized.

First, the partly sectarian nature of the conflict weakened the national bond among the Lebanese. It led to an intensification of sectarian feelings, the eviction of tens of thousands of people from their homes and villages, and the de facto partition of many parts of the country along sectarian lines. The emphasis on sectarian rather than national loyalty deepened political divisions and affected Lebanese social and cultural life adversely. Instead of a harmonious interaction among sets within one state, the war situation emphasized conflicting sectarian aspirations. The sectarian trend came to dominate at all levels – social, cultural, economic and political – and the significance of any national policy became correspondingly less meaningful. Indeed, the fiscal crisis caused by the declining power of the central government, and the difficulties faced in implementing development expenditures in accordance with envisaged national development criteria, were all manifestations of the weakening national character of governmental policies. The semblance of one state remained, but the de facto rule of various militias implied at least partial fractionalization or regionalization of economic and social policies.

Second, the conflict accelerated the growth of squatter populations, drawn from the tens of thousands of people displaced from their homes. Beirut and other urban centres experienced unchecked population growth without a parallel growth of the requisite urban infrastructure. Housing shortages, illegal occupancy of private and public property, and deteriorating health and social conditions emerged as pressing issues. As we saw in Chapter 1, even before the 1975–76 war there had been an unchecked movement of the rural population towards the urban centres, especially Beirut, bringing with it all the familiar social problems of rural migration to the cities. The war intensified this movement and further aggravated already existing social problems.

Third, the reduction in the stature and authority of the central government occurred at a time when the country's social problems were rapidly multiplying. The fiscal situation compelled the government to curtail expenditure, not only on reconstruction but also on social and economic services. Moreover, the disruption of governmental operations hindered its administrative ability to cope with socio-economic issues, even when financial resources were available. The bulk of fiscal expenditure covered current items, principally wages and salaries, fuel subsidies, and transfers to cover deficits of public bodies (e.g. the Electricité du Liban). Eventually interest payments on internal debt grew substantially.[110]

The government's reduced role in health and social services was partly offset by private social activities. Private health and medical facilities were set up in various regions (a manifestation of the 'regionalization' of social policy), but they could not match the central government's potential resources and were insufficient for public needs.

Fourth, the reduction in real wages, noted earlier, did not only imply a lower standard of living for wage earners, many of whom were forced to seek multiple jobs to make ends meet. It also contributed to a worsening of income distribution in favour of the richer groups in society. The latter included, of course, warlords and the other 'nouveaux riches' of the war. Put differently, the burden of economic adjustment was borne primarily by the wage earners and fixed income groups. They had to withstand the impact of the drop in their real income and consumption, as well as in domestic savings. The affluent segments of society (i.e. those who chose not to leave the country) were much less affected in terms of their living standards, outside the normal constraints and inconveniences of the ongoing war, which affected all classes. More generally, the business and professional class, despite incurring occasional losses, were generally capable of coping with the difficult economic/financial situation: some, indeed, accumulated further riches in the process. As we saw above, many were able to seek employment abroad or move their business to other countries. Some could simply afford to leave the country altogether.

5 Reflections on the war period

In retrospect, the experiences of the civil war point to a number of distinctive features of national economic performance during this period which are worth highlighting. They may be grouped under three headings: (i) economic resilience in the context of political fragmentation and military conflict; (ii) maintenance of an open economy in the face of external deterioration; and (iii) stability of the sectarian political set-up despite war and internal political upheavals and their economic consequences.

5.1 Economic resilience and political fragmentation

Despite almost sixteen years of political fragmentation and military conflict, the national economy, while deteriorating and suffering tremendous losses, did not collapse: no mass lay-offs and no voluntary mass closures of production units took place, and not until 1983 were huge transfers of capital abroad registered. Economic activities were disrupted but economic functions continued to be carried out, and the production cycle was maintained, under increasingly difficult conditions. It is as though Lebanese enterprise – business, education, banking, industry, agriculture and other sectors – was, to a large extent, adamant that it would adapt to the evolving situation. Economic resilience, more successful before 1982 than after it, was maintained despite the heavy human and economic losses that were incurred: loss of life, emigration, forced internal migration, destruction of housing units, plants and infrastructure, loss of income and physical assets, and, after 1982, dramatic currency depreciation and inflation. In turn, the enfeebled public sector attempted to cope with the deteriorating economic situation, sometimes successfully. Overall, national economic performance was superior to national political performance.

Several factors explain Lebanese economic resilience under conditions of protracted military/political conflict. The most important, in my view, is the self-reliant and enterprising nature of the private sector, aided by a more active governmental policy during the war period. Another factor is the clinging of civil society – across sects – to a 'national' home, emigration and forced internal migration notwithstanding. To many Lebanese the Palestinian uprooting of 1947 and 1967 was instructive. They did not wish to be similarly uprooted: a strong propensity to protect one's own property and sustain a sense of national belonging prevailed. Ironically, this might in part have been fostered by the emergence of quasi-independent sectarian regions that provided relative safety from the atrocities of the war.

Traditionally enterprising, the Lebanese private sector had operated in the pre-war period with minimal or very limited governmental intervention and no explicit overall policy direction. In the context of rapid growth and relative stability, economic policy implicitly rested on the principle of permitting the private sector to lead national development. As noted in Chapter 1, a free foreign exchange system based on a flexible exchange rate was maintained; fiscal policy was conservative, and monetary policy was activated only in the first half of the 1970s, when inflationary pressures appeared and the pound tended to appreciate substantially. The private sector, therefore, had not been dependent on direct state support or an active economic policy. Hence, with the outbreak of war and the consequent enfeeblement of the state and its various organizations, the private sector was able to cope with the impact of withdrawn or weakened state support. As far as the government was concerned, the private sector could – at least initially – continue to operate as before, particularly as the governmental bureaucracy kept functioning, albeit at a lower level of efficiency than previously. When the provision of normal governmental services (in particular electric power) was interrupted, the private sector filled the gap. The reliance of the private sector on its own initiative, already strong before the war, became stronger during the war.

At the same time, as pressure mounted, governmental macroeconomic policy became more active and, during certain periods, better coordinated. Fiscal policy was constrained but monetary policy was active throughout and the banking sector – considered vital to the national economy – benefited from governmental support whenever it faced serious crises. Furthermore, reconstruction policy attempted to counter the damage to infrastructure, and during certain periods helped sustain industrial development. The traditional self-reliance of the private sector received a boost from a more active governmental policy at a time when it needed it, disagreements between the commercial banks and the Central Bank concerning monetary policy notwithstanding. It is true that macroeconomic policies (especially fiscal policy) were constrained by the existing situation. But even with the constraints it faced, macroeconomic policy served the interests of the national economy, and hence the private sector, more than any absence of such policies would have done. The emerging economic consequences of the war helped raise the awareness of the national authorities of the need for proper policy formulation to cope with these consequences. They also came to recognize that this stance would be consistent with the workings of a liberal and market-oriented economy such as Lebanon's.

5.2 Maintenance of an open economy

It is striking that despite the deteriorating external position, in particular after 1982, Lebanon continued to maintain a free foreign exchange system and a flexible exchange rate. This consistent policy position rested on the notion (implicit or explicit) that the burden of balance of payments adjustment should be carried by the exchange rate, i.e. external pressures should be resolved via the depreciation of the Lebanese pound. Central Bank intervention was aimed at smoothing out rate fluctuations and not at countering basic market trends, which would have implied the depletion of the bank's foreign exchange reserves with only temporary support for the pound. Under the circumstances, a flexible rate policy carried with it its own costs, including a rising price level, intermittent loss of confidence in the national currency and consequent dollarization of the economy, and a fall in the real value of wages and salaries. These costs were implicitly judged to have been less than the potential costs associated with the introduction of exchange controls and/or restrictions (see below).

One major drawback of a deteriorating Lebanese pound was that it did not act as an adequate adjustment mechanism. The overall trade balance and more broadly the current account balance do not necessarily respond positively to a depreciation of the pound. For one thing, the Lebanese import bill far exceeds the export bill in a situation where the trade account is dominant in the overall current account. For another, certain important invisibles such as immigrant remittances are not price sensitive. In the case of the tourist sector, a traditionally important earner of foreign exchange, war conditions virtually eliminated its role. But even if the overall current account responded positively to a depreciating pound, traditionally it is short-term capital movements which determine the overall balance of payments outcome. Especially under the conditions that prevailed in the war period, a deteriorating national currency usually acted as an additional incentive to switch Lebanese pound balances into foreign exchange balances, whether held within the Lebanese banking system or transferred abroad.

Nevertheless, the alternative policy option of imposing restrictions and/or controls on transfers abroad, along with additional import restrictions, would have carried with it greater national economic costs. Three reasons for this may be advanced. The first is that under the existing political/administrative set-up, effective implementation of any restrictions would have been an almost impossible task. Their intended return would have been minimal if any. Second, given Lebanon's traditional policy of an open economy, the imposition of restrictions would have made the Lebanese economy lose one of its primary economic attributes with consequent loss of confidence on the part of savers and investors, both resident and non-resident. It is highly unlikely that, had restrictions been imposed, their removal at a later date could have made up for the damage that, in the meantime, their imposition would have engendered. Third, the experiences of many countries have shown that external restrictions are, in most instances, an inappropriate, or a less efficient, response to a deteriorating external situation than the adoption of appropriate domestic and exchange rate policies aimed at coping with economic imbalances, albeit with full recognition that necessary domestic adjustment carries with it its own short-term costs.

For all the above reasons, Lebanon's external economic policy stance throughout the war period was the least costly. The authorities may not have thought through the intricacies of alternative external policy responses to the situation. It was akin to an article of faith, on their part, that a free foreign exchange system should be maintained and a flexible exchange policy should continue in force. Because of this faith, the issue of whether restrictions should be imposed was never given any serious consideration.

5.3 Stability of the sectarian political set-up: economic consequences

It is also noteworthy that war and political fragmentation could not under-mine the Lebanese sectarian political set-up. Domestic and external political forces converged in their belief that a settlement of the conflict in Lebanon, at least for the foreseeable future, could be based only on maintaining the sectarian features of the political system. Adjustments in the sectarian distribution of political power were advocated (eventually agreed in the Taif Accord), but abolishing the sectarian attributes of the political system was never a serious political alternative (see section 6 below).

What concerns us here is not the debate as to whether, in the absence of a fully fledged secular society, the elimination of political sectarianism will or will not lead to long-term political stability. Rather, we should dwell briefly on the economic consequences of the stability of the sectarian political set-up. Two opposing views will be outlined here, leaving our final assessment to Chapter 5.

There are those who argue that political sectarianism is essential to the survival of Lebanon's multi-religious society and distinctive political attributes. A stable sectarian political set-up, they contend, assures political and hence economic liberalism, an essential feature of the Lebanese economy from which it has greatly benefited. This argument may have lost some of its weight with the emergence of globalization. Perhaps more importantly, to the extent that a sectarian balance gives rise to political stability it is conducive to economic development. In the context of war conditions, the stability of the political set-up, the argument may be further extended, lessened the fear of a possible one-sect hegemony as one outcome of the war. In turn, this arguably helped check the rate of emigration and capital transfers abroad.

On the other hand, there are those who believe that political sectarianism has induced sectarian political patronage, an inefficient public administration, corruption in the civil service and non-accountability of holders of public office, not to mention the occasional, sometimes severe, political conflicts associated with sectarian political tugs-of-war. Poor political governance led to wasteful spending, misallocation of public sector resources, and inefficient public administration and procedures. All these developments exacted an im-portant economic toll. Even if the private sector was able to generate adequate rates of economic growth in the pre-war period, the ineptness of the politi-cal system did not ensure a more appropriate income distribution or social equity, a more balanced regional development or the proper preservation of the country's natural resources and environment. This has continued in the post-war period with tremendous potential adverse economic consequences for future growth. Those who advocate the elimination of political sectarianism argue that such a step would enhance political governance and lay stronger foundations for political stability. It would enable Lebanon to overcome a situation of quasi-political equilibrium associated with a sectarian system. This could only enhance the quantitative and qualitative aspects of national economic performance.

Indeed, the relationship between sectarianism and economic development has not been thoroughly researched, despite the tremendous impact of sectarianism on political life. Any assessment will have to be based on the relationship of sectarianism to long-term domestic political stability and governance, and also on the alternative to the dismantling of the sectarian political system. This matter will be taken up in Chapter 5.

6 The attempted reconciliation: the Taif Accord

The settlement of sixteen years of war in Lebanon by the Taif Accord was based on the reaffirmation of the principle of sectarian power-sharing, albeit according to a modified formula. The accord drew on earlier reform plans that for various domestic and external reasons could not be implemented, especially the Syrian-sponsored 1985 Tripartite Agreement between the Lebanese Forces, Amal and the Progressive Socialist Party militias. This agreement proposed a number of constitutional reforms that were subsequently incorporated in the Taif Accord.[111]

Although after a long civil war the parties to the conflict were exhausted and ready to reach a settlement, it took external pressure to bring this about. The Iraqi invasion of Kuwait in August 1990 prompted outside powers (both Arab and Western) involved in or concerned with the Lebanese conflict to help settle it as a prelude to the allied campaign led by the USA to drive the Iraqi forces out of Kuwait (February 1991). Syria, a main actor in Lebanon's civil war, was one of the Arab countries that supported this campaign. As noted earlier, with tacit US approval General Aoun was unseated by direct Syrian/Lebanese military action in October 1990, paving the way for the re-unification of the Lebanese state and public administration.

The Taif Accord rendered the formula for sectarian power-sharing between the Christian and Muslim communities more equitable by enhancing the position of the Sunnite prime minister as well as that of the Shiite speaker of the House, while curtailing some of the privileges that the Maronite President of the Republic had enjoyed. For example, the new (Taif) constitution stipulates that the prime minister shall be designated by the President of the Republic on the basis of binding consultations with members of parliament. The prime minister is thus no longer beholden to the president (as had been the case before) for his appointment. The Council of Ministers, which collectively was given executive authority under the new constitution, is chaired by the prime minister unless the president chooses to attend its meetings, in which case the president chairs.[112] Furthermore, instead of the small advantage previously enjoyed by the Christian community in parliament, the accord specifies equal representation for the two communities. This same principle of equal representation continues to apply in the Council of Ministers.[113]

The essence of the political set-up thus remained unchanged from pre-war days. While the accord specifies the body (to be chaired by the President of the Republic) that is supposed to initiate the process of national dialogue with the aim of reaching national agreement on the elimination of political sectarianism, it does not set a time frame for this purpose. Indeed, thirteen years after the end of the conflict, this body has yet to be officially created. It is a moot question whether agreement on the elimination of political sectarianism will be reached in the foreseeable future.

By readjusting the basis for sectarian power-sharing, the Taif Accord envisaged a more collegiate political governance among the major communities and hence, in principle, a firmer basis for domestic political stability. One major manifestation of this presumed collegiality is the enhancement of the power of the Council of Ministers, which is supposed to act as a collective governing body. In contrast with parliamentary legislation that is approved by majority vote, the new constitution specifies that decisions of the Council of Ministers are be to be arrived at by consensus, and only failing that by majority vote. For 'fundamental' questions facing the country, if consensus is not reached, decisions would require a two-thirds majority. Significantly, the Taif Accord allowed for the temporary presence of Syrian troops to help the Lebanese state establish its authority; eventual Syrian withdrawal from Lebanon was to be mutually agreed upon. As would be expected, Syria has come to exercise substantial political influence in Lebanon.

However, the experience of collegiate governance up until 2002 has generally not been successful, and frequent criticisms of the manner in which the Taif Accord has been implemented have been voiced from within and outside the political spectrum. Still, no matter how imperfect its implementation, the accord was the means for ending the civil war, and thus served an important objective. It is an open question whether it can constitute the ultimate political framework for ensuring political stability in the long run. What concerns me here, as well, is the impact of the post-Taif political system on long-term economic development. I shall take up these matters in the following chapters.

Table 2.1 Estimates of financial resources accruing to militias during the civil war* (Source 1)

Arms trade	Looting	Exploitation[1]	Smuggling	Bribes and extortion[2]
Average: US$400 million Minimum: US$100 million Maximum: US$800 million Annually, 1975–90 Earnings from arms trade exceeded US$150 million Annually, 1975–90	Gross value of looted property US$2 billion, of which US$500 million accrued to looters 1975–90	Profits US$50 million Annually, 1975–90	Illegal exports of fuel US$40 million Total, 1980–89 Earnings from illegal exports of subsidized wheat US$20 million Total, 1987–90	US$200 million Annually, 1975–90

Ports	Drugs	Political money and military resources	Total
Loss of tariff revenues of legal ports[3] Minimum: US$15.5 million Maximum: US$19.5 million Annually, 1975–90 Average earnings from unloading, loading and transport in illegal ports US$2 million, annually, 1980–89 and US$8 million, annually, 1987–89 Illegal earnings[4] US$2.1 billion Total, 1975–90	Total exports[5] US$1.7 billion Total as of 1985	US$10 billion 1975–91	Turnover of the black economy US$14.5 billion 1975–90 US$900 million[6] Annually, 1975–90

Table 2.1 Estimates of financial resources accruing to militias during the civil war (Source II)

Pillaging[7]	Ransoms[8]	Embezzlement from banks[9]	Drugs and contraband	Confiscation of army arsenal	Total
Minimum: US$5 billion *Maximum:* US$7 billion *Total, 1975–90*	US$500 million *Total, 1975–90*	US$250 million *1982–83[10]*	Earnings from trade in drugs *Minimum:* US$700 million *Maximum:* US$1 billion *Annually, 1975–90*	Value unknown[11]	Total earnings US$15 billion *1975–90*

Sources: Source I: *Annahar*, 15 October 1990, p. 8; Source II: George Corm, 'The War System: Militia Hegemony and the Reestablishment of the State', in Deirdre Collings (ed.), *Peace for Lebanon? From War to Reconstruction*, Lynne Rienner, Boulder, CO, 1994, pp. 215–30.

Notes: 1. Exploitation includes import and sale of expired medical supplies, sale of pirated products as originals, banknote forgeries (especially US dollars), etc. 2. Source I also reports that during the period 1975–90 illegal commissions on governmental projects and purchases totalled US$600 million and accrued to 200 government officials. 3. Due to the existence of illegal ports. 4. Earnings created by avoiding payment of port charges and customs fees, both of which had generated abnormal profits for industrialists, merchants and importers. 5. Another source, Jean François Couvrat and Nicolas Pless, *Das verborgene Gesicht der Weltwirtschaft*, Münster, 1993, estimates profits accruing from the drug business at US$2 billion for the period 1975–90. 6. Another source, N. Richani, *The Political Economies of the War Systems in Lebanon and Colombia*, unpublished paper presented at the World Bank Conference on the Economics of Civil Wars, Oslo, 11–13 June 2001, estimates money circulating in the war economy at US$900 million per year between 1978 and 1982, of which US$400 million was circulated by the PLO, US$300 million was donated by foreign sources to different militias, and US$200 million was acquired by militias from internal Lebanese sources through various means, including extortion, drug trafficking and contraband. 7. Includes pillaging of the Beirut port (1976), looting of the downtown district (1975/6) and confiscation of property. 8. Revenues from imposed tolls and taxes are not quantified. 9. In April 1976, the British Bank of the Middle East was subject to armed robbery. Estimates of cash stolen range from US$20 million to US$50 million (source: F. N. Tarabulsi: 'De la violence. Fonctions et rituels', in: *Stratégie II, Peuples Méditerranéens* 64–65 (July–December 1993, pp. 57–86). 10. This figure pertains to the reserves embezzlement from the First Phoenician Bank and Capital Trust Bank. 11. Source II mentions that in the period 1982–83 the Lebanese army purchased about US$1 billion worth of arms from the United States, presumably as replacements for the confiscated arms and equipment.

* Reproduced from S. Makdisi and R. Sadaka, 'The Lebanese Civil War: Background, Causes, Duration and Post-conflict Trends'.

Table 2.2 Lebanon: real and nominal GDP, 1974–90 (in LL millions, unless otherwise indicated)

	Nominal GDP	CPI (1974 = 100)	Real GDP at 1974 prices	GDP using trend growth rates		
				$e = 6\%$	$e_1 = 4\%$	$e_2 = 2\%$
1974	8,137	100	8,137	....	....	....
1975	7,500	109.91	6,824	8,584	6,789	5,340
1976	4,099	141.64	2,894	9,110	7,066	5,448
1977	8,199	168.93	4,853	9,669	7,354	5,558
1978	8,799	186.09	4,728	10,262	7,654	5,670
1979	11,150	230.33	4,841	10,891	7,967	5,785
1980	14,000	284.99	4,912	11,559	8,292	5,902
1981	16,800	340.16	4,939	12,268	8,630	6,021
1982	12,599	403.55	3,122	13,020	8,982	6,143
1983	16,573	432.60	3,831	13,818	9,349	6,267
1984	28,171	508.97	5,535	14,665	9,730	6,393
1985	59,329	862.40	6,880	15,565	10,127	6,522
1986	108,096	1,685.20	6,414	16,519	10,541	6,654
1987	740,743	9,893.90	7,487	17,532	10,971	6,789
1988	1,356,000	25,229.45	5,375	18,607	11,419	6,926
1989	1,350,000	43,445.10	3,107	19,748	11,885	7,066
1990	1,973,000	73,342.00	2,690	20,958	12,370	7,208

$${}^{90}_{75}y^r_t = 78,434 \quad {}^{90}_{75}y^e_t = 222,774 \quad {}^{90}_{75}y^{e_1}_t = 149,124 \quad {}^{90}_{75}y^{e_2}_t = 99,691$$

Source: IMF, *Lebanon – Economic Recovery, Stabilization and Macroeconomic Policies*, 8 August 1994.

Table 2.3 Lebanon: GDP by activity for selected years (in per cent)

	1973	1988	1990
Agriculture	9.3	10.6	7.2
Manufacturing	14.4	20.5	14.3
Construction	4.4	10.0	7.1
Non-financial services[1]	27.1	17.5	19.2
Financial services	4.0	8.0	8.7
Trade	31.7	28.1	28.3
Administration[2]	9.1	5.3	15.2

Sources: For 1973: Ministry of Planning; for 1988: S. Makdisi, I. Chatila, K. Hamda and M. Sader, *Lebanon, the Gross Domestic Product and Gross National Product for 1988*, UNDP, 1991; for 1990: S.Makdisi et al., *Extrapolations of GDP for 1989–90*, UNDP.
Notes: 1. Includes rent; 2. Including electricity and water.

Table 2.4 Lebanon: indices of real wages and average labour productivity (1990 = 100)

	Real minimum wage	Real average wage	Labour force (in millions)	Average labour productivity
1974	448	–	0.747	370
1975	460	–	0.771	301
1977	400	747	0.759	217
1980	386	678	0.742	225
1981	383	653	0.747	225
1982	374	644	0.753	141
1983	414	661	0.758	172
1984	404	618	0.764	246
1985	284	438	0.769	304
1986	261	376	0.796	274
1987	111	162	0.824	309
1988	113	162	0.853	214
1989	169	169	0.883	120
1990	100	100	0.914	100

Source: IMF, *Back to the Future, Postwar Reconstruction and Stabilization in Lebanon*, Occasional Paper no. 176, 1999.

Table 2.5 Lebanon: net foreign assets of the banking system, exchange rate developments and consumer price index, 1975–90 ($ million)

	Net foreign assets of the			Nominal exchange rate		Effective rate		Consumer price index (1974=100)
	BDL[1]	Banks	Total	Ave.	End period	Nominal	Real	
1975	1,218	937	2,155	2.295	2.4	–	114	110
1976	1,300	592	1,892	2.908	2.9	–	118	142
1977	1,547	1,071	2,618	3.069	3.0	–	117	169
1978	1,814	989	2,803	2.955	3.0		113	186
1979	1,484	1,658	3,142	3.243	3.3	18,273	112	230
1980	1,592	2,124	3,716	3.436	3.6	17,264	118	285
1981	1,502	2,757	4,259	4.309	4.6	16,283	120	340
1982	2,597	1,918	4,515	4.723	3.8	16,694	133	404
1983	1,897	1,678	3,575	4.523	5.5	18,923	152	433
1984	668	1,556	2,224	6.506	8.9	14,571	131	509
1985	1,071	1,540	2,611	16.42	18.1	6,080	88	862
1986	484	2,012	2,496	38.38	87.0	2,451	67	1,685
1987	362	2,255	2,617	224.7	455	442	69	9,894
1988	972	2,255	3,227	409.2	530	167	66	25,229
1989	931	2,000	2,931	496.5	505	143	93	43,445
1990	650	1,919	2,569	695.1	842	100	100	73,342

Sources: International Financial Statistics, Yearbook 1997 and December 1998; IMF, *Lebanon – Economic Recovery, Stabilization and Macroeconomic Policies* (SM/94/207), 8 August 1994. *Note:* 1. Excluding gold.

Table 2.6 Lebanon: public sector operations for selected years, 1974–90 (in billions of Lebanese pounds, at current prices)

	1974	1980	1982	1983	1984	1985	1986	1987	1988	1989	1990
Revenue	1.70	2.50	2.70	4.40	2.50	4.34	6.07	20.1	21.4	63.8	126
Tax direct	0.21	0.30	0.50	1.30	0.40	0.65	1.15	1.8	7.1	14.8	37.1
indirect	0.72	1.00	0.60	1.40	0.70	0.54	0.58	0.7	1.2	3.6	3.7
(of which customs receipts)	0.48	…	0.40	1.30	0.50	0.4	0.42	0.5	0.9	1.8	2.2
Non-tax											
BDL profits	0.77	1.20	1.00	1.00	0.80	0.97	2.5	11.1	3.9	28.5	64.7
Other non-tax revenues	…	…	0.60	0.70	0.60	2.16	1.84	6.5	9.3	16.9	20.9
Expenditure	1.22	5.10	9.30	11.3	13.4	25.5	34.3	144	276	511	794
Wages and salaries	0.52	1.20	2.10	2.00	3.40	4.4	6.74	20.6	61.6	96.9	215
Interest payments											
Domestic	…	0.20	1.40	1.90	2.40	6.59	10.7	23.5	78.8	152	204
Foreign	…	–	–	–	–	0.05	0.18	1.1	1.3	0.7	0
Fuel subsidy (Electricité du Liban)	…	…	0.80	1.80	1.00	5.82	5.1	46.8	39.6	99.3	46
Transfers and advances	…	2.80	2.30	1.60	2.10	3.17	4.7	40.8	64.4	106	248
Other current expenditures	…	…	…	…	…	1.34	3.74	5.5	11.7	24.4	48.5
Development	0.26	0.90	1.30	2.30	2.60	2.1	1.4	5.1	18.5	32.7	33.1
Deficit (-)/Surplus (+)	0.48	-2.60	-6.60	-6.90	-11	-21	-28	-123	-255	-448	-668
Deficit/expenditures (%)	-40	51	71	61	81	83	82	86	92	88	84
Revenues/expend. (%)	140	49	29	39	19	17	18	14	8	12	16

Sources: BDL annual reports for the years 1988, 1990, 1991, and 1992 and IMF, Lebanon – Economic Recovery, Stabilization and Macroeconomic Policies, 8 August 1994.

Table 2.7 Lebanon: commercial bank deposits and cross-border deposits, 1975–90 (US$ billion)

	Lebanese pound deposits in $ equivalents	Foreign currency deposits	Total deposits (in dollar equivalents)	Dollarization ratio (2)/(3) (%)	Cross-border deposits
1975	2.75	1.27	4.02	32	...
1976	2.28	0.93	3.21	29	...
1977	3.11	1.20	4.3	28	...
1978	3.83	1.20	5.04	24	...
1979	3.93	2.14	6.07	35	...
1980	4.48	2.94	7.42	40	...
1981	4.64	3.83	8.46	45	1.95
1982	8.46	3.5	11.9	29	4.47
1983	7.48	3.06	10.5	29	4.94
1984	5.44	2.83	8.27	34	5.39
1985	4.01	2.48	6.49	38	5.77
1986	1.06	2.81	3.87	73	6.50
1987	0.27	3.22	3.49	92	7.35
1988	0.86	3.40	4.25	80	7.23
1989	1.58	3.29	4.87	68	7.98
1990	1.19	3.32	4.51	74	9.46

Sources: Bank of Lebanon, *Annual Report* (various issues); *International Financial Statistics Yearbook 1992.*

Table 2.8 Lebanon: monthly average exchange rate, 1975–90 (LL/per US dollar)

	Jan.	Feb.	Mar.	Apr.	May	Jun.	Jul.	Aug.	Sep.	Oct.	Nov.	Dec.
1975	2.287	2.268	2.243	2.237	2.229	2.225	2.266	2.273	2.253	2.415	2.390	2.450
1976	2.500	2.470	2.474				3.225	3.285	3.309	3.178	2.841	2.895
1977	2.993	3.053	3.038	3.041	3.059	3.071	3.119	3.120	3.115	3.097	3.073	3.047
1978	2.989	2.966	2.939	2.937	2.926	2.899	2.916	2.944	2.958	2.968	2.991	3.031
1979	3.057	3.160	3.143	3.180	3.250	3.260	3.244	3.250	3.270	3.315	3.407	3.377
1980	3.272	3.305	3.388	3.428	3.418	3.407	3.411	3.423	3.435	3.477	3.574	3.694
1981	3.750	3.920	3.990	4.020	4.210	4.300	4.390	4.670	4.620	4.600	4.610	4.630
1982	4.690	4.850	4.850	4.960	4.960	5.120	5.150	5.090	4.680	4.280	4.130	3.920
1983	3.830	3.990	4.160	4.150	4.180	4.260	4.360	4.700	4.890	5.100	5.240	5.410
1984	5.670	6.060	5.530	5.640	5.800	6.020	5.950	6.290	6.990	7.850	7.630	8.640
1985	10.150	14.180	17.740	17.460	16.500	15.680	15.730	17.390	18.570	18.010	17.510	18.100
1986	20.230	21.780	19.680	24.040	28.440	40.390	42.960	43.070	43.600	47.090	59.480	69.740
1987	85.02	100.33	106.38	116.68	119.47	134.71	168.00	229.05	272.64	389.05	498.21	477.36
1988	465.87	381.02	366.36	370.43	369.79	355.96	351.66	363.71	400.97	458.97	512.95	513.12
1989	530.47	512.20	475.62	516.75	505.93	507.12	513.38	536.54	504.97	453.46	427.36	474.22
1990	544.61	552.25	558.99	585.55	635.30	664.03	661.71	771.39	1,079.87	870.36	706.65	790.45

Source: Bank of Lebanon, *Bulletin trimestriel* (various issues).

Table 2.8a Lebanon: monthly exchange rate, 1975–90 (max.–min.)/ave. quotations (in per cent)

	Jan.	Feb.	Mar.	Apr.	May	Jun.	Jul.	Aug.	Sep.	Oct.	Nov.	Dec.
1975	2.4	2.0	1.3	0.5	0.6	0.1	3.3	1.6	4.0	4.1	2.1	...
1976	...	...	...	...	...	...	...	...	...	...	...	...
1977	2.7	3.7	2.8	0.7	0.8	0.6	2.8	1.8	0.9	1.4	0.9	2.5
1978	1.6	3.0	1.7	1.3	1.1	1.3	1.7	4.2	0.6	2.9	3.6	3.3
1979	4.3	5.1	1.8	2.2	3.4	3.6	0.7	0.4	1.2	1.6	3.7	7.4
1980	1.2	1.6	3.1	2.4	1.5	1.2	0.9	0.6	0.7	1.8	3.4	6.2
1981	6.4	4.3	2.3	2.7	6.2	3.5	3.6	5.6	6.5	3.7	1.5	3.0
1982	3.2	3.7	3.5	1.8	1.6	6.6	3.1	11.4	14.3	3.7	5.6	5.4
1983	6.8	2.5	4.8	1.0	3.1	2.1	8.5	6.4	3.7	8.2	3.2	4.1
1984	9.2	8.4	10.8	8.3	4.7	3.0	4.4	10.5	9.9	21.0	7.5	11.3
1985	30.5	30.0	20.3	12.6	8.7	6.7	1.8	14.3	8.6	11.5	11.1	8.6
1986	30.4	25.5	16.4	13.5	24.3	32.8	15.7	17.5	11.5	18.6	29.3	42.5
1987	10.0	32.1	27.2	8.1	7.1	14.4	23.4	45.7	13.4	80.9	15.3	13.9
1988	15.0	14.7	1.8	8.0	3.5	2.8	0.7	22.0	15.0	28.1	13.2	7.6
1989	8.5	15.0	16.3	9.3	6.7	2.6	4.3	3.3	15.8	8.8	7.8	13.7
1990	13.8	4.3	3.4	6.5	10.7	8.3	5.4	44.3	38.9	50.6	12.0	31.6

Source: Based on BDL exchange rate data.

Table 2.8b Lebanon: coefficient of variation of the exchange rate,* 1977–90

	1977	1978	1979	1980	1981	1982	1983	1984	1985	1986	1987	1988	1989	1990
Jan.–Dec.	1.3	1.2	3	3.2	7.6	8.6	11.6	15.7	14.3	41.9	67.2	15	6.5	22.4
Feb.–Jan.	1.3	1.6	2.4	3.8	6.6	10.4	12.2	20.8	9.1	45.3	61.9	16.6	6.8	...
Mar.–Feb.	1.6	2.5	2.2	4.9	6.2	11.2	13.5	33.3	9.7	48.4	55.2	17.3	7.4	...
Apr.–Mar.	2	2.9	2.1	5.9	5.6	11.5	12.9	44	10	47.2	48.4	16.6	7.8	...
May–Apr.	2.3	3.3	2	6.6	4.9	11.4	12.1	46.3	13.4	45.7	41.7	16.3	8.9	...
Jun.–May	2.5	3.8	2.1	7.7	4.4	11.1	11	44.7	18.7	42.7	34.5	15.3	11	...
Jul.–Jun.	2.8	4	2.1	8.4	4.3	10	9.8	41.5	31.6	42.1	27.3	13.5	13	...
Aug.–Jul.	2.8	3.9	2	8.9	4.2	8.1	8.1	37.4	37.2	43.9	20.7	10.7	14.1	...
Sep.–Aug.	2.5	3.8	1.8	9.8	4.4	6.3	7.5	33.5	39.1	50.1	16.2	7.5	17.6	...
Oct.–Sep.	2.2	3.5	1.6	9.7	4.3	7.2	8.8	30	39.2	54	12.9	4.2	28.5	...
Nov.–Oct.	1.7	3.3	1.7	9.1	5.3	9.1	12.1	26	38.5	63.1	13.3	4.4	27.8	...
Dec.–Nov.	1.3	3.3	2.2	8.4	6.7	10.7	13.1	20.3	40	70.2	13.9	6.4	24.8	...

Source: Based on BDL exchange rate data.
Note: * Defined as annual standard deviation divided by the mean. A twelve-month moving average is used.

CHAPTER 3

The post-war period: aspirations versus reality. 1 Political background, growth and macroeconomics

1 Introductory remarks

Whatever the nature of the political governance that has come to prevail in the post-war period (see below), various positive steps have been implemented since the end of the civil war. The government and the public sector were immediately reunified after the departure of General Aoun. Three parliamentary elections were held in 1992, 1996 and 2000 respectively. The 1992 election, the first since 1972, was bitterly opposed and boycotted by traditional, mainly Christian, political parties and groupings, which included both supporters of the Taif Accord and those that stood against it. They protested against the passage of an electoral law that in their view was biased towards pro-government parties, and what they saw as both governmental and outside interference in the election process. The second and third parliamentary elections witnessed increasingly wider participation, calls for a boycott being confined to political groups originally opposed to the Taif Accord. Militias were partially disarmed, although some more thoroughly than others, and their de facto rule practically terminated, but a tenacious armed resistance, especially on the part of Hezbollah, against the Israeli occupation of the southern strip of the country was permitted to continue. With mounting resistance to this occupation, the Israelis were eventually forced to withdraw in late May 2000 from the territories they had occupied since 1978, and their surrogate militia, the South Lebanon Army, immediately collapsed. Their withdrawal was widely celebrated in Lebanon: 25 May was declared an official holiday as Resistance and Liberation Day.

In general, the revival of the state and its institutions gradually took place, although not with total success. Attempts at ensuring the return of displaced citizens to their original place of residence were made. By the beginning of the present decade, however, only a partial return had taken place. Some of those displaced had emigrated, and others had either been unwilling or unable to return.

For various domestic and external reasons that I cannot go into here, the experience of collegiate governance since the end of the conflict has so far failed to reflect what was envisaged for it in the Taif Accord. In particular, the Council of Ministers has not come to assume the enhanced role assigned to it in the constitution as the collective governing body. Instead, what has come to be called the 'Troika', a grouping comprising the president, the speaker and the prime minister, has tended, especially since 1992, to dominate political life, and to become the effective decision-making body, albeit often in close consultation with the Syrian leadership, especially when it came to matters of concern to both countries, for example in foreign affairs and domestic security.

What is noteworthy is that disagreements among members of the 'Troika' on domestic issues, which sometimes took the form of public accusations, were not necessarily settled within the Council of Ministers or parliament but outside these institutions. Often Syrian mediation would become necessary to settle emerging disputes. With Syria thus playing the role of the influential arbiter, domestic political flare-ups as well as dormant, unresolved or partly resolved political issues have not been permitted to totally disrupt the domestic political process, uneven as it has sometimes been.[1]

All this not only reduced the stature of the Council of Ministers but, given the juxtaposition of vested sectarian, political and business interests, also contributed to the deterioration in the quality of political governance. This should not necessarily lead to the conclusion that the Taif Accord itself has proved to be an inadequate transitional instrument of long-term political reform. What it does mean is that, irrespective of its intended reforms, the performance record of Lebanese political institutions and public sector bodies, at best, did not basically differ from that of pre-war years: many may even argue that it has regressed. It is as though the devastating sixteen-year civil war simply served to effect a readjustment in sectarian power-sharing and not much else.[2] Some observers choose to attribute the lack of progress in political governance to the inappropriate implementation of the Taif Accord, rather than to any inherent deficiencies in the accord itself.[3] Others see the problem as lying in both the implementation and the accord itself. They take the view that the practical implementation of the accord violated what it was meant to stand for, and that in any case it does not provide the proper basis for long-term political stability.[4] Still, the Taif Accord does not lack advocates.

Whatever the judgement on the accord, political governance in the post-Taif era has not reflected greater awareness or sensitivity than before on the part of the political body of what constitutes public interest, and thereby a greater readiness to actively promote it. Indeed, one could perhaps say that it has reflected less awareness and sensitivity. Suffice it to mention in this respect the continued inefficiency of the public sector and its total subjugation to political/sectarian patronage. All attempts at administrative reform have so far failed. Social inequities have increased. Natural resources and the

environment continue to suffer from lack of protection, if not systematic destruction. Urban and rural planning is inadequate. Corruption has increased,
as acknowledged not only by opposition groups but also occasionally by
responsible officials themselves.

This state of affairs is not what ordinary Lebanese citizens who had to
face the tragedies of the civil war had hoped for. The gap between their
aspirations and the reality of the situation is glaring. In Chapter 5 I will argue
that the questions of governance and firm political stability in Lebanon should
go beyond formal agreements on power-sharing among the major religious
communities, requiring fundamental domestic reforms as well as the creation
of a new political culture.

Since the end of the civil war Lebanon has been recovering at the economic
level: reconstruction projects have been implemented and price stability has
been restored. Economic policy, especially in the monetary field, has become
increasingly more active and, in contrast with the pre-war period, explicit
in its targets and instruments, while certain sectors, notably banking, have
achieved substantial progress. However, economic recovery has been achieved
at a huge economic cost. As will be seen in section 3 below, as a result of
the policies that have been put into effect, the Lebanese economy came to
be burdened with a major public debt that, among other things, threatened
domestic financial stability and eventually forced the government to seek
outside help to avert a potential financial crisis. Of equal concern is the
quality of recovery and development. As already noted, the socio-economic
and environmental record of post-war development suffers from a number of
major failures that remain to be addressed and appropriately resolved. Unless
this task is successfully accomplished the long-term national development of
Lebanon will not be as promising as many had dared hope.

My assessment of post-war development until 2002 is divided into two parts.
The first, taken up in this chapter, begins with brief introductory remarks on
the evolving political context followed by a discussion of macroeconomic and
developmental performance. The second part, presented in the following chapter, discusses first the labour market and then focuses on the qualitative aspects
of development: governance and selected socio-economic issues. It concludes
with a note on how and why the reality of the post-war situation did not
measure up to the hopes and aspirations of Lebanese citizens.

2 The political context: a brief overview

Initially the national authorities were preoccupied with issues of security
and the re-establishment of the state apparatus. This was the task of the
first two governments headed by Salim al Hoss (1989–90)[5] and Omar Karami
(1991–May 1992) respectively. Intended to be governments of national
reconciliation, they included only representatives of the major factions that

had supported the Taif Accord, including the Lebanese Forces. Opposition groups – represented mainly by followers of General Aoun and others who had opposed the Taif Accord – were excluded from cabinet representation, though they continued to be active politically. Given the inherited difficult economic and financial situation, these governments also addressed economic, financial and reconstruction issues (see below, section 3).

The first government resigned on 20 December 1990. One main reason for this reported in the press was a political desire, expressed by the office of the president, to form a new government more representative of national unity which, among other things, would address the issue of disbanding the militias.[6] The second government was forced to resign on 6 May 1992 under the pressure of organized public demonstrations, which some observers asserted were instigated to protest against mounting economic/financial pressures associated with the rapid depreciation of the national currency that began a few months earlier.[7]

The third post-Taif government, headed by Rashid al Solh, followed the resignation of the Karami government. One of the primary tasks of the new government was to arrange for parliamentary elections. The last elections had taken place in 1972. Since that time, parliament had taken the extraordinary step of renewing its own term of office every four years as long as prevailing conditions were judged not suitable for the holding of parliamentary elections. The Solh government was also concerned, however, with implementing financial measures aimed at gradually restoring financial stability.

The Solh government resigned in late October 1992, following the election of a new parliament. The fourth post-war government was headed by Rafic Hariri (a Lebanese billionaire/politician), who came to play a major role in post-war Lebanese politics and reconstruction projects. Hariri remained prime minister, heading three consecutive governments, until the election of Emile Lahhoud as President of the Republic in November 1998. Thus, while in the period 1989–92 three governments were formed headed by three different prime ministers, in the subsequent period, from November 1992 until November 1998, three governments were formed by the same prime minister. The successive cabinets that Hariri headed did not lead to any significant changes in the governing political coalition or in the government's economic, financial and reconstruction policies, despite mounting criticisms by opposition political groups and others.

The first government following the election of Emil Lahhoud as president in 1998 was headed by Salim al Hoss. After the parliamentary elections of September 2000, however, Rafic Hariri again headed a new government.[8] Following the US/British occupation of Iraq in March/April 2003, he tendered his resignation on 13 April, only to be asked, once more, to head the new government.[9]

Bearing in mind that under the Taif Accord the distribution of power between the president, the speaker of the house and the prime minister became much more diffuse, in comparison with the pre-Taif era, it is perhaps not surprising that the domestic scene, especially after 1992, periodically witnessed political tugs-of-war between the holders of the three highest political offices in the country. The Taif's readjusted formula of power-sharing, which enhanced the powers of the latter two, allowed greater space for political manoeuvring motivated by political and other interests between the holders of the highest three political offices. This was reinforced by their different interpretations of their respective prerogatives and functions as promulgated by the Taif Accord. As noted earlier, their disagreements were not necessarily always resolved within the Council of Ministers or parliament, but often outside these institutions, within the framework of what came to be called the 'Troika' set-up, and often with Syrian mediation. It is not surprising, therefore, that frequent criticisms were made of the operational side of the Taif Accord as being at variance with what it was intended to achieve.[10]

While disputes or persistent unresolved issues affected the domestic scene negatively, at times severely, they were not permitted to destabilize the existing political set-up. (Controversial issues included, among others, the nature of Syrian–Lebanese relationships; the conditions governing the return of the displaced to their original place of residence; administrative decentralization; the electoral law; and the consequences of the military operations of Hezbollah against Israeli occupation.)[11] That these, or other controversial issues, some of which were resolved in due course, were not allowed to disrupt the political process was due in large part to substantial Syrian influence, publicly claimed and recognized.[12]

In turn, this raises a fundamental question concerning the long-term workability of the new Lebanese political set-up in the absence of an outside (in this case Syrian) steadying hand.[13] Is it in the nature of post-civil-war Lebanese political reality that extensive reliance on outside (Syrian) support is necessary for the existing system to sustain itself? In the pre-war years outside influences on internal domestic issues were also present, but not to the extent experienced in the post-war period. The economic and political implications of this question will be dealt with in Chapter 5.

The Lebanese political environment was also strongly influenced by the unsettled regional situation, mainly the recurrent military clashes with the Israeli army and its surrogate militia in the south as a consequence of their occupation of southern territory, the so-called security zone.[14] With certain exceptions, most of these clashes were confined to the southern borders.[15] The unsettled regional situation influenced the domestic political situation (e.g. Hezbollah's military operations in the south, exceptional treatment of the occupied territory under the electoral laws, and frequent political warnings that, in the absence of a settlement, Israel would always try to undermine Lebanon's political stability). No doubt the regional situation acted as an incentive to further cement Syrian–Lebanese relationships at various levels, and it is partly in this context that Syrian influence on the domestic political scene should be read. Further, while the unsettled regional situation impacted adversely on the investment climate in Lebanon, this impact is not easily quantified. Whatever its magnitude was, it did not prevent Lebanon from attracting expatriate capital as well as foreign investment, albeit mostly from the Arab countries.[16]

As of the time of writing, the Arab–Israeli conflict is yet to be settled. In the meantime, and despite the liberation of the south, its ramifications will continue to affect the Lebanese political scene.

3 Growth and the macroeconomic and financial situation

3.1 Growth trends

With the end of the civil war in October 1990, and excluding 1991, the rate of growth (according to official estimates) witnessed a rising trend in 1992–94, estimated at about 8 per cent for the latter year, only to be followed by a declining trend in 1995–2000, estimated at about 3 per cent for 1998 declining to 1 per cent for 1999 and less for 2000, picking up a little in 2001 and 2002[17] (see Table 3.1 and Figure 3.1). Looking at the period as a whole, the year 1991 should be excluded as the very substantial rise in the level of real GDP registered for that year (over 30 per cent) reflected a rebound from the dramatic fall in the levels of GDP during the previous two years in consequence of the ongoing military conflicts, mainly in the eastern suburbs of Beirut. Nevertheless, the level of real GDP for 1991 remained below the levels attained in 1987 and 1988. For the period 1992–2002, the annual growth rate averaged a little less than 4 per cent.[18]

Several factors explain this trend. The rising growth trend in 1992–94 was induced by increasing public sector expenditure and private sector investments. The latter peaked in 1995, both as a flow and as a proportion of GDP (about 9 per cent), with the construction sector accounting for the largest proportion of the total. The increased total expenditure in 1992–94 took up existing slack in the post-war economy, and private sector expectations were initially positive regarding future prospects. In later years the picture began to change: the pace of private investment (including foreign direct investment) slowed down as the fiscal situation continued to deteriorate.

Figure 3.1 indicates that after 1992 until the early part of this decade the public debt tended to increase rapidly both in dollar terms and as a ratio of GDP. The reason is that successive governments could not bring the relatively large budget deficit under control. Indeed, it tended to worsen from 1993 to 1997, and budget deficits continued to run at high levels through 2002 (see below, section 3.2). As a result, the government resorted to ever-increasing borrowing, primarily from commercial banks, at relatively high domestic interest rates. While the commercial banks stood to gain from this phenomenon, the resulting 'crowding-out effect' contributed to a slowing down in private sector investment and hence economic growth. The extent to which this effect may have played a role is not readily quantifiable, as it was and remains partly cushioned by the substantial dollarization of the domestic economy.

The private sector preferred to assume dollar loans, which carried a lower rate of interest than loans contracted in Lebanese pounds: for 1993–2002 credit in foreign currency comprised 87 per cent of total credit to the private sector (see Table 3.4). However, the banks' capacity to extend dollar loans was subject to two limitations: the first was the maximum net loans/deposit ratio in foreign currency imposed by the Central Bank.[19] The second was the distribution of deposits between foreign currency (primarily dollars) and pounds.[20] As most credit was foreign currency denominated (mainly US dollar) total credit expansion was primarily governed by the level of foreign currency deposits subject to the prevailing net loan to deposits ratio.

Other factors that contributed to the decline in the rate of growth were the prevailing regional political uncertainties and clashes associated with the Arab–Israeli conflict referred to above, such as the Israeli attack in April 1996 on the Unifil headquarters near the village of Qana, in which more than a hundred civilians were killed. This climate of uncertainty, while it did not halt the in-flow of private capital and investments, acted as a restraining factor in this regard. Furthermore, the decline in the oil revenues of the Gulf region from 1990 until 1999, in comparison with the levels prevailing in the late 1970s and early to mid-1980s, affected regional investments by the Gulf countries and the in-flow of expatriate remittances from the region negatively.[21] In addition,

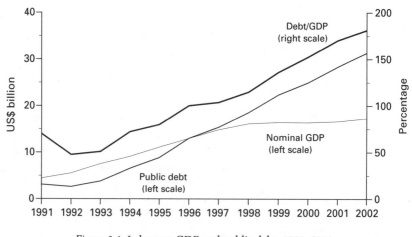

Figure 3.1 Lebanon: GDP and public debt, 1991–2002
Source: Based on Table 3.1.

while the rehabilitation of the country's infrastructure had a positive impact on the investment climate, lack of progress in reforming the administration and establishing transparency and accountability, not to mention increasing corruption, influenced this climate negatively. Admittedly, it would be difficult to quantify their impact. Together the above factors contributed, after 1995, to a substantial decline in foreign direct investment and gross capital inflows.[22]

Over the period 1991–2000, the broad sectoral composition of GDP did not appear to undergo significant trend changes. According to available data, trade and services continued to account for the larger proportion, ranging from 53 to 62 per cent of the total with a gradually rising trend over the period.[23] The share of trade alone ranged between 26 and 30 per cent. Within the services sector, however, it would seem that the share of financial services (financial institutions and insurance) increased, averaging about 18 per cent for 1999–2000. The share of manufacturing ranged between 10 and 13 per cent, and that of agriculture between 9 and 12 per cent. Official estimates carried out for two years, 1994 and 1995, reveal a similar sectoral composition except for manufacturing: trade and services accounted for close to 50 per cent of the total; manufacturing for 17 per cent and agriculture for 12 per cent.[24]

3.2 Financial developments
Exchange rate developments and inflationary trends

Figure 3.2 exhibits the exchange rate and inflation trends in the period 1991–2002.

After relative exchange rate stability in 1991, two major factors contributed to the quick depreciation of the pound, and consequently the rise in the rate of inflation, in the first half of 1992. The first was the government's decision towards the end of 1991 to raise public sector wages substantially (by about 200 per cent) without accompanying revenue increases. This step was taken while the budgetary deficit was running at high levels (over 80 per cent of governmental expenditure). The immediate consequence of the wage increase, financed by borrowing, was to inject additional liquidity into the economy. Pressures on the pound mounted, which the Central Bank initially attempted to counter through intervention on the foreign exchange market, keeping the pound stable at LL879 to the US dollar (see Table 3.3). With its reserves being continuously depleted, the bank could no longer maintain a policy of rate stabilization. On 21 February 1992 the governor issued a public statement to the effect that, henceforth, the bank had decided to halt its support of the pound but it would continue to monitor exchange rate developments carefully. The pound, as expected, immediately began to depreciate.

The second factor pertained to additional pressures that subsequently arose from adverse speculation against the pound, in large measure induced by heightened domestic political tension. This was associated with strong opposition by certain political parties and groupings to the national parliamentary elections that the government had decided to hold in the summer of 1992. Numerous reports and commentaries that appeared in the press at the time referred to this matter, and some noted that the adverse speculation was deliberate, not simply to generate profits but, under conditions of a worsening exchange rate, to force postponement of the national elections and/or a change of government.[25] Those opposing the elections, it was reasoned, thought that the relatively low level of foreign exchange reserves at the disposal of the Central Bank would not permit it to counter continuous adverse speculation against the pound, although attempts in this direction were made.

The policy issue that the Central Bank faced was not whether to permit the pound to fluctuate but how to minimize the amplitude of fluctuations under the prevailing tense political conditions. The government, whose primary task was to organize the parliamentary elections, attempted to cope with the inherited fiscal imbalances and the turbulence in the foreign exchange market. As noted below, it succeeded in introducing a fiscal programme that, among other things, led to a reduction in the budgetary deficit over a relatively short period. Nevertheless, the months preceding the conclusion of the elections continued to witness turbulence in the foreign exchange market for the reason mentioned above. The pound depreciated from an average of LL889 per US dollar in the second half of 1991 to LL1,296 per dollar during the first half of 1992 and LL2,129 in the second half of the year (see Table 3.3). This was accompanied by substantial rate volatility around its trend.

The parliamentary elections took place in the summer. With their conclusion in early October 1992, and the election of a new parliament, the

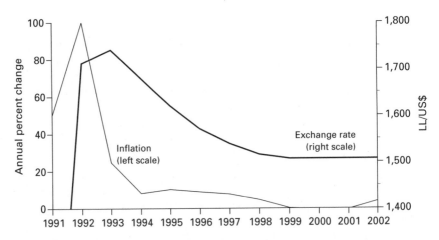

Figure 3.2 Lebanon: exchange rate versus inflation, 1991–2002 (annual averages)
Source: Based on data in Table 3.3.

foreign exchange market began to calm down and the pound gradually to appreciate. This development supported the notion that previous speculation was, to a large extent, connected to efforts on the part of opposition groups to disrupt the election process. With the formation of the first post-parliamentary government (headed by Rafic Hariri), the appreciation of the pound tended initially to accelerate rapidly. The government decided to follow a policy of very gradual appreciation of the pound *vis-à-vis* the US dollar, a crawling up peg policy that was maintained throughout 1993–98 despite, at times, sustained and substantial pressure on the pound, which the Central Bank countered by intervening on the foreign exchange market and maintaining relatively high real interest rates (see below, section 3.3). Very narrow margins around parity were maintained to discourage speculation. The monthly rate of appreciation during this period averaged about 0.3 per cent. The Hoss government formed in late 1998 following the presidential elections of that year discontinued the policy of gradual appreciation in favour of a fixed rate *vis-à-vis* the US dollar, a policy that has since been maintained.

What is noteworthy is the upward trend of the real exchange rate of the pound. Given a nominal rate that is either gradually appreciating or fixed *vis-à-vis* the dollar, the deceleration in the Lebanese rate of inflation led to a substantial appreciation in the real exchange rate of the pound. According to IMF estimates this appreciation was close to 75 per cent by the end of 1998, with likely adverse consequences on the competitiveness of Lebanese national production.[26] This appreciation tended to stabilize over the subsequent three years, and with the weakening of the dollar in 2002 the real effective rate tended to depreciate somewhat. Nevertheless, over the period 1998–2002 the pound is estimated to have appreciated in real terms by over 10 per cent.[27]

Inflation significantly followed exchange rate developments, exhibiting two trends (see the following section). The first was the rise in the inflation rate from about 50 per cent for 1991 to about 100 per cent for 1992, followed by its deceleration over the subsequent period as a whole. The inflation rate stood at an estimated 5 per cent for 1998, close to or less than 1 per cent for 1999–2001 but rising to an estimated 4 per cent for 2002 following the introduction of the value added tax in February of that year (see Figure 3.2 and Table 3.3). But as in the case of GDP estimates, the price indices constructed to measure price changes suffer from statistical limitations and, in any case, are not comprehensive measures of the inflation trend.

Relationship between the exchange rate and inflation

While in an open economy such as Lebanon's exchange rate behaviour has a direct impact on the domestic price level, conversely, the significance of the relationship and the degree of this impact may differ under conditions of relative stability and inflation respectively. It was observed in Chapter 1 that the stability of the exchange rate in the pre-1975 period contributed, among other factors, to the maintenance of relative price stability. It was also observed in Chapter 2 that the depreciation of the pound was translated quickly into increases in domestic prices. Did a significant relationship between the two variables also exist during the post-civil-war period of relative currency stability, beginning late 1992, when the pound was anchored to the dollar? More specifically, did the crawling up peg policy followed by the Central Bank until 1998 contribute to the reduction in the rate of inflation? Investigating this period, a recent econometric study finds that there was a strong positive correlation between the rate of change in the exchange rate and the change in inflation differential (i.e. between the US and Lebanese inflation rates). Further, the appreciation of the pound significantly influenced the inflation spread for up to one month. The effect seems to die out after a few months, bearing in mind that other factors also affected the inflation rate (e.g. liquidity injections). On the other hand, inflation did not seem to influence the exchange rate significantly. Thus there was a unidirectional relationship – namely from the pound to inflation but not conversely. Specifically, a 1 per cent appreciation in the pound caused the Lebanese inflation rate to decline by 0.03 per cent, assuming the US inflation rate remained unchanged.[28]

However, as pointed out below, under conditions of large fiscal imbalances such a policy carried with it substantial economic costs. Furthermore, it should be emphasized that the complete openness of Lebanon's capital account leaves the exchange rate subject to internal and/or external influences of either an economic or a non-economic nature. The Lebanese experience indicates that the ability to maintain relative exchange rate stability requires not only an appropriate macroeconomic environment but also stable political conditions. Otherwise, even if the underlying economic situation is stable, political disturbances may exert substantial adverse influences on the exchange rate.

Persistent dollarization of the economy

Despite the gradual economic recovery in the post-civil-war period, the extent of dollarization in the domestic economy remained substantial. Four indicators of dollarization are: (i) the ratio of deposits denominated in foreign exchange (primarily the US dollar) to total deposits; (ii) the ratio of credit extended in foreign exchange (again primarily the US dollar) to total credit; (iii) the ratio of dollar denominated to total cheques cleared at the Central Bank; and (iv) the actual use of the dollar as a currency in circulation, i.e. as a percentage of total currency holdings.

During the period 1991–2002, with the exception of 1996, the ratio of foreign currency deposits to total deposits at year-ends ranged between 61 and 73 per cent, standing at over 69 per cent at end 2002 (see Figure 3.3 and Table 3.4). It is noteworthy that from 1993 to 1996, when it bottomed at 56.5 per cent, there was steady decline in this ratio, influenced by significantly rising real interest rates on TBs in domestic currency during this period. These ratios were lower than those prevailing in 1986–1990 (except for 1989), but much higher than the ratios prevailing in the pre-1986 years. In other words, the conversion from Lebanese pound denominated deposits to foreign currency denominated deposits, engendered by the rapid and substantial depreciation of the pound after 1984, reaching a peak in 1987, was only partially reversed in the post-civil-war period. Even then the ratios of foreign currency deposits to total deposits remained high.[29]

Several factors explain the persistent phenomenon of dollarization as manifested by the relatively high ratio of foreign currency deposits to total deposits. They include:

(1) Latent fear of depreciation of the pound despite its relative stability since the end of 1992; this fear was sustained by the persistence of high levels of fiscal deficits, measured as a ratio of GDP, throughout the period under consideration. Their financing, primarily via the issuance of domestic treasury bills, led to the rapid rise in public debt, which at the end of 2002 had risen to over 180 per cent of GDP. The rapid rise in public debt (see Table 3.5), alongside persistent budget deficits, accentuated concerns over the ability of the authorities to bring the fiscal situation under control and fed latent fears related to the possible depreciation of the pound.

(2) Domestic and regional political uncertainties associated with the continuing Arab–Israeli conflict, along with continued resistance to the Israeli occupation of southern Lebanon and various Israeli military incursions, which occasionally took the form of major air attacks on Lebanese civilian targets. While we cannot quantify the adverse impact of this conflict, it had a negative, though not a decisive, effect on foreign investments in Lebanon and influenced the composition of investments undertaken. In particular, most investments

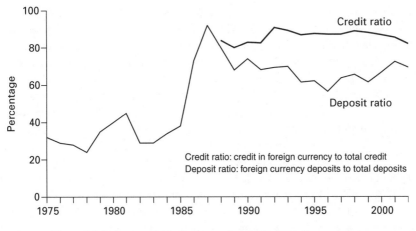

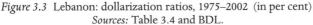

Figure 3.3 Lebanon: dollarization ratios, 1975–2002 (in per cent)
Sources: Table 3.4 and BDL.

were either in real estate or relatively short-term financial obligations. Under more normal circumstances, a greater flow of private investment towards other real sectors and/or longer-term ventures might have taken place.

(3) The so-called 'ratchet effect' which, in a specified function, refers to the asymmetric relationship between the dependent variable and one of the independent variables. In the Lebanese context, given the significant relationship between depreciation/inflation and dollarization, this refers to the observed faster switch to dollar accounts under conditions of mounting inflation and depreciation of the currency compared to the reverse switch to Lebanese pound accounts after the currency was stabilized and inflation brought under control. The emerging literature on dollarization stresses that adapting to dollar accounts carries with it certain costs associated with strategies to 'beat' inflation, labelled as financial innovations. Having incurred costs (e.g. efforts of learning) in adapting to the holding of dollar accounts over a relatively long period of time, households become reluctant to de-dollarize quickly when relatively stable conditions are re-established, or as quickly as when moving from domestic currency denominated accounts to dollar denominated accounts. Analysis of the dollarization phenomenon in Lebanon points out that the 'ratchet effect' did play a role.[30] However, it is likely to have been less important than in other countries which, unlike Lebanon, did not traditionally maintain a free foreign exchange market or permit the opening of foreign currency accounts. In the case of Lebanon, even before the civil war a relatively high ratio of deposits with the banking system was denominated in foreign currencies, primarily US dollars: for the period 1970–74 it averaged about 22 per cent and for the previous five years, 1965–69, about 20 per cent.

On the credit side, the degree of dollarization is even more striking. The ratio of bank claims in foreign currency to total bank claims on the private sector during the period 1991–2002 ranged between 83 and 91 per cent. As observed earlier, for the debtor loans in foreign currency carried a lower rate of interest than loans denominated in Lebanese pounds, although the debtor carried the risk of a possible pound depreciation.[31] For banks, loans in foreign exchange eliminated the foreign exchange rate risk. As in the case of deposits, however, the relative stability of the exchange rate did not lead to a reduction in the large share of credit in foreign currency in total claims on the private sector. This is not surprising. The currency mix of loans is basically governed by the currency mix of bank deposits, which did not change substantially, as well as by the specified ratio of loans in foreign currency to liquid assets. Throughout, the budget deficit was absorbing an increasing amount of the available credit in Lebanese pounds: the share of the public sector rose from about 67 per cent at the end of 1991 to about 82 per cent at the end of 2001, dropping slightly to 78 per cent at the end of 2002.

Data on the currency composition of cheques cleared at the Central Bank are available only since 1996. They indicate that the ratios of dollar denominated to total cheques were lower than the credit ratios but higher than the deposit ratios, being closer to the former than the latter. This is not surprising in so far as the currency mix of cleared cheques to a large extent reflects the currency mix of transactions. For the period 1996–2002 the proportion of dollar denominated cheques ranged between 64.4 and 87.4 per cent at an average of 78.2 per cent.

The use of the dollar, not only as a store of value but also as a means of exchange and a unit account, cannot be quantified. There are no data on the use of the dollar as a currency in circulation. Nevertheless, it became widespread, and the Lebanese economy effectively became and remains a two-currency economy. Payments were and are effected in either currency and when conversions were (are) made, the prevailing rate of exchange was (is) used. When the pound exhibited a depreciating trend, increasingly pricing of goods and services was made in dollar terms, although stores had always been required to price their goods in the national currency. As exchange rate stability was established there was a return to pricing in the national currency (and frequently in both currencies at the same time), and it is possible that the use of the dollar as a currency in circulation may have declined somewhat in the second half of the 1990s. Nevertheless, it continued (and continues) to circulate alongside the Lebanese pound. In the absence of enforced legislation that bans the use of the dollar as a currency in circulation, payment in either currency has become (until further notice) a normal and accepted mode of transaction.[32]

The fiscal dimension: perseverance of large budgetary deficits and rising public debt

Table 3.2 indicates the evolution of the public sector's fiscal position over the period 1991–2002. The overall deficit (excluding grants) measured as a proportion of GDP declined from 1991 to 1993 but rose to higher levels in subsequent years. According to official data, this proportion declined from an estimated 16 per cent for 1991 to 12 per cent for 1992 and 9 per cent for 1993, averaging for the three years about 12 per cent. It rose in subsequent years, peaking at 28 per cent for 1997, and standing at 18 per cent for 2001 and an estimated 16 per cent for 2002. For the period since 1993 the deficit averaged 20 per cent of GDP.

Similarly, as a proportion of public sector expenditure, the deficit declined during the period 1991–93, standing for the latter year at 40 per cent. In subsequent years the trend was reversed: the proportion peaked at about 63 per cent for 1997, declining to 49 per cent for 2001 and an estimated 41 per cent for 2002.[33] These estimates exclude unpaid government obligations, however, which were significant (see below). The primary deficit (i.e. after excluding interest payments) declined from about 11 per cent of GDP for

1991 to about 3 per cent for 1993 but then rose, peaking at 12 per cent for 1997. It stood at 8 per cent for 2000 and 1 per cent for 2001, turning into an estimated surplus of 3 per cent for 2002.

Thus, contrary to policy declarations, the national authorities were not successful, from 1993 to 2002, in containing the rise in fiscal deficits and thereby the public debt to levels that would not undermine the stability of the macroeconomic environment, as they came to fear by the end of this period (see section 3.5). The rise in governmental spending on both current and capital activities could not be matched by the required increase on the revenue side. In particular, the persistence of budgetary deficits implied an increasing proportion of governmental revenue was claimed by the servicing of the growing debt. For the period 1998–2002, interest expenditure averaged a little more than 81 per cent of total treasury revenue. Further, the rehabilitation of the country's infrastructure, which was regarded as an important reconstruction objective, added further budgetary burdens. While reconstruction projects were backed by foreign funding, most of the cost was covered by domestic sources[34] (see below, section 3.4).

In consequence, gross public debt rose substantially throughout this period: from the equivalent of $3.1 billion at the end of 1991 (about 70 per cent of the estimated GDP for that year) to the equivalent of $18.5 billion at the end of 1998 (115 per cent of GDP) and to $31.3 billion at the end of 2002 (181 per cent of GDP), excluding arrears to the private sector, which were relatively substantial (see Table 3.5). By the end of 1999, they had amounted to about $511 million or over 8 per cent of the actual expenditure for that year and an estimated 3 per cent of GDP for the same year,[35] decreasing to an estimated $350 million by the end of 2001, or roughly 6 per cent of total expenditure and 2 per cent of GDP for that year.[36] The rise in total public debt accelerated beginning in 1994, along with an increase in the share of debt denominated in foreign currencies which rose from less than 2 per cent at the end of 1991 to about 22.5 per cent at the end of 1998 and 46.4 per cent at the end of 2002.

Treasury bills have been the primary instrument of domestic debt financing, with commercial banks holding the largest share. Their share rose from over 61.5 per cent at the end of 1991 to 74.5 per cent at the end of 2001 and about 70 per cent at the end of 2002. The share of TBs held by commercial banks in total domestic debt increased substantially from over 58 per cent at the end of 1991 to about 74 per cent at the end of 1992; subsequently until 1999, it ranged between 68 and 74 per cent, declining to about 66 per cent at the end of 2000 and 53 per cent at the end of 2001. The reason for this decline is that increasingly commercial banks became reluctant to subscribe to additional TBs, by way of financing budgetary deficits, forcing the Central Bank to hold a larger share instead. At the end of 2002 the share of commercial banks rose to about 68 per cent of total domestic debt, partly because the government was able to convert a proportion of its domestic debt into foreign debt and to reach agreement with the Central Bank to effectively forgive a limited amount of its outstanding TBs.[37] As for foreign debt, beginning in 1994 it increasingly came to take the form of eurobonds, whose share stood at 82 per cent at the end of 2001 and 88 per cent at the end of 2002 (see Table 3.5).

In an attempt to reduce the annual debt burden, the Central Bank resorted to stretching the average maturity of treasury bills, which rose from thirty-five weeks at the end of 1994 to fifty-seven weeks at the end of 1998 and sixty-six weeks at the end of 2001; and beginning in 1995, the government decided to partly switch to foreign borrowings via the issuance of government bonds denominated in US dollars and the euro, which led to a rise in the proportion of public debt denominated in foreign currency. But this measure did not significantly influence the rapid rise in the interest burden that the budget had to carry. According to official data, it rose from the equivalent of about 17 per cent of governmental expenditure for 1991 to 48 per cent for 2002. As a proportion of GDP, interest payments rose from 5 per cent to about 18 per cent respectively. Interest on foreign debt rose from $9 million at the end of 1994 to $504 million at the end of 2001 (3 per cent of GDP and about 8 per cent of public sector expenditure for that year).

Costs of exchange rate stabilization under conditions of large fiscal deficits

While the anchoring of the Lebanese pound to the US dollar (albeit with its consistent very gradual appreciation) helped decelerate the rate of inflation, under conditions of persistent large fiscal deficits this policy carried with it substantial economic costs. We have already referred to the 'crowding-out effect' of governmental borrowing from the commercial banks. To ensure the required level of borrowing from the banking system, the authorities had to maintain high nominal interest rates on TBs (see Table 3.6a) and eventually rising real rates of interest. In turn banks linked their interest rate charges to the yield on TBs, thereby maintaining high borrowing costs for the private sector. An additional undeclared reason for the high interest rates was latent fear that should the interest rate on Lebanese pounds be lowered significantly, and consequently the differential between the interest rate on the dollar and the pound narrowed, this step might induce conversion of Lebanese dominated financial assets into dollar denominated assets. Further, adverse domestic political and economic developments were sometimes reflected in heavy and sustained pressures on the pound, which the Central Bank was forced to counter by sustained intervention on the foreign exchange market in support of the pound. At times this intervention was at the cost of a substantial decline in its net foreign reserves.[38] And as noted above, the rigid nominal exchange rate policy that was implemented led to a much faster rise in the real exchange rate of the pound, which may have affected negatively the competitiveness of Lebanese production. Regional uncertainties apart, the combined effect of governmental macroeconomic policies eventually contributed to the decline in the growth rate experienced in the period 1995–2002, in turn negatively influencing employment prospects and encouraging emigration.

At the policy level, anchoring the pound to the US dollar greatly limited the scope for an independent monetary policy, particularly in the context of capital account openness. Capital flows are highly sensitive to interest rate movements and, as demonstrated above (i.e. with reference to currency substitution), to exchange rate expectations. Under these circumstances, the use of interest rate policy becomes highly constrained in supporting fiscal and/or growth objectives; if rates were lowered to lighten the interest burden on the budget and/or stimulate investment, there was always the danger of an increased switch to dollar balances or increased capital outflow, bearing in mind, of course, the prevailing level of interest abroad. Given the limitations facing Lebanese exchange rate and monetary policies, fiscal policy became the primary independent policy instrument at the disposal of the national authorities. In other words, controlling the budget deficit arose as a primary policy concern in order to ensure the creation of a sound macroeconomic environment.[39] As of the beginning of the present decade, this was a major fiscal challenge still confronting Lebanese policy-makers. The basic policy issue centred on how to reconcile the requirements of sound financial stability with those of reconstruction and growth. Governmental policies eventually led to a mixed result at the macroeconomic level: a stable exchange rate (often supported by substantial Central Bank intervention) and deceleration of the inflation rate accompanied by large fiscal deficits, rapidly rising pubic debt and a declining rate of growth.

However, the major policy failure in controlling the large fiscal deficits meant that the stabilization of the exchange rate hinged, to a large extent, on the maintenance of relatively high interest rates. In turn, domestic borrowing to cover the fiscal deficit increasingly added to the debt burden carried by the budget, rendering it more difficult to cope with this deficit.[40] Furthermore the consistent crawling up peg policy of the Lebanese pound *vis-à-vis* the US dollar until 1998 created the impression that this was the 'natural' state of affairs. While the impact of a depreciation of the pound, small as it might have been, was never tested by the authorities, there developed a latent fear on their part that any depreciation would be interpreted as a loss of control over the destiny of the pound, propelling a switch from pounds to dollars, even though basic economic fundamentals remained unchanged. The impression of an ever-appreciating pound until 1998 was fostered by the national authorities not only to dissuade speculation against the pound but also specifically to maintain subscriptions to Lebanese government TBs that would permit the roll-over of existing public debt and more generally the holding of Lebanese pound accounts. As observed earlier, despite its benefits the policy of anchoring the pound to the dollar under conditions of fiscal instability turned out to be a costly option, and did not succeed in de-dollarizing the national economy. Concurrently with the discontinuation of the policy of gradual appreciation of the pound in late 1998 in favour of a strictly fixed rate *vis-à-vis* the US dollar, governmental efforts became increasingly focused on how to cope with the fiscal deficit and the rising public debt through stricter fiscal policies.

By the beginning of the present decade the economy was relatively stagnant, fiscal deficits were running high, the public debt burden was rapidly mounting, the pound was under pressure, and the Central Bank's foreign exchange reserves were being depleted; in addition, international rating agencies downgraded the rating of major Lebanese banks on account of their high exposure to governmental debt. The authorities were faced with a major fiscal/exchange rate policy issue. While the need for major corrective fiscal action was generally recognized as a prerequisite for any macroeconomic reform, there was less agreement on the need for an exchange rate policy adjustment, i.e. on whether to continue maintaining the policy of strict anchoring of the pound to the dollar, or permit greater rate flexibility, which could result in the depreciation of the pound. Government policy has so far been to maintain the first option, a major concern of the responsible authorities being the adverse political and social consequences that a depreciation would bring in its wake, irrespective of the question of its economic merit.

To succeed in maintaining the existing exchange rate policy, it became increasingly clear to the authorities that a fundamental reversal in fiscal policy had to be initiated, whereby the fiscal deficits would be contained and the rise in public debt not only halted but over the medium term reduced, and that to achieve this objective major outside financial assistance was needed.[41] Accordingly, the 2003 budget proposal submitted to parliament (approved in January of that year) included a major reduction in the deficit (to 25 per cent of expenditure). During 2002 moves in the direction of privatizing certain public enterprises were planned, beginning with the two cellular companies. There also occurred an in-flow of non-resident Gulf portfolio investment, attracted by the rise in the twenty-four-month TB rate (see Table 3.6a), and a subsequent increase in resident demand for treasury bonds. These developments reflected a change in market sentiment occasioned by improved prospects for the convening of the so-called Paris II meeting later that year, which the Lebanese government (in particular the prime minister) actively lobbied for with the strong support of the French president, its declared objective being the mobilization of outside financial assistance for Lebanon to cope with the accelerating rise in its public debt. President Chirac called for this meeting on 23 November 2002 and potential donor countries and international financial institutions were invited to consider ways and means of support for Lebanon.[42] It is interesting to observe that the appeal by the government for outside assistance was based on the assertion that, on their own, the corrective fiscal measures it planned to implement would not be sufficient to cope with the problem of the rapidly rising public debt, and that unless the requested assistance was forthcoming, the country's financial and social stability would be undermined. Put differently, this was akin to an admission that if the exchange rate policy were to remain unchanged, the dynamics of the rising public debt could not be addressed by solely domestic measures[43] (see below, p. 128).

Clearly, successive Lebanese governments should have acted much earlier to reduce the fiscal deficit to manageable proportions in order to gain greater flexibility in macroeconomic management, in particular as concerns interest rate and exchange rate policies. This would have helped the government to properly manage its public debt and lessen the negative effects of the Arab–Israeli conflict on private investment, while pursuing the goals of macroeconomic stabilization. The relative decline in the fiscal deficit achieved over the period 1991–93 was not sustained. Indeed, it was reversed. The required proper coordination of reconstruction, monetary and fiscal policies was lacking. To that should be added the costs associated with inadequate governance manifested in the inability to enhance the role of institutions and allow for an independent judiciary, along with increased corruption.

While the Lebanese government has chosen to maintain, at least for the time being, the policy of a fixed exchange rate *vis-à-vis* the dollar, a successful containment of the fiscal and public debt problems would give the authorities wider policy options. But if in the future a more flexible exchange rate policy were deemed necessary, then it is essential that such a step be perceived by investors and savers, at large, as a desirable policy adjustment. Such a perception could be successfully fostered if any adjustment in exchange rate policy were undertaken as part of a continued overall economic and financial reform that carries with it clear signals intended to bolster confidence, especially that of the business community, in the domestic economy.

More importantly, the question of macroeconomic policy reform is but one element in a wider national agenda of political and institutional reform, the essential prerequisites for sound and sustainable economic development. We take up this question in Chapter 4.

3.3 Monetary policy and banking performance
Monetary policy
Monetary policy was mainly concerned with the financing of the deficit while attempting to maintain exchange rate stabilization. For this purpose several instruments were employed, the principal one being treasury bills (TBs) sold mainly to commercial banks and the public which effectively linked domestic interest rates to yields on TBs. Other instruments included reserve requirements, the imposition of the specified ratios of treasury bills to deposits, and exceptionally ceilings on credit expansion. Monetary policy did not attempt to influence the composition of credit, and in practice could not

be used effectively to stimulate growth. In short, stabilization in the context of persistent large fiscal deficits was its overriding objective. As pointed out in the previous section, such a policy carried with it significant economic costs.

Prior to May 1993 interest rates carried by TBs were set by the Ministry of Finance in consultation with the bank of Lebanon. Subsequently, the bank began to sell three-month TBs in a multiple price auction, later extended to six-, twelve- and twenty-four-month TBs. Treasury bills have throughout been used to fulfil three related aims: the first was to provide financing for the fiscal deficit from outside the Central Bank, thereby minimizing Central Bank accommodation. The second was to absorb the injected liquidity and counter the monetary impact of current fiscal deficits on the national economy. At times the Central Bank took in TBs by amounts that exceeded the requirements of deficit financing in order to sterilize additional liquidity. The third was to generally bolster demand for the pound. Prior to 1993 interest rates were raised during periods of pressure on the pound, e.g. during the first three-quarters of 1992, but then were reduced when the pound tended to stabilize. Beginning in February 1993, monetary policy was geared towards maintaining relatively high (although over time gradually declining) interest rate levels, both during periods when the pound was not under pressure and when it was in demand.[44] Additionally, in specific periods of increased pressure on the pound (e.g. the first three-quarters of 1995) interest rates on TBs were substantially raised in an attempt to avoid or lessen currency conversions from pounds to dollars (see Figure 3.3 and Table 3.6a). When, during such periods, there was a strong tendency to discount treasury bills denominated in Lebanese pounds, the Central Bank resorted to raising the Repo rate (repurchase agreement) on TBs dramatically in order to discourage such a move. At the same time, substantial intervention on the foreign exchange market in support of the pound was carried out.

What is noteworthy is that interest rate and exchange rate policy was coordinated in a manner that generally aimed at keeping the effective return on TBs attractive to investors inside and outside Lebanon. In this context, the consistent policy of gradual appreciation of the national currency (after September 1992 until 1998) amounted to an additional return, measured in dollar equivalents, on Lebanese funds invested in TBs. For purposes of illustration, Figure 3.4 and Table 3.6c contrast, for the period 1993–98, changes in the effective yield on twelve-month TBs (TBY) with the effective (dollar equivalent) yield on the same TBs calculated as TBY plus the percentage appreciation/depreciation of the pound over corresponding twelve-month periods (DETBY). A twelve-month moving scale is used to discern a continuous correlation between the two variables. Three observations are in order: (i) both yields were kept at a relatively high level though, over the period as a whole, they tended to decline; the differential between the pound interest rate and the interest on three-month dollar deposits was consequently also kept relatively wide but again gradually declined over time; (ii) the DETBY levels were higher than the TBY levels, which clearly indicates the impact of the consistent pound appreciation on yields calculated in dollar equivalents; and (iii) as the decline in the rate of inflation outpaced that of nominal interest rates, the real interest eventually tended to rise, which in turn affected domestic investment flows adversely. Basically similar results would obtain had we contrasted the TBY and DETBY trends for TBs with alternative maturities.

Thus, while after its jump in February 1993 the effective yields on TBs were gradually reduced until the end of 1994, the managed appreciation of the pound countered this drop when the yield on the same TBs is measured in dollar equivalents. Similarly, with increased pressure on the pound beginning in 1995 interest rates were again raised throughout the first nine months of the year. Nevertheless, the Central Bank continued its policy of gradual appreciation of the pound and both TBY and DETBY increased substantially. From October 1995 until the end of 1998 the nominal interest was gradually reduced, accompanied by the gradual appreciation of the pound that cushioned the decline in DETBY.

During the latter part of 1999 until 2002 both the exchange and interest rates and hence the effective yields were generally kept stable. With economic activity continuing to decline, accompanied by a rising interest burden, the Ministry of Finance in the Hoss government was anxious to reduce interest rates to relieve the debt burden, but also as an incentive to promote investment and spending by the private sector. The Central Bank, however, tended to counsel against any significant interest rate reduction, being concerned about its impact in inducing conversions from pound to dollar balances. Indeed, on 8

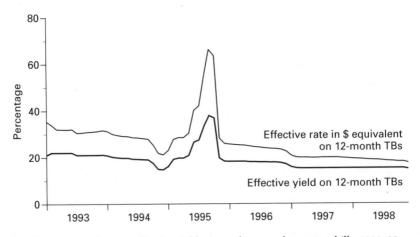

Figure 3.4 Lebanon: effective yields on twelve-month treasury bills, 1993–98 (in per cent) *Source:* Based on data in Table 3.6c.

April 2002 the effective rate on two-year TBs was raised from 14.64 per cent to 16.34 per cent on the open market operations of the Central Bank as a further step in defence of the pound. With improved prospects in the second half of the year noted above, it was reduced in September to its previous level.

Over the period, the structure of TBs changed in favour of longer-maturity TBs. At the end of 1992, three-month TBs comprised 24 per cent of the total, falling to 2.4 per cent at the end of 2001 and 1.26 per cent at the end of 2002. By comparison, the share of two-year TBs rose from 31.0 to 85.8 and 89.9 per cent respectively (see Table 3.6b). This was accomplished at the cost of an increasing interest burden, as interest rates on longer-term debt (especially two-year TBs) were greater than on shorter-term debt. With a view to reducing the interest burden, the government chose, beginning in 1994, to launch medium-term eurobonds (mostly three- and five-year maturities) with nominal interest rates ranging from 8.6 to 10.13 per cent. At the end of 2001 foreign currency denominated debt stood at $9.5 billion (33.8 per cent of the total), rising to $14.5 billion at the end of 2002 (46.5 per cent of the total), compared with $0.577 billion at the end of 1991 (18.5 per cent of the total) and $0.362 billion at the end of 1992 (14.7 per cent of the total). As to the type of domestic debt-holder, it was noted above that resident commercial banks held the largest proportion.[45]

The imposition of required TB ratios, first introduced in March 1986, was intended to ensure availability of domestic finance to cover fiscal deficits. This requirement was eliminated in March 1997. In practice, until the late 1990s banks would have subscribed voluntarily to the high-yielding TBs, particularly in the absence of equally (risk-adjusted) profitable outlets, and indeed prior to 1997 they often held TBs in excess of the required ratios. However, as the TB portfolio of major commercial banks expanded as a result of their continued financing of the fiscal deficit, by 2000 they had become increasingly reluctant to hold additional TBs whether denominated in pounds or dollars/ euros, especially given that the spiralling public debt posed a threat to the stability of the pound. The government had to coerce the banks to renew and/or subscribe to new TBs. Whenever commercial bank subscription to TBs fell below the required deficit financing, the Central Bank stepped in to make up for the shortfall.

In contrast with the 1980s, reserve requirements remained unchanged at 13 per cent of bank deposits in Lebanese pounds, of which 3 per cent could be held in special treasury bills carrying 6 per cent interest (modified in February 1998).[46] Until 5 January 2002 deposits in foreign exchange had been exempt from reserve requirements.[47] As in recent years such deposits comprised the greater proportion of total deposits, the effective role of reserve requirements in controlling credit expansion was, until then, limited. On the above date the Central Bank introduced a 15 per cent reserve or, more correctly, deposit requirement against foreign exchange deposits. The main objective of this measure was not necessarily to control credit expansion in dollars. Rather it was to ensure that such deposits, voluntarily placed with the Central Bank and carrying rates of interest that varied with maturity up to three years, could not be withdrawn should the banks choose to do so under market pressure, thereby leading to a loss in the gross foreign exchange holdings of the bank. At the time this requirement was introduced, the pound was under pressure and the government was facing increasing reluctance on the part of commercial banks to subscribe to its new issues of eurobonds; accordingly the Central Bank was concerned about its ability to defend the pound. It may be added that, in a highly dollarized economy such as Lebanon's, another concern of the bank was that in order to play its role as lender of last resort it should have access to a sufficient level of foreign reserves.

For the purpose of slowing down the flow of Central Bank credit to the government (in conjunction with a targeted reduction in the fiscal deficit), ceilings on governmental borrowing from the Central Bank were recommended in April 1992 by a government-appointed committee of economic experts, and later adopted, in revised form, by the Solh government in July 1992 as part of its fiscal programme to reduce the deficit by controlling governmental expenditure (for a brief discussion of these measures, see below). The governments that followed did not choose to apply explicit ceilings on governmental borrowings from the Central Bank but managed, as we have seen, to ensure that the commercial banks and public financed most or a large part of the fiscal deficit.

Banking developments, performance and challenges

The structure of the banking system did not undergo major changes during this period. While decreasing over the period as a result of mergers, the number of operating commercial banks continued to be large, standing at sixty in mid-2002, with the traditional concentration of bank activity. What is noteworthy, however, are the successive measures taken by the monetary authorities and the Banking Control Commission to strengthen the banking system, whose performance was generally robust. Many challenges remain, a major one being the development of the very weak Beirut capital market and more generally promoting financial deepening. In what follows, we shall first briefly summarize major developments in the banking sector during the 1991–2002 period and then discuss the challenges that lie ahead.

The wave of bank failures that took place in 1989–90 (see Chapter 2) prompted the government to adopt law no. 110 (14 November 1991), which represented the first attempt at regulating the banking sector after sixteen years of civil war. Essentially it defined the basis for auto-liquidation of banks in trouble (within a period ending on 31 December 1993) and created a special banking tribunal (whose term ended on the same date) for the prompt settlement of claims and litigation related to these banks. The law also raised deposit guarantee by the National Institute for Deposit Guarantee from LL1 million to LL5 million (equivalent to about $2,900 at the end of 1993).[48]

Later, with the objective of encouraging bank consolidation, law no. 192 of 4 January 1993 was adopted, with a duration of five years, extended in 1998 for another five years (law no. 679 of 26 March 1998). The law provided for limited concessional loans from the Central Bank, if deemed necessary, for the completion of the mergers. The bank was also authorized to exempt the acquiring bank from income tax on a portion of its income provided it did not exceed the cost of merger and subject to an upper ceiling of LL2 billion ($15.6 million as at the end of March 1992). Over the period 1993–2001 as many as thirty-two mergers and/or acquisitions took place, thereby reducing significantly the number of operating banks. Further, a few foreign banks opened or reopened branches in Beirut.

Bank concentration in terms of deposits and credit continued to dominate the banking scene. At the end of 2001 the alpha group, comprising the largest banks,[49] accounted for 78 per cent of total deposits and 74 per cent of loans in the banking system. There was an even greater concentration among the beneficiaries of bank credit. For example, it is estimated that at the end of 1998 the biggest 292 debtors (0.04 per cent of total beneficiaries) accounted for 37.5 per cent of total loans and 3,020 debtors (3.37 per cent of the total) for 74 per cent.[50] Similarly, a few sectors, namely trade, services and construction, absorbed the largest proportion of bank credit: about 64 per cent of the total at the end of 2002.

The number of private medium- and long-term (investment) banks stood at eight at the end of 2002. However, while their activities may have gradually expanded, their combined share of the banking market remains very limited. At the end of 2001 their combined claims on the private and public sectors amounted to about 5 per cent of commercial bank claims on the two sectors.[51] At the same time, in line with global trends, domestic banks, especially the larger ones, have, since the mid-1990s, been veering in the direction of universal banking. A number of them established wholly owned investment banks, and most have been developing new activities such as retail banking alongside improved services, with the objective of strengthening their competitive position not only domestically but also with an eye on emerging regional opportunities.

The rules regarding foreign ownership of banks were liberalized. In early 1991 a law was adopted which stipulated that a third of total shares (instead of the one half that had been in force) must be owned by Lebanese citizens or Lebanese companies owned by Lebanese citizens or joint stock companies in which at least a third of the shares were held by Lebanese citizens. The objective of this law was to attract foreign, mainly Arab, banking capital to Beirut.

Overall, the banking sector performed strongly, better than the real economy. For the period 1991–2002 its combined claims on the private sector (measured in current US dollars) increased at an annual average rate of about 19.6 per cent, and for deposits at about the same rate. Hence their ratios to GDP rose over the period. At the end of 2002, the ratio of bank claims on the private sector to GDP stood at 87 per cent, and that of deposits at 246 per cent (see Table 3.4). These are very high ratios, even by comparison with industrial countries.[52] Profitability indicators for the period 1991–2001, as measured by return on average assets (ROAA) and average equity (ROAE), point to robust results up to 1998, after which they tended to decline. The asset ratio increased from 0.5 per cent for 1991 to 1.46 per cent for 1994 and maintained a similarly high rate until 1997 (1.47 per cent), after which it progressively declined to 0.78 for 2001. The relatively high ratios prior to 1998 are attributable to the relatively high spreads on Lebanese pounds (i.e. between TB yields and deposit rates). Afterwards, as the deposit base and bank lending increasingly shifted to dollars, the spread narrowed. The return on average equity increased substantially from 1991 to 1992 (88.3 per cent) but then declined gradually to 21.1 per cent for 1997 and 11.6 per cent for 2001. The explanation for this lies in the increased capitalization of Lebanese banks, including the ploughing back of profits, and in recent years to a limited decline in net income. But the major banks continued to generate a high level of profits.[53]

It should be borne in mind, though, that the overall average performance of the banking sector conceals variations among various categories of banks. The alpha group generally outperformed the smaller banks, some of which faced difficulties and chose to merge with stronger banks. On the other hand, Lebanese bank operations have suffered from a maturity mismatch, shorter-term deposits being invested in longer-term instruments such as TBs. The risks associated with this policy stemmed from a possible rise in the domestic interest rate, thereby adding to the burdens of banks in the shorter term and/or a possible depreciation of the pound that would have induced conversion of short-term pound denominated assets into dollar denominated assets, thus leaving the banks exposed to severe Lebanese pound illiquidity. In practice these dangers have been (and are) partly mitigated through the Repo facility extended by the Central Bank at times of liquidity squeezes, but of course at a high cost. Further, aware of these risks, banks have maintained rolling TB maturities spread across different short- and longer-term bills, and have also kept relatively high margins on call money.[54]

With the objective of strengthening the banking sector, the Central Bank and the Banking Control Commission implemented several important measures. First, insolvent banks were liquidated and troubled banks were required to take remedial measures (decree no. 110/91 on bank reform of 7 November 1991). Later, bank mergers were encouraged (law no. 192 of January 1993). Equally importantly, the bank regulatory environment was improved. Several prudent regulations were successively put in place:

among others, capital adequacy ratios were set in conformity with the Basle Committee guidelines, the level of minimum bank capitalization was raised, limits on foreign currency exposure were placed, provisioning for loans classified according to risk was enforced, internal audit procedures were enhanced, and credit risk management was improved.[55] Furthermore, in April 2001 a law was passed criminalizing money laundering.

By the beginning of this decade, the challenges facing the Lebanese banking sector could be grouped under three headings: (i) coping with an inadequate macroeconomic environment; (ii) the need to further strengthen the banking sector, develop bank policies and enhance the monitoring system; and (iii) fostering financial deepening.

The macroeconomic dimension related to the control of the persistent fiscal deficit and the consequent rise in public debt as one major prerequisite for the maintenance of a basically sound and stable macroeconomic situation. The prevalence of large fiscal deficits had the effect of diverting substantial bank resources from the private sector to the government and constraining the role of interest rate policy in stimulating investment. Equally important, the perception of potential macroeconomic instability signalled by the inability to control the deficit contributed to the weakening of business confidence in the domestic economy. In particular, the issue of exchange rate stability gained, over time, greater attention as the authorities failed to address the fiscal problem and contain the rapid rise in public debt after 1994. Specifically, there was latent fear that unless the fiscal situation was successfully addressed, the prevailing exchange rate of the pound might not be sustainable despite the proclaimed commitment of the authorities to the policy of exchange rate stability.[56] Such latent fears negatively affected the demand for assets denominated in pounds: the rate of dollarization of deposits remained high throughout the period under consideration, steadily increasing after 1996; and they are likely to have weakened willingness to invest in Lebanon, although in the absence of reliable quantitative measures it is not possible to gauge the extent to which this was so. Whatever the case, Lebanese banks had become more secure against exchange risks because of limits placed on currency exposure and the fact that most of their credit remained dollar denominated.[57] Nevertheless, depreciation of the pound would have put pressure on bank customers (individuals and companies) who derived in part, if not entirely, their earnings in Lebanese pounds while being indebted in foreign currency. The banks would have had to face and try to contain such pressures. In the prevailing banking context of the latter part of the 1990s and the early years of this decade, the greater the degree of dollar indexation, the smaller would have been the potential adverse impact of any depreciation. But the fact remains that a sizeable segment of business earnings, and more of salaries, were pound denominated, and the immediate impact of a depreciation would have been a loss of real income. Also, a significant depreciation would have had an important adverse impact on banks' profits.[58] Businesses would have been able to reindex to the dollar (as happened during the civil war), the brunt of the adjustment being again borne by the salaried segment of the population. In practice, the Lebanese authorities having been able to exclude exchange rate adjustment as one of the required corrective policy measures, those segments of the population who would have had to bear the brunt of this adjustment have been spared this experience.

The Lebanese banking system is dynamic and generally well informed and well connected to the global banking industry. Human resources in the banking sector have been steadily developing and banks have been attempting to continually modernize technologically. Being privately owned and operating in an open and competitive economy has spurred Lebanese banks to modernize and maintain continuous contact with advances in the banking industry abroad.

At the same time, in the early years of this decade there came to the fore specific issues that needed to be addressed with the objective of strengthening the sector's position and competitiveness in an increasingly open world economy and financial system. Three will be briefly noted here. The first is the move towards greater transparency in bank operations and statements, particularly as concerns the small banks, a move that the Banking Control Commission will need to enforce.[59] Such a step will further enhance the confidence of savers and investors, both resident and non-resident, in the Lebanese banking system. The second is the further development of newer areas of banking activities, such as retail, private and investment banking, which a number of banks initiated, especially in the second half of the 1990s. The third is credit product diversification, whereby banks will move from the strictly traditional forms of commercial banking into such areas as personal, car and mortgage loans. This will render bank portfolios more diversified and hence less risky as a variety of instruments with differing maturities are developed. Again, modest moves in these areas have been undertaken in the 1990s and early this decade: medium-term lending expanded and personal loans and corporate bond issues have appeared.

The development of Lebanese banking will have to go hand in hand with continuous improvements in bank monitoring on the part of the Central Bank and the Banking Control Commission, bearing in mind that substantial progress in this area has been achieved.[60] As a result the overall banking structure has improved significantly, and the sector has become stronger. However, there are several areas where banking control will need to be further strengthened, e.g. more effective monitoring of maturity mismatches, procedures pertaining to loan portfolio examinations, reassessing the system of penalties for non-compliance (in many cases no penalties are set), raising minimum capital requirements, and strengthening internal audit procedures.[61] More generally, stricter compliance with the Basle Core Principles is required.[62]

The Lebanese financial sector remains primarily rooted in commercial banking, with a strong orientation towards short-term credit operations. Other financial intermediaries, e.g. banks specializing in medium- and long-term credit (investment banks), and financial institutions dealing in asset management, have been established. But as noted above, their activities remain very limited and small in comparison with traditional commercial banking. And while Lebanese banking has been gradually developing in the direction of universal banking, Lebanon's capital market remains weak. The market, officially reopened in September 1995 (after a twelve-year closure), is still in its infancy, and is yet to take off in any significant way. As at the end of 2002 there were only thirteen companies listed on the stock exchange (up from four when the market was reopened) with a market capitalization of only $1.4 billion (roughly 8 per cent of the estimated GDP for that year).[63] This ranked it as the smallest of the Arab stock exchanges in operation.

The development of the capital market and more generally the promotion of financial deepening are important policy challenges.[64] The literature on financial development and economic growth amply illustrates the important role of financial markets and institutions in providing growth opportunities, broadly via better mobilization of savings and improvement of resource allocation. And whereas the comparative effects of different types of financial intermediation (e.g. market-based, universal banking, specialized banks) on economic growth are not necessarily universally agreed, it is recognized that their development (whether concomitantly or sequentially, i.e. the development of the banking system preceding that of financial markets) is an essential ingredient for the sustained growth of developing countries.[65]

For Lebanon, the development of a well-regulated Beirut capital market – at the level of institutions and instruments – will not only open up additional savings outlets and enhance investment opportunities at home but will also permit Beirut to develop as a regional capital market in an increasingly open region. It will also provide Lebanese banks with better opportunities to build more diversified, mature and profitable balance sheets typical of higher-rated banks operating in more developed markets. Progress in this direction is being made – for example, medium-term lending, personal loans and corporate bond issues have appeared, which should eventually lead to stronger balance sheets. Retail, investment and private banking are areas that hold promise and are expected to widen the scope and nature of Lebanese banking. In a series of circulars issued in the second half of the 1990s the Central Bank regulated the listing of Lebanese banks on the stock market, the opening by commercial banks and financial institutions of fiduciary accounts, the issuance of bonds and GDRs (Global Depository Rights) by banks and financial institutions, the issuance of mutual funds for public subscription, and the issuance by banks of long-term certificates of deposit (CDs).[66] However, a number of further steps need to be taken, including regulations that will, among others, ensure full disclosure and transparency among listed companies, widening their ownership base, a revision of existing regulations to enhance the ability of joint stock companies to issue debt instruments, and strengthening of internal controls and the introduction of hedging instruments. As the capital and banking markets are being developed, it is essential to keep in mind that their sound development goes hand in hand with the macrofinancial and economic development of the country in line with the emphasis that international organizations, such as the IMF, have recently been laying on the importance of macro-prudential indicators in assessing the health and stability of financial systems.[67]

3.4 Reconstruction programmes and expenditures

The preoccupation of respective governments in the period 1991–92 with issues of political reconciliation and normalization leading to the 1992 parliamentary elections did not preclude their involvement in questions of reconstruction and (as discussed above) the restoration of relative financial stability. On the reconstruction front, the CDR was reactivated and the preparation of reconstruction plans was initiated. By 1992 a National Emergency Reconstruction Programme (NERP) was finalized for the emergency reconstruction phase, which was to be followed by a medium-term reconstruction phase.[68] The NERP (encompassing fifteen sectors in groups of five) was designed as a $2.25 billion three-year multi-sectoral programme (1993–95), aimed at having maximum impact on restoring economic activity and alleviating social hardship.[69] Subsequently CDR developed a broader and longer-term (1993–2002) investment programme by building on the NERP. It is referred to as Horizon 2000.[70]

In the period January 1994–May 2002 the CDR published twelve progress reports. None was issued for the earlier years, 1990–93. Principally they include a review of the major reconstruction programmes that have been initiated in various sectors and their respective stages of implementation. Three salient features of the reconstruction process are revealed in this official documentation.

The first is the early prominence (progress report of January 1994) given to the 'Base Scenario' that embedded the so-called Horizon 2000 ten-year programme in a macroeconomic framework (model), with an envisaged total expenditure of $11.7 billion, capable of assessing its likely impact on major economic aggregates. This scenario envisaged: (i) a growth rate in the ten-year period 1992–2002 whereby real GDP was to be restored by 1995 to its 1974 level; (ii) moving the current budget position into approximate balance by 1995, after which fiscal surpluses (before investment) were to be generated to constitute the principal source of financing public recovery expenditures as well as debt service payments; (iii) public debt stock was to peak at 84 per cent of GDP by 1995, followed by a progressive decline to 39 per cent by 2002;

the stock of foreign debt was projected to peak at 37 per cent of GDP by 1996 before declining to 16 per cent by 2002; and total debt service payments (amortization and interest) were anticipated to rise to 11 per cent of GDP by 1994 and then decline to 5 per cent by 2002.[71] Subsequent reports did not refer to actual macroeconomic performance in comparison with the predictions of the Base Scenario, presumably because of the growing divergence between the actual and intended performance.

Second, several adjustments and additions were made to the Horizon 2000 programme during 1994, which raised its total from $11.7 to $18.0 billion over a thirteen-year period stretching over 1995–2007. Annualized, this implied an average annual increase of 18 per cent in public investment.[72] This was to be accompanied by a growing emphasis on administrative and socio-economic reform, alongside intended encouragement of the private sector to participate in the reconstruction projects, taking the form of Build Own Transfer (BOT).[73]

Third, in later years the reported activities of the CDR began to focus on balanced regional development and the protection of the environment.[74] The progress report of 9 March 1999 acknowledged that this latter sector had long been neglected (p. 2).

In practice, implementation of the reconstruction plan fell substantially short of its announced targets, with a growing divergence, over time, between actual results and intended targets. The 1995 real GDP is estimated to have stood at about 60 per cent of the 1974 GDP instead of reaching its level as planned.[75] In 1995 current expenditure, instead of being in balance with domestic revenues, was equivalent to over 150 per cent of such revenue; by 1997 the proportion had climbed to roughly 210 per cent, falling back to about 150 per cent for 1999 but then rising again to an estimated 233 per cent for 2002.[76] The ratio of public debt to GDP stood at 78 per cent at the end of 1995 (as against a projected peak of 84 per cent), but then instead of declining as planned rose to 114 per cent at the end of 1998 and about 180 per cent at the end of 2002. Similarly, outstanding foreign debt stood at an estimated 15 per cent of GDP at the end of 1996 (as against a projected peak of 37 per cent) and then continued its upward trend to an estimated 74 per cent at the end of 2002. Debt service payments amounted to about 10 per cent of GDP at the end of 1994 but then, instead of declining as projected, rose to a little less than 14 per cent at the end of 1998, 17 per cent at the end of 2001 and an estimated 18 per cent at the end of 2002.

Table 3.7 indicates that the total of contracts awarded for CDR projects for the period 1992–2001 amounted to about $6.21 billion, backed by foreign funding comprising about 40 per cent of the total. By the end of 2001 a little over $3 billion (about 50 per cent of the total) had been completed, the rest being in the process of implementation.[77] The grant element in external financing was about 15 per cent, with soft loans comprising an additional 41 per cent.[78] The sectors that benefited mostly from the reconstruction projects were electricity, telecommunications, ports/airports, solid waste management and roads, in that order. Together they accounted for about 70 per cent of the total contracts awarded during 1992–2001.

The large gap between the number of awarded and completed contracts was partly due to the nature of the projects being implemented and the time element involved. However, it also seems to reflect inability and/or unwillingness to utilize all available foreign financing, along with administrative and/or political and/or financial constraints that hampered the execution of reconstruction projects.[79] Annual CDR reconstruction expenditure varied substantially, with a rapidly accelerating annual rhythm after 1994 peaking in 1997, after which it tended to decline. As the greater proportion of capital expenditure was domestically financed, it is not surprising that these were the years that also witnessed a rapid increase in fiscal deficits, which also peaked in 1997, as both a proportion of expenditure and of GDP. Indeed, total capital expenditure (inclusive of CDR foreign-financed expenditure) showed a similar trend, peaking in 1997, maintaining a similar level in 1998 and then declining substantially until 2002.[80]

3.5 Attempts at coping with macroeconomic imbalances: an overview

The 1991–92 period: normalization and fiscal progress versus overall exchange rate volatility and rising inflation

With the reunification of the government in October 1990 after the forced removal of General Aoun, major national tasks faced the authorities: at the political level, reunifying public administration, national reconciliation in the context of the Taif Accord, disarming the various militias and strengthening national security, and the return of war refugees to their original places of residence. At the economic level, fiscal stability had to be gradually restored, orderly foreign exchange conditions maintained and plans to initiate the process of reconstruction prepared, not to mention coping with various socio-economic issues engendered by the civil war. I touched above on the broad political process of normalization (incomplete as it was) initiated in this period, culminating in the parliamentary elections of summer 1992 and the heightened political tensions that followed the decision to hold them. The elections, although opposed by a number of mainly Christian parties and groupings, were officially considered as a necessary step in the normalization process: renewed political representation in parliament in the wake of the civil war and the Taif Accord. Their boycott by the above parties rendered the newly elected parliament less representative of the potential electorate than might otherwise have been the case. However, the parliamentary elections of 1996, again boycotted (to a much lesser extent than before) by anti-Taif groupings, did not lead to a significantly different political representation in parliament. Nor did the 2000 parliamentary elections, which effectively were not boycotted by any major political group. Parliamentary representation, it would thus seem, was governed by factors more influential than the boycott (which declined significantly over time) of parties opposed to Taif or disgruntled with the emerging post-Taif political process. Major objections to the electoral law have been raised by opposition and other groups. Among others, they point out that it was not drawn up in strict conformity with the Taif Accord, and furthermore, electoral districts have been modified from one election to another to suit the electoral interests of those in power, leaving aside the role of 'political' money in influencing the outcome.[81]

In what follows we outline the response of the authorities at the economic level. Overall the national authorities succeeded in starting the process of gradually coping with the fiscal situation, initiating certain reconstruction projects and planning for longer-term financial recovery and reconstruction. While the fiscal deficit, as a proportion of GDP, was gradually reduced over this period (the forced resignation of the Karami government on 6 May 1992 notwithstanding) and fiscal planning was introduced, rising domestic political tensions helped generate turbulence on the foreign exchange market that increased pressure on the pound, leading to its depreciation at a time when the Central Bank's reserves had not yet been reconstituted to adequate levels; this in turn led to rising inflation.

Higher Council for Economic Policy Coordination This committee was set up in March 1991 for the purpose of reviewing and coordinating the economic, financial and developmental objectives of the state. It was chaired by the then prime minister and included the ministers of finance, economy and trade, foreign affairs, transportation, the governor of the Central Bank, the president and one of the two vice-presidents of the CDR, an economic adviser, and the third vice-governor of the Central Bank. A subcommittee comprising the economic adviser, the vice-president of the CDR and the third vice-governor of the Central Bank was charged with the task of preparing the agenda for the committee's meetings after consultation with the prime minister and other members.[82]

The committee met regularly. Among the major issues on which it deliberated, the fiscal situation was given primary attention, with the objective of reducing the budget deficit.[83] Means of raising the level of revenues including the possibility of introducing new taxes (e.g. sales tax, capital gains tax, tax on professions, etc.) as well as issues of tax collection were discussed.[84] More generally, the committee considered alternative tax options and the feasibility of implementing them. Other issues it considered pertained to priorities of reconstruction, coordination of Lebanese efforts to solicit foreign assistance, reviewing the policy recommendations of international and private consulting organizations in the light of the government's economic and reconstruction objectives, possible Central Bank participation in financing selected private sector projects, and possible use of gold reserves to reduce public debt or finance public sector projects (under prevailing conditions, it was decided not to resort to this option). The committee also met with delegations of international organizations to discuss the evolving economic and financial situation.

For policy purposes, coordination of economic, financial and developmental policies is of paramount importance. The committee's regular meetings proved to be very useful in providing a framework in which the policy-makers concerned could discuss the policy issues at hand on the basis of position papers prepared for this purpose. At the same time, given the composition of the committee and its relatively large membership, its discussions were not always as focused as might have been desired, and it came to be recognized that the format of committee deliberation should be modified to render it more efficient. As it turned out, the government of Prime Minister Karami had to resign in May 1992, and with its resignation the committee ceased to function. A new government, headed by Rashid Solh, took office on 14 May 1992 (see below).

Report of the committee of economic experts It was noted above that the Lebanese pound began to depreciate rapidly following the decision of the Bank of Lebanon on 21 February 1992 to halt its intervention on the foreign exchange market, and that this depreciation was accompanied by a concomitant rise in domestic prices. As a result of the deteriorating monetary situation, the Karami government decided on 11 March 1992 to appoint a committee of economic experts from outside the public sector, and charged it with the task of preparing an economic/financial work plan that would outline measures to redress the prevailing situation and lay the foundations for economic recovery. As specified in the cabinet decision, the plan was to be drawn up in the light of available national resources and the committee was to submit its report to the cabinet within a period of one month after it was set up.[85]

The committee submitted its report on 21 April 1992. Entitled 'Foundations of Economic Stability in Lebanon: a General Framework',[86] it focused mainly on policy measures intended simultaneously to restore financial stability and stimulate economic growth in the light of the reconstruction programmes then under preparation. The report emphasized that the achievement of these goals required the fulfilment of two important conditions. The first was the implementation of the proposed measures *in toto*, and the second securing the necessary political will and ability to implement the proposed reforms. Only then would the recommended measures restore confidence in the national economy and effectively initiate the process of reform.

At the fiscal level, the report recommended: (a) the imposition of an upper ceiling for governmental expenditure accompanied by suggested measures to reduce the fiscal deficit for 1992; (b) imposing a ceiling on governmental borrowing from the Central Bank; (c) reforming and simplifying the tax system, including, among other measures, reducing and consolidating the various progressive income taxes into two tax brackets: 10 and 15 per cent respectively; and (d) a drastic reform of the tax administration along with overall administrative reform.

At the monetary level, the report recommended, among other things: (a) the continuation of the tight monetary measures presently in force which might be relaxed as the fiscal situation improved; (b) the maintenance of an exchange rate that reflected fundamental market forces while attempting to maintain orderly market conditions; and (c) speeding up the process of bank reform, including the enforcement of the 'Basle Agreement' pertaining to capital adequacy ratios and raising the level of bank capitalization. The importance of coordination between fiscal, monetary and reconstruction policies was stressed.

Of the various proposed measures to stimulate economic growth, the following may be noted: (a) the reduction in income tax rates referred to above accompanied by strict enforcement of tax collection and strengthening of tax administration; (b) enhancement of the resources of the Housing Bank (specific recommendations were made); and (c) privatization of specific public sector entities (e.g. telecommunications, solid waste management) in accordance with well-defined criteria and an appropriate regulatory framework. The report also dealt with several other areas, notably emerging social issues, institutional reform and the investment climate.

The Karami government approved the proposed recommendations, but, as noted, shortly afterwards, on 6 May 1992, it was forced to resign in the wake of demonstrations, which some claimed were orchestrated, in protest against the deteriorating economic and social conditions.

Parliamentary elections and the 14 July 1992 fiscal measures The government that took over after the 6 May 1992 crisis set for itself two major tasks: (i) preparing for the post-Taif parliamentary elections, the first since 1972; and (ii) coping with the inherited difficult fiscal situation in the context of an unsettled foreign exchange rate situation, associated, in large measure, with heightened political opposition to the elections. We have discussed exchange rate developments above. The primary aim of the fiscal measures adopted by the government on 14 July 1992 was twofold: (i) to bring the fiscal situation gradually under control through a planned reduction in the large fiscal deficit and central bank financing; and (ii) thereby restore fiscal credibility which, in turn, would positively influence the foreign exchange market and enhance Lebanon's position in negotiating for international economic assistance. The fiscal measures were intended as an initial move, in the context of a coordinated economic policy that would permit the government to restore financial balance.

To reduce the fiscal deficit the government imposed ceilings on total public sector expenditure for the second half of 1992, and on governmental borrowing from the Central Bank, and sought, among other measures, to enhance governmental revenues through stricter enforcement of tax collection, raising taxes on gasoline and adjusting upwards the 'customs dollar rate'.[87] The Council of Ministers also decided to initiate the process of privatization with regard to specific sectors. It charged a ministerial committee with submitting recommendations in this regard, based on the reports of specialized committees for each of the sectors to be privatized wholly or partially. This longer-term process was not, however, taken up by the newly formed government in the wake of the parliamentary elections that took place over the summer of 1992. Indeed, the whole issue of privatization was postponed until May 2000, when legislation was approved by parliament for the creation of the Higher Privatization Council which set the modality for the privatization process.

Notable progress was made in reducing the fiscal deficit in a relatively short period of time: from about 64 per cent of governmental expenditure for the first half of the year to 54 per cent for the second half. Nevertheless, for the reasons mentioned earlier, the turbulence in the exchange market continued to prevail until the conclusion of the parliamentary elections and the formation of a new government.

The 1993–2002 period: exchange rate stabilization and decreasing inflation versus large budgetary deficits and rising public debt

The general focus of successive governments during this period was to maintain exchange rate stability and rehabilitate the country's damaged infrastructure (discussed in detail above). The former objective was achieved, along with a substantial reduction in the rate of inflation, and a number of major infrastructure projects were completed over this period. But, as analysed above, in the context of persistent large fiscal deficits the attainment of these objectives carried with it substantial economic costs. Efforts were also made to stimulate investment and attract foreign resources. However, the persisting regional conflict, the burden of which was partly shouldered by Lebanon, and perhaps more importantly inability or unwillingness to control the fiscal deficit, and hence the rapid rise in public debt and the debt burden, dampened the in-flow of private investment and eventually contributed to the decline in the rate of economic growth; and, as already noted, by 2002 the Lebanese government was forced to seek substantial foreign support in an attempt to stabilize the fiscal situation and reverse the rise in public debt.

Major governmental policy measures during the period may be briefly outlined as follows.

1. To ensure exchange rate stability the pound was anchored to the US dollar (with a gradually appreciating trend for the pound). The policy instruments used to defend it were Central Bank intervention on the foreign

exchange market and relatively high real domestic interest rates. For the period 1993–98, the differential between the effective yield on three-month TBs and the average interest rate on dollar deposits in Lebanon averaged 10.5 per cent, dropping from a high of about 15 per cent for 1993 to about 7 per cent for 1998 and 6.7 per cent for 2001.[88]

2. At the end of 1993, parliament approved law no. 282 of 30 December 1993 which simplified the income tax brackets and reduced tax rates, maintaining a degree of progressivity in the tax structure. Income taxes on wages and salaries were scaled down to five brackets (from thirteen) with tax rates ranging from 2 to 10 per cent (previously 2 to 32 per cent); income taxes on financial establishments were set at a flat 10 per cent and on profits of commercial and industrial enterprises from 3 to 10 per cent, grouped into four brackets (previously profits from all three categories were regrouped into thirteen brackets with a tax range from 6 to 50 per cent); taxes on returns from certain capital accounts (e.g. return on stocks) were set at a flat 5 per cent, but other returns, such as those from savings accounts and treasury bills, remained exempt. The announced purpose of these modifications was to stimulate investment and render Lebanon more attractive to foreign investments, and also to induce greater compliance with due income tax payments on the part of business enterprises and independent professional groups. Some modifications were introduced in the 1999 Budget Law (approved by parliament) whereby the upper income tax bracket was raised to 21 per cent (excluding certain categories of professionals) and corporate income tax to 15 per cent.

Despite the 1999 income tax modifications, the issue of social equity was not given much consideration, the apparent progressivity of the income tax rates notwithstanding. According to two studies, the effects of the new tax system on income distribution were minimal.[89] Available data for 1997–2001 indicate that the proportion of corporate taxes of total revenue stood at 8 per cent for 1997, dropping to less than 7 per cent in the following three years and rising again to 8 per cent in 2001. When taxes on wage and salaries are added, the proportion of income taxes rises gradually from 8.5 per cent to 11.0 per cent, owing mainly to the gradual increase in the proportion of taxes on wages and salaries over the period.[90] It would seem that the intended enhancement of income tax compliance on the part of business enterprises was not as successful as was hoped for.[91]

Other tax measures included the elimination of the 'customs dollar rate', increases in taxes on gasoline, increases in governmental fees on various services and, effective February 2002, the introduction of a 10 per cent value added tax after tariff rates on a wide range of imports had been reduced the previous year. This was followed a year later, i.e. effective 31 January 2003, by the introduction of a 5 per cent tax on interest income from all deposits, resident and non-resident. During the period 1997–2001 the proportion of indirect taxes of total revenue, while declining a little, remained very high, ranging from 89 to 92 per cent. At the same time, there occurred a significant shift to non-tax revenue (fees and similar levies) whereby its proportion of the total rose from 23 per cent for 1997 to 36 per cent for 2001. With the introduction of VAT in early 2002 this proportion is expected to decline. Studies carried out on the tax system point out that middle-income groups, primarily salaried people, increasingly bore the brunt of taxation, and not surprisingly that indirect income taxation is regressive.[92]

The impact of income tax reduction on investment and, in particular, the in-flow of foreign investment cannot be readily determined. Other factors weigh in. Declining rates of growth, alongside a mounting public debt and lack of progress in the political and administrative domain, contributed, among other factors, to the declining in-flow of investment noted earlier, irrespective of any inducements the income tax reductions were intended to carry. Briefly, the evolving macroeconomic environment became increasingly less attractive, while the prevailing political/administrative conditions acted as a further restraining factor to the in-flow of private foreign investment.

3. The authorities took measures to reduce the interest burden of public debt and extend its maturity. For this purpose foreign currency denominated medium-term government bonds (mainly dollar or eurobonds) were issued. They carried a lower rate of interest than Lebanese pound denominated debt and helped extend the average maturity of the outstanding public debt. Other steps were also taken to extend the maturity of domestic currency denominated debt. Whenever financial market conditions allowed, the Central Bank attempted to increase the maturity structure of public debt denominated in Lebanese pounds. And, in particular, during periods of financial pressure, the bank used swap operations in the secondary market for TBs to smooth its maturity profile so as to avoid the refinancing of large numbers of maturing bills at certain peak dates. It swapped maturing TBs and newly issued short-term TBs held by banks and the public with newly issued longer-term twelve- and twenty-four-month bills at a discount. The burden associated with the difference between secondary and primary market yields on longer-term TBs was assumed by the Central Bank.[93] While the flotation of foreign currency bonds contributed to a slowing down of the rate of increase in the interest burden, it increased the foreign currency exposure of public debt: at the end of 2002 foreign currency denominated debt comprised 46.4 per cent of the total.[94] An underlying assumption of governmental action on this front was that the stability of the Lebanese pound would be sustained. With prevailing high TB yields, the national authorities succeeded in inducing commercial banks (in recent years reluctantly) and to a lesser extent the public to carry the TBs, thereby providing financing for the fiscal deficit. At the same time, as mentioned above, TBs were the instrument used to control liquidity and partly build up foreign exchange reserves. Whenever the required financing

of the deficit was not covered by the issuance of TBs to commercial banks and public, the Central Bank covered the remaining shortfall.

4. In terms of development and reconstruction the Horizon 2000 plan was completed in 1994, incorporating an earlier three-year emergency reconstruction plan completed in 1992. While actual expenditures fell substantially short of planned targets, a number of major rehabilitation projects were completed. Nevertheless, as analysed above, by 1999/2000 the rate of growth had stagnated, with a limited improvement in 2001/2, accompanied by an escalating rise in public debt.

5. By the late 1990s the authorities came to face the twin problem of a slow performing economy burdened by a rapidly rising public debt and a relatively high debt service. The first government formed after the presidential elections of 1998 (headed by Salim al Hoss) planned to cope with emerging difficult economic/fiscal conditions by means of a financial adjustment programme that was intended to control the rise in public debt and provide the incentives for renewed economic growth.[95] As part of the intended programme, a privatization law was approved by parliament which, among other things, set up the Higher Privatization Council, charged with the task of guiding the intended privatization of some public sector enterprises. However, generally domestic political tensions and lack of political harmony within the ranks of the cabinet forestalled governmental efforts in this regard; and by late summer 2000 a new government (headed by Rafic Hariri) was formed following the parliamentary elections of that year.

6. In turn the new government attempted to revitalize the economy by further opening up the already open domestic economy, being partly motivated by the requirements of the association agreement with the European Union (it was signed in spring 2002) and eventual membership of the WTO. Among other measures, import duties were lowered, a policy of open skies was implemented, and rationalization of two public sector enterprises (the state TV station and MEA, the national carrier) was carried out.[96] Further, with continuing large fiscal deficits and rising public debt levels, the government introduced new taxes and tried to control non-interest expenditure. Also the process of privatization was started by enacting three laws pertaining to three public enterprises.[97] While some progress was made on the fiscal front, the situation had reached a point where the government was forced to admit that without substantial outside financial support the spiralling public debt could not be brought under control, thereby setting the stage for its appeal for such support at an international meeting in Paris called by French President Jacques Chirac on 23 November 2002[98] (see below, pp. 128–9).

Throughout the years from 1993 to 2002 attempts at administrative reform failed and institutional development was never a focus of serious governmental action. The issue of governance remained one of the principal challenges facing the country.

Appeal for outside financial support: the Paris II meeting of November 2002[99]

This meeting included a number of donor countries and international institutions which assembled to consider financial assistance to the Lebanese government in an effort to help it stabilize the rising public debt and eventually gradually bring it down. The document presented by the Lebanese government to the meeting requested a total assistance package of $5 billion (to take various forms), intended concomitantly to help the government reduce the interest debt burden it had been shouldering, arrest the rapid rise in total public debt, and eventually reduce it to more manageable levels. The appeal was essentially based on three major elements: the record of recent economic and fiscal reform steps undertaken by the government, plans to implement further measures in the future and, perhaps most important of all, public admission that without substantial outside support the planned government measures would not be sufficient to address the problem at hand, with dire economic, social and implicitly political consequences that would threaten Lebanon's domestic stability. This last admission is tantamount to a public acknowledgement of the inappropriate fiscal policies that for many years had been in place, and equally government delay in taking the required corrective measures to avert a major governmental fiscal crisis.

I referred above to recent measures that had been initiated by the government. Of the planned measures, the government had approved in preparation for the Paris II meeting a budget for 2003 (approved by parliament in January 2003) that incorporated expenditure cuts and revenue-enhancing measures, including new taxes and fees. The stated aim was to reduce the budgetary deficit from 41 per cent of expenditure for 2002 (16 per cent of GDP) to around 25 per cent of total expenditure (8–9 per cent of projected GDP); and further increase the primary surplus, in comparison with 2002, to the equivalent of 4 per cent of GDP. In addition (according to the document submitted to the Paris II meeting) measures were planned to privatize or reprivatize the cellular phone system (bid offerings made for the licence with or without governmental sharing), and to transform the fixed phone system and power sectors into commercial entities with or without strategic partners. The proceeds derived from these measures were supposed to be used only for debt reduction purposes. And furthermore, the Central Bank planned to enter into voluntary reverse swap arrangements with Lebanese commercial banks, intended to reduce the rates carried by the existing stock of public debt (carried out in December 2002). These measures were expected to lead in 2003 to a reduction in outstanding public debt, some decline in the rates on domestic debt and limited easing of spreads on foreign currency borrowing.

But, according to the document, in the absence of external support, together the above measures would not be sufficient to reverse the debt dynamics beyond 2003. The objective of debt reduction in the medium term can be accomplished only if the requested external support were forthcoming.

It could take several forms, such as sovereign guarantees and investment by governments and central banks in Lebanese foreign currency bonds which would allow Lebanon to borrow on the markets of the supporting countries at low spreads and using the proceeds to substitute this lower-interest external debt for existing high-interest debt. The request was made for long-term borrowing with a grace period of five years and a repayment period of ten years. With external support and a projected pick-up in the rate of growth to 4 per cent by 2007, the net public debt was projected to decline to 92 per cent of GDP at the end of that year.

Donor countries and institutions meeting in Paris on 23 November 2002 agreed to provide a package of financial and developmental assistance totalling $4.4 billion, of which about $1.3–1.4 billion was to be in the form of long-term loans for development projects and the rest, $3.0–3.1 billion, to support the efforts of the Lebanese authorities in tackling the immediate debt problem.[100] It is too early to pass judgement on the medium-term economic impact of the Paris II meeting.[101] But two of its salient features are worth noting. The first is the immediately recognizable political dimension of the meeting. France played a leading role in marshalling European support for the Lebanese government lest it fall prey to an unsustainable fiscal/debt situation with whatever political ramifications this may carry with it. The second is the quasi-role assigned to the IMF, under whose direct umbrella financial rescue packages are normally undertaken and in the context of which donor countries stand ready to assist. The reason could be that a full agreement between the Lebanese government and the IMF on the required financial/economic reforms (if at all feasible) might take a longer period of time than was available to withstand the pressures that the Lebanese economy had been facing.[102] At the same time, the IMF was requested to provide semi-annual assessments of the progress made by the Lebanese government in implementing the measures outlined in the document submitted to Paris II.

The major reason for the failure of successive governments to implement some of the necessary macroeconomic corrective measures prior to Paris II is attributable to low-level institutional performance (see Chapter 4) which had blurred the distinction between public and private interests, constrained the proper formulation and management of economic policy and effectively permitted responsible officials not to be accountable for their policy actions. However, the issue of fiscal/monetary reform is part of the wider issue of national reform which embraces political governance and the quality of development. If faulty macroeconomic policies are reversible in the short or medium run, this is not necessarily the case when it comes to the deterioration in the quality of development. With or without outside financial support, national political and economic reform can succeed in the long run only if the requisite conditions for its success are met (see Chapter 5).

Table 3.1 Lebanon: GDP and public debt, 1991–2002 (in million US dollars)

	1991	1992	1993	1994	1995	1996	1997	1998	1999	2000	2001	2002*
Nominal GDP	4,452	5,546	7,535	9,110	11,119	12,992	14,862	16,165	16,458	16,399	16,660	17,300
Public debt (end period)	3,114	2,635	3,821	6,557	8,870	13,008	15,390	18,555	22,365	24,969	28,340	31,334
(In per cent)												
Rate of real growth	...	4.5	7.0	8.0	6.5	4.0	4.0	3.0	1.0	0.0	2.0	2.0
Debt/GDP	69.9	47.5	50.7	72	79.8	100.1	103.6	114.8	135.9	152.3	170.1	181.1

Sources: Ministry of Finance, Bank of Lebanon.
Note: * Official projections

Table 3.2 Lebanon: fiscal operations, 1991–2002 (billion LL)

	1991	1992	1993	1994	1995	1996	1997	1998	1999	2000	2001	2002[1]
Government revenues	522	1,060	1,855	2,241	3,033	3,533	3,753	4,449	4,868	4,749	4,643	5,830
Government expenditures	1,196	2,220	3,069	5,379	6,342	7,958	10,067	9,062	8,910	10,932	9,170	9,915
(o/w interest payments)	206	519	784	1,488	1,875	2,653	3,482	3,352	3,625	4,197	4,312	4,755
Budget deficit/surplus	-674	-1,160	-1,214	-3,138	-3,309	-4,425	-6,314	-4,613	-4,042	-6,183	-4,527	-4,085
Primary deficit/surplus[2]	-468	-641	-430	-1,650	-1,434	-1,772	-2,832	-1,261	-417	-1,986	-215	670
Budget deficit/GDP (%)	16	12	9	21	18	22	28	19	16	25	18	16
Primary deficit or surplus/GDP (%)	11	7	3	11	8	9	12	5	2	8	1	3
Budget deficit/expenditure (%)	56	52	40	58	52	56	63	51	45	57	49	41

Sources: IMF, *Lebanon – Economic Recovery, Stabilization and Macroeconomic Policies* (SM/94/207, 8 August 1994) and Ministry of Finance.
Notes: 1. Official projections; 2. Fiscal balance excluding interest payments

Table 3.3 Lebanon: monthly exchange rates and the consumer price index, 1991–2002
Exchange rate (monthly average) (LL per US dollar)

	Jan.	Feb.	Mar.	Apr.	May	Jun.	Jul.	Aug.	Sep.	Oct.	Nov.	Dec.	Annual ave.
1991	974.23	1,081.50	980.40	942.13	921.80	909.13	897.29	892.97	892.42	886.67	881.16	879.08	928.23
1992	879.00	929.26	1,175.00	1,443.00	1,621.11	1,730.50	1,855.80	2,382.25	2,527.75	2,248.10	1,911.76	1,850.62	1,712.84
1993	1,827.65	1,777.89	1,748.40	1,742.06	1,734.95	1,732.28	1,730.10	1,727.14	1,724.57	1,720.88	1,717.48	1,713.18	1,741.38
1994	1,708.40	1,703.14	1,697.08	1,692.31	1,687.03	1,681.83	1,678.20	1,673.65	1,668.32	1,663.21	1,658.50	1,649.26	1,680.08
1995	1,644.62	1,640.76	1,636.43	1,632.78	1,627.28	1,622.43	1,618.50	1,615.23	1,612.26	1,607.64	1,601.30	1,597.74	1,621.41
1996	1,593.45	1,589.53	1,585.43	1,581.34	1,577.10	1,572.90	1,568.60	1,564.00	1,559.90	1,557.25	1,554.95	1,552.90	1,571.45
1997	1,550.81	1,548.71	1,546.75	1,544.60	1,542.60	1,540.65	1,538.60	1,536.45	1,534.34	1,532.10	1,529.95	1,527.92	1,539.45
1998	1,526.13	1,524.42	1,522.35	1,520.73	1,519.33	1,517.35	1,515.10	1,512.90	1,510.75	1,508.80	1,508.50	1,508.29	1,516.22
1999	1,508.00	1508.00	1,508.00	1,508.00	1,508.00	1,508.00	1,508.00	1,508.00	1,507.64	1,507.50	1,507.50	1,507.50	1,507.85
2000	1,507.50	1,507.50	1,507.50	1,507.50	1,507.50	1,507.50	1,507.50	1,507.50	1,507.50	1,507.50	1,507.50	1,507.50	1,507.50
2001	1,507.50	1,507.50	1,507.50	1,507.50	1,507.50	1,507.50	1,507.50	1,507.50	1,507.50	1,507.50	1,507.50	1,507.50	1,507.50
2002	1,507.50	1,507.50	1,507.50	1,507.50	1,507.50	1,507.50	1,507.50	1,507.50	1,507.50	1,507.50	1,507.50	1,507.50	1,507.50

Table 3.3 cont. Exchange rate (end of month) (LL per US dollar)

	Jan.	Feb.	Mar.	Apr.	May	Jun.	Jul.	Aug.	Sep.	Oct.	Nov.	Dec.	End of year
1991	1,110.00	1,060.00	938.00	932.00	915.00	904.50	893.00	893.00	891.50	883.50	879.50	879.00	879.00
1992	879.00	1,070.00	1,280.00	1,600.00	1,680.00	1,705.00	2,165.00	2,390.00	2,420.00	1,965.00	1,874.00	1,838.00	1,838.00
1993	1,825.00	1,742.00	1,742.00	1,741.00	1,733.00	1,731.00	1,729.50	1,725.50	1,723.50	1,719.00	1,715.50	1,711.00	1,711.00
1994	1,706.00	1,700.50	1,694.50	1,690.50	1,684.00	1,680.00	1,676.50	1,671.00	1,666.00	1,661.00	1,656.00	1,647.00	1,647.00
1995	1,643.00	1,639.00	1,634.50	1,631.50	1,624.50	1,620.50	1,616.50	1,613.50	1,610.50	1,604.50	1,599.00	1,596.00	1,596.00
1996	1,591.50	1,588.00	1,583.50	1,580.00	1,575.00	1,571.00	1,566.50	1,562.00	1,558.50	1,556.00	1,554.00	1,552.00	1,552.00
1997	1,549.75	1,547.75	1,545.75	1,543.50	1,541.75	1,539.75	1,537.50	1,535.50	1,533.25	1,531.00	1,529.00	1,527.00	1,527.00
1998	1,525.50	1,523.50	1,521.25	1,520.25	1,518.50	1,516.25	1,514.00	1,512.00	1,509.75	1,508.50	1,508.50	1,508.00	1,508.00
1999	1,508.00	1,508.00	1,508.00	1,508.00	1,508.00	1,508.00	1,508.00	1,508.00	1,507.50	1,507.50	1,507.50	1,507.50	1,507.50
2000	1,507.50	1,507.50	1,507.50	1,507.50	1,507.50	1,507.50	1,507.50	1,507.50	1,507.50	1,507.50	1,507.50	1,507.50	1,507.50
2001	1,507.50	1,507.50	1,507.50	1,507.50	1,507.50	1,507.50	1,507.50	1,507.50	1,507.50	1,507.50	1,507.50	1,507.50	1,507.50
2002	1,507.50	1,507.50	1,507.50	1,507.50	1,507.50	1,507.50	1,507.50	1,507.50	1,507.50	1,507.50	1,507.50	1,507.50	1,507.50

Table 3.3 cont. Consumer Price Index (1990 = 100)

	Jan.	Feb.	Mar.	Apr.	May	Jun.	Jul.	Aug.	Sep.	Oct.	Nov.	Dec.	Year ave.	YTY % chg
1991	136.80	139.20	154.70	155.10	146.80	147.80	146.10	146.80	147.20	159.20	160.60	160.90	150.10	50.00
1992	183.00	192.00	219.50	239.50	271.90	278.80	302.60	358.80	413.60	409.80	379.10	351.50	300.01	99.87
1993	369.40	371.50	371.90	375.00	376.70	370.50	372.90	376.70	376.30	378.10	383.90	367.70	374.22	24.74
1994	375.30	394.30	411.10	407.70	407.40	399.40	401.50	412.90	414.60	409.80	415.30	411.10	405.03	8.23
1995	412.50	434.60	443.90	447.70	440.80	451.50	455.90	462.80	450.40	451.50	452.20	456.30	446.68	10.28
1996	467.00	461.80	474.20	475.90	477.00	502.80	499.70	496.60	504.50	498.70	491.10	486.60	486.33	8.88
1997	500.70	513.20	519.40	518.70	530.40	539.70	538.70	545.50	528.30	517.60	516.60	519.40	524.02	7.75
1998	519.40	529.70	543.80	542.40	544.90	552.40	556.20	558.30	563.10	560.00	554.20	549.70	547.84	4.55
1999	549.00	549.30	559.30	548.00	547.60	555.50	558.00	558.30	550.70	543.80	535.60	534.90	549.17	0.24
2000	...	...	...	...	...	...	...	...	...	...	...	...	...	-0.40
2001	...	...	...	...	...	...	...	...	...	...	...	...	...	-0.40
2002	...	...	...	...	...	...	...	...	...	...	...	...	...	4.00*

Source: Bank of Lebanon.
Note: * Estimate

Table 3.4 Lebanon: commercial bank deposits and claims on the private sector, 1991–2002 (in billion US dollar equivalent)

End of:	1991	1992	1993	1994	1995	1996	1997	1998	1999	2000	2001	2002
Lebanese pound deposits	1.99	2.02	2.77	4.76	5.64	8.60	9.13	10.50	13.03	12.46	11.03	13.06
Foreign currency deposits	4.29	4.59	6.46	7.59	9.33	11.20	16.10	20.00	20.91	25.17	29.11	29.58
Total deposits	6.28	6.61	9.23	12.40	14.97	19.80	25.23	30.50	33.94	37.63	40.14	42.64
FC deposits/total deposits (%)	68.3	69.4	70.0	61.5	62.3	56.6	63.8	65.6	61.6	66.9	72.5	69.4
Total deposits/GDP (%)	141	119	123	136	135	152	170	189	206	229	241	246
Lebanese pound credit	0.39	0.24	0.37	0.62	0.80	1.05	1.30	1.37	1.64	1.92	2.13	2.69
Foreign currency credit	1.85	2.38	3.08	4.12	5.67	7.13	8.82	11.00	12.28	12.84	12.59	12.41
Total credit	2.24	2.62	3.45	4.74	6.47	8.18	10.12	12.37	13.92	14.76	14.72	15.10
FC credit/total credit (%)	82.6	90.8	89.3	86.9	87.6	87.2	87.2	88.9	88.2	87.0	85.5	82.2
Total credit/GDP (%)	50	47	46	52	58	63	68	77	85	90	88	87
Nominal GDP	4.45	5.55	7.54	9.11	11.12	13.00	14.86	16.16	16.46	16.40	16.66	17.30*
Exchange rate (end of year)	879	1,838	1,711	1,647	1,596	1,552	1,527	1,508	1,507.5	1,507.5	1,507.5	1,507.5

Source: Bank of Lebanon.
Note: * Official projections

Table 3.5 Lebanon: outstanding debt by type of debt holder, 1990–2002 (LL billions)

end of:	1990	1991	1992	1993	1994	1995	1996	1997	1998	1999	2000	2001	2002
Domestic debt	1,482.8	2,229.7	4,178.2	5,803.8	9,347.5	11,997.2	17,228.8	19,787.1	21,685.7	25,382.8	27,161.2	28,213.8	25,302.3
Central bank	611.7	276.3	284.0	453.7	104.6	194.7	124.0	374.6	281.4	115.0	1,726.2	6,250.6	722.8
Direct loans	529.3	198.9	123.5	0	0	0	0	0	0	0	0	0	0
Loans to public entities	8.3	9.3	21.2	61.6	77.7	102.7	100.4	100.6	103.8	111.9	113.9	117.5	114.0
TBs	74.1	68.1	139.3	392.1	26.9	0	0	274.0	13.5	3.1	1,597.8	6,111.0	601.4
Repurchase agreements	0	0	0	0	0	0	0	0	164.1	0	14.5	22.1	7.4
Commercial banks	688.4	1,309.3	3,098.5	4,245.4	7,345.0	8,453.1	12,638.3	13,532.4	16,132.8	18,965.4	18,736.1	15,829.8	17,211.3
TBs	681.1	1,302.3	3,082.9	4,242.1	7,341.0	8,396.6	12,532.2	13423.6	15,986.9	18,501.1	17,968.0	14,913.7	17,156.5
Other loans	7.3	7.0	15.6	3.3	4.0	56.6	106.1	108.8	145.9	157.2	83.0	54.2	54.8
Factoring	0	0	0	0	0	0	0	0	0	307.1	685.1	861.9	0
Other domestic debt (TBs)	182.7	644.1	795.7	1,104.7	1,897.9	3,349.4	4,466.5	5,880.1	5,271.5	6,302.4	6,698.9	6,133.4	7,368.2
Foreign debt	458.0	507.1	665.4	734.5	1,451.6	2,158.9	2,959.5	3,712.7	6,279.0	8,331.9	10,479.6	14,402.0	21,918.6
(o/w: eurobonds)	0	0	0	0	671.9	1,149.4	1,278.8	1,632.7	3,914.5	5,746.1	7,867.0	11,787.5	19,263.9
Total debt (in billion	1,940.8	2,736.8	4,843.6	6,538.3	10,799.1	14,156.1	20,188.3	23,499.8	27,964.7	33,714.7	37,640.8	42,615.8	47,220.9
dollar equivalent)	2.30	3.11	2.64	3.82	6.56	8.87	13.00	15.39	18.54	22.36	24.97	28.27	31.32

Source: Bank of Lebanon.

Table 3.6a Lebanon: monthly treasury bill effective rates, 1991–2002 (percentages)

3-month TBs

End of	Jan.	Feb.	Mar.	Apr.	May	Jun.	Jul.	Aug.	Sep.	Oct.	Nov.	Dec.
1991	18.84	18.84	19.94	18.84	18.84	18.30	17.21	16.61	16.61	15.58	15.04	15.04
1992	15.04	21.01	23.84	23.84	23.84	23.84	23.84	34.18	34.18	19.12	13.00	13.00
1993	13.00	21.01	21.01	19.50	18.53	18.48	18.55	18.49	18.06	17.88	17.51	17.22
1994	17.04	16.50	16.33	16.19	16.07	15.30	14.90	14.46	14.47	13.60	12.77	13.49
1995	13.62	15.30	16.55	16.55	17.75	19.94	20.50	22.83	25.30	24.56	17.61	16.01
1996	15.97	15.82	15.81	15.81	15.72	15.56	14.94	14.74	14.61	14.61	14.39	14.29
1997	14.08	13.87	13.75	13.70	13.62	13.40	13.16	13.09	13.09	13.09	13.09	13.09
1998	13.09	13.09	13.09	13.09	12.98	12.82	12.69	12.50	12.48	12.38	12.38	11.77
1999	11.73	11.73	11.73	11.73	11.73	11.73	11.73	11.73	11.42	11.18	11.18	11.18
2000	11.18	11.18	11.18	11.18	11.18	11.18	11.18	11.18	11.18	11.18	11.18	11.18
2001	11.18	11.18	11.18	11.18	11.18	11.18	11.18	11.18	11.18	11.18	11.18	11.18
2002	11.18	11.18	11.18	11.18	11.18	11.18	11.18	11.18	11.18	11.18	11.18	11.18

6-month TBs

End of	Jan.	Feb.	Mar.	Apr.	May	Jun.	Jul.	Aug.	Sep.	Oct.	Nov.	Dec.
1991	22.22	22.22	24.71	22.22	22.22	21.60	20.38	19.77	19.77	18.57	16.80	16.80
1992	16.80	22.87	25.34	25.34	25.34	24.34	25.34	35.28	35.28	21.29	15.00	15.00
1993	15.00	22.01	22.01	20.50	20.50	20.08	20.10	20.11	19.85	19.79	19.79	19.65
1994	19.53	18.55	18.04	17.97	17.85	17.47	17.43	17.15	17.21	16.00	14.54	14.83
1995	15.37	16.83	18.00	18.00	18.87	21.70	22.43	25.13	27.91	27.37	19.01	17.21
1996	17.20	17.16	17.16	17.16	17.07	16.99	16.97	16.95	16.92	16.92	16.55	16.15
1997	15.56	14.61	14.49	14.45	14.37	14.21	14.02	13.97	13.97	13.97	13.97	13.97
1998	13.97	13.97	13.97	13.97	13.97	13.97	13.88	13.70	13.66	13.52	13.52	13.21
1999	13.00	13.00	13.00	13.00	13.00	13.00	13.00	13.00	12.52	12.12	12.12	12.12
2000	12.12	12.12	12.12	12.12	12.12	12.12	12.12	12.12	12.12	12.12	12.12	12.12
2001	12.12	12.12	12.12	12.12	12.12	12.12	12.12	12.12	12.12	12.12	12.12	12.12
2002	12.12	12.12	12.12	12.12	12.12	12.12	12.12	12.12	12.12	12.12	12.12	12.12

12-month TBs

End of	Jan.	Feb.	Mar.	Apr.	May	Jun.	Jul.	Aug.	Sep.	Oct.	Nov.	Dec.
1991	24.98	24.98	28.18	25.00	25.00	24.22	22.69	21.94	21.94	20.47	19.47	19.47
1992	19.47	23.44	29.01	29.01	29.01	29.01	29.01	34.20	34.20	24.98	20.99	20.99
1993	20.99	22.01	22.01	22.00	22.00	22.00	20.99	20.99	21.00	21.02	21.05	21.07
1994	20.80	20.18	19.92	19.72	19.66	19.31	19.22	19.14	19.04	17.45	14.94	14.73
1995	16.08	19.18	19.66	19.66	20.83	26.45	27.37	33.30	37.85	36.86	19.69	18.26
1996	18.18	18.15	18.15	18.15	18.04	17.96	17.93	17.85	17.80	17.78	17.57	17.02
1997	15.84	15.27	15.20	15.20	15.20	15.20	15.20	15.20	15.20	15.20	15.20	15.20
1998	15.20	15.20	15.20	15.20	15.20	15.20	15.20	15.20	15.20	15.20	15.20	14.84
1999	14.84	14.84	14.84	14.84	14.84	14.84	14.84	14.77	13.66	13.43	13.43	13.43
2000	13.43	13.43	13.43	13.43	13.43	13.43	13.43	13.43	13.43	13.43	13.43	13.43
2001	13.43	13.43	13.43	13.43	13.43	13.43	13.43	13.43	13.43	13.43	13.43	13.43
2002	13.43	13.43	13.43	13.43	13.43	13.43	13.43	13.43	13.43	13.43	13.43	13.43

24-month TBs

End of	Jan.	Feb.	Mar.	Apr.	May	Jun.	Jul.	Aug.	Sep.	Oct.	Nov.	Dec.
1991	....											24.59
1992	24.59	28.82	30.50	30.50	30.50	30.50	30.50	33.59	33.59	29.07	26.00	26.00
1993	26.00	26.00	26.00	26.00	26.00	26.00	24.99	24.99	24.99	24.99	23.99	23.99
1994	21.99	20.89	20.34	20.07	20.07	20.07	20.07	20.07	18.53	17.18	15.73	15.84
1995	16.66	18.57	18.81	18.81	19.79	24.06	26.68	28.26	28.05	29.96	26.34	23.39
1996	23.28	23.25	23.25	23.25	23.17	23.08	23.01	22.94	22.83	22.79	22.10	20.54
1997	17.87	16.79	16.73	16.73	16.73	16.73	16.73	16.73	16.73	16.73	16.73	16.73
1998	16.73	16.73	16.73	16.73	16.73	16.73	16.73	16.73	16.73	16.73	16.73	16.66
1999	16.66	16.66	16.66	16.66	16.66	16.36	16.19	15.95	14.92	14.64	14.64	14.64
2000	14.64	14.64	14.64	14.64	14.64	14.64	14.64	14.64	14.64	14.64	14.64	14.64
2001	14.64	14.64	14.64	14.64	14.64	14.64	14.64	14.64	14.64	14.64	14.64	14.64
2002	14.64	14.64	14.64	16.34	16.34	16.34	16.34	16.34	14.64	14.64	14.64	14.64

Source: Bank of Lebanon.

Table 3.6b Lebanon: distribution of treasury bills by maturity, 1994–2002 (percentage)

3-month TBs

End of	Jan.	Feb.	Mar.	Apr.	May	Jun.	Jul.	Aug.	Sep.	Oct.	Nov.	Dec.
1994	9.33	7.77	5.64	5.41	5.09	3.98	3.74	3.90	3.88	3.31	3.22	2.83
1995	3.19	4.00	6.14	8.05	8.13	11.14	12.72	15.10	11.30	9.03	6.35	7.18
1996	6.38	6.85	8.28	9.40	11.00	10.31	9.08	7.35	6.58	7.02	6.31	5.25
1997	3.91	3.25	3.05	3.30	3.99	3.82	3.23	2.71	2.53	1.78	0.88	2.14
1998	2.69	2.56	2.49	0.98	1.78	2.57	2.86	2.01	1.34	1.07	0.94	1.55
1999	1.72	2.38	1.96	1.86	1.56	1.72	1.45	1.21	1.27	1.74	2.00	2.22
2000	1.67	1.56	1.56	2.06	1.85	1.91	1.17	1.15	1.46	2.03	2.94	2.86
2001	3.17	2.70	2.56	2.69	2.22	2.43	1.98	1.94	1.66	1.57	2.03	2.41
2002	3.16	3.01	2.88	1.78	1.35	1.55	1.80	1.99	1.73	1.29	1.11	1.26

6-month TBs

End of	Jan.	Feb.	Mar.	Apr.	May	Jun.	Jul.	Aug.	Sep.	Oct.	Nov.	Dec.
1994	16.95	15.74	15.69	13.63	12.86	12.33	11.84	11.74	11.29	11.63	11.66	11.06
1995	11.01	10.82	9.15	9.05	9.28	10.05	9.63	8.95	9.11	8.04	7.51	8.33
1996	9.76	11.10	11.57	11.10	9.97	9.71	10.28	11.79	12.65	16.74	16.73	16.23
1997	15.62	14.95	13.91	12.18	11.61	11.44	11.42	11.17	10.80	8.34	6.50	6.48
1998	5.54	5.53	6.02	4.96	4.87	4.03	4.13	4.06	4.00	3.92	3.58	3.98
1999	4.31	4.67	4.89	5.07	5.39	5.20	5.52	5.44	5.28	5.78	6.07	6.57
2000	6.34	6.40	6.68	6.81	6.56	6.32	6.65	6.40	6.31	6.34	6.69	6.09
2001	5.48	5.45	5.29	5.28	4.71	4.81	4.64	4.57	4.20	3.28	3.46	3.96
2002	4.41	4.72	4.97	4.63	4.42	3.98	3.59	3.50	3.64	3.76	3.52	4.09

12-month TBs

End of	Jan.	Feb.	Mar.	Apr.	May	Jun.	Jul.	Aug.	Sep.	Oct.	Nov.	Dec.
1994	26.20	26.16	26.93	27.51	28.04	28.85	28.71	28.53	28.29	28.64	28.90	29.00
1995	28.37	27.37	26.00	25.41	24.89	23.31	23.43	23.60	27.89	38.13	43.79	43.32
1996	43.93	44.16	44.58	45.77	45.85	45.63	44.93	43.56	38.45	27.50	24.88	24.10
1997	23.32	23.66	24.34	25.07	25.18	25.24	24.80	24.43	23.86	23.26	23.85	23.59
1998	24.20	23.47	22.83	20.94	19.59	18.77	18.72	18.75	19.57	17.05	16.04	15.37
1999	15.22	15.27	16.15	16.42	14.72	13.93	12.82	12.67	12.60	12.99	13.46	13.36
2000	13.81	13.61	12.80	12.91	13.19	13.27	13.28	13.01	12.73	12.87	13.56	13.69
2001	13.83	14.01	13.97	13.80	13.75	13.27	12.60	12.20	11.72	9.86	8.52	7.80
2002	6.91	6.91	6.50	6.49	6.36	6.42	6.31	6.33	6.27	6.17	5.44	6.05

24-month TBs

End of	Jan.	Feb.	Mar.	Apr.	May	Jun.	Jul.	Aug.	Sep.	Oct.	Nov.	Dec.
1994	47.53	50.33	51.74	53.45	54.01	54.84	55.71	55.83	56.54	56.41	56.21	57.12
1995	57.43	57.80	58.72	57.48	57.70	55.49	54.22	52.35	51.70	44.80	42.35	41.16
1996	39.93	37.89	35.57	33.73	33.18	34.36	35.70	37.30	42.32	48.74	52.07	54.42
1997	57.15	58.14	58.69	59.45	59.22	59.51	60.55	61.69	62.81	66.63	68.77	67.79
1998	67.57	68.44	68.66	73.11	73.76	74.62	74.29	75.18	75.09	77.97	79.43	79.10
1999	78.75	77.68	77.01	76.66	78.33	79.15	80.22	80.67	80.85	79.49	78.47	77.86
2000	78.18	78.43	78.96	78.22	78.41	78.50	78.91	79.44	79.51	78.65	76.82	77.37
2001	77.52	77.84	78.18	78.22	79.32	79.49	80.78	81.29	82.43	85.29	85.98	85.83
2002	85.52	85.37	85.65	87.11	87.88	88.05	88.30	88.17	88.37	88.78	89.93	88.60

Source: Bank of Lebanon.

Table 3.6c Lebanon: effective yields on twelve-month TBs, 1993–98 (percentage)

		Jan.	Feb.	Mar.	Apr.	May	Jun.	Jul.	Aug.	Sep.	Oct.	Nov.	Dec.
1993	TBY	20.99	22.01	22.01	22.00	22.00	22.00	20.99	20.99	21.00	21.02	21.05	21.07
	DETBY	35.40	33.85	32.10	31.97	31.85	32.05	30.48	30.61	30.85	31.00	31.17	31.60
1994	TBY	20.80	20.18	19.92	19.72	19.66	19.31	19.22	19.14	19.04	17.45	14.94	14.73
	DETBY	31.16	30.04	29.50	29.11	29.04	28.47	28.36	28.14	27.81	25.33	21.76	21.06
1995	TBY	16.08	19.18	19.66	19.66	20.83	26.45	27.37	33.30	37.85	36.86	19.69	18.26
	DETBY	22.99	27.72	28.47	28.52	30.33	40.24	42.06	54.84	66.30	63.50	28.23	25.87
1996	TBY	18.18	18.15	18.15	18.15	18.04	17.96	17.93	17.85	17.80	17.78	17.57	17.02
	DETBY	25.58	25.39	25.23	25.08	24.74	24.44	24.23	23.91	23.68	23.62	23.30	22.48
1997	TBY	15.84	15.27	15.20	15.20	15.20	15.20	15.20	15.20	15.20	15.20	15.20	15.20
	DETBY	20.74	19.90	19.81	19.78	19.73	19.74	19.75	19.76	19.77	19.75	19.60	19.46
1998	TBY	15.20	15.20	15.20	15.20	15.20	15.20	15.20	15.20	15.20	15.20	15.20	14.84
	DETBY	19.34	19.21	19.05	18.92	18.81	18.66	18.48	18.31	18.17	18.03	18.00	17.49

Source: Based on Table 3.6a.
Notes: TBY: Treasury Bill Yield; DETBY: Dollar Equivalent Treasury Bill Yield

Table 3.7 CDR contracts awarded from 1 January 1992 to 31 December 2001 (figures in USD millions)

Sectors	Total		Completed		In progress		
	No.	Amount	No.	Amount	No.	Amount	Prog.
Physical infrastructure							
Electricity	65	1,385.1	57	920.5	8	464.6	95%
Telecommunication and posts	88	776.6	85	502.3	3	274.3	93%
Roads, highways	232	876.5	139	513	93	363.5	56%
Social infrastructure							
Education and sports facilities	671	506.7	563	265.3	108	241.4	50%
Public health	184	217.6	122	77.5	62	140.1	67%
Social affairs	15	2.5	14	2.5	1	0	45%
Integrated development	51	36.5	28	18.5	23	18	26%
Basic services							
Water supply	145	437.1	85	136.2	60	300.9	66%
Waste water	145	278.0	104	167.7	41	110.3	16%
Solid waste	60	650.8	36	103.9	24	546.9	52%
Productive sectors							
Agriculture and irrigation	155	85.3	72	30.8	83	54.5	50%
Ports and airports	68	663.4	43	116.6	25	546.8	84%
Government buildings	144	104.1	129	92.2	15	11.9	62%
Management and implementation	325	179.6	261	126.7	64	52.9	39%
Other	31	9.4	28	5.1	3	4.3	84%
Grand total	2,379	6,209.2	1,766	3,078.8	613	3,130.4	68%

Source: Council for Development and Reconstruction.

Note: For contracts in progress, the amounts represent the original contract value, while progress represents the percentage of executed works

The post-war period: aspirations versus reality. 2 Labour market, governance and socio-economic issues

1 Labour market and wage policy

The settlement of the civil war and the consequent reunification of the country led to the opening up of regions hitherto largely closed to one another. The goods and labour markets were gradually reunified, the former having been only partially fragmented at the national level during the war. At the same time, a good proportion of the displaced population either could not or chose not to return to their original places of residence. To an extent the legacy of the war acted as a restraining, but over time declining, factor on the growing geographical mobility of the labour force. In principle, as the domestic political situation further improved and stabilized, mobility among the regions increased. In practice, the main trend of labour movement was towards Beirut and its suburbs, given their economic and social pull.

Before turning to the formal labour market, a word on the informal sector is in order. It is defined as including small-scale firms, the self-employed and unpaid workers, all of whom are not included within the regulatory domain set by the government, including the commercial register, tax and social security coverage. While no systematic studies have been carried out to quantify the informal sector's size or impact on the labour market and national income, available evidence suggests it has remained significant in the post-war period. To illustrate, it is estimated that the self-employed and unpaid workers constituted in 1996 about 28 per cent of the total active population, the majority being male workers. Small-scale industrial enterprises, employing fewer than ten people, continue to make up a sizeable proportion of the total. And for 1995 it is estimated that over 50 per cent of the active population were not covered by any type of health insurance.[1] The economic consequences of the informal sector are various: loss of tax revenue and underestimation of national production, not to mention influences on the formal labour market. What matters is that the absence as yet of in-depth studies of the informal sector and of its size across various economic activities constitutes a gap in any analysis dealing with labour market developments. To the extent possible, account should be taken of the influences of the informal sector on the formal labour market (as in the case of Syrian workers, the majority of whom do not have work permits). With this in mind, we turn to the supply and demand side of the evolving labour market in the post-civil-war period.

On the aggregate supply side, the labour market has been influenced by three important developments: (i) the evolution of the global rate of economic activity;[2] (ii) the emigration of Lebanese manpower; and (iii) the in-flow of non-Lebanese manpower. The global rate of economic activity is estimated to have increased in the 1990s standing at about 35 per cent for 2001 compared with 30 per cent for 1987 and 27 per cent for 1970.[3] Both male and female economic activity rates increased, reaching 48.8 and 16.5 per cent respectively (bearing in mind that the estimates for the female activity rate do not include female employment in informal sector activities).[4] The female active population for 2001 was estimated at 25.6 per cent of the total active population, up from 9.5 per cent for 1970. What should be noted is the increasing level of education of the Lebanese workforce. By 1997 over 16 per cent were holders of university degrees (compared to about 4 per cent in 1970) with a higher portion being registered among female than male workers.[5]

During the period 1991–2001 emigration of Lebanese manpower (persons seeking work abroad) has been estimated at about 111,000[6] (an average of 10,000 annually), most of those emigrating being educated with various skills. At the same time, the de facto open-door policy with respect to the in-flow of non-Lebanese (especially Syrian) manpower, mostly unskilled or semi-skilled, became more pronounced than before, especially in the years 1994–96, which witnessed rapid expansion in the construction sector. Some estimates put the Syrian workforce in the mid-1990s at about 450,000 (one third the active population for 1997), declining to about 225,000 by the beginning of 2000,[7] in tandem with the slowing domestic economy. Official attempts to regulate the in-flow of non-Lebanese manpower were nominal, though in 2001/2 stricter compliance with regulations concerning work permits (effectively for non-Syrian workers) was put in place.

On the demand side of the labour market, there occurred, in the first half of the 1990s, a noticeable increase in the demand for labour which tended to slow down subsequently as the rate of growth began to decline, beginning in 1995. Two areas where the increased demand manifested itself were the construction and services sectors. But whereas the former required a growing proportion of unskilled/semi-skilled labour, the latter required increasing numbers of skilled workers and professionals.

Despite emigration, excess supply of Lebanese manpower has persisted throughout the post-war period, tending to increase after 1995. A recent study estimates that by the year 2000 the cumulative excess supply, i.e. the unemployed (after allowing for emigration) stood at about 180,000 workers or 12.5 per cent of the active population for that year,[8] up from the officially estimated 8–9 per cent for 1997 (the question of unemployment is touched upon in section 2.2 below). Analysis of the supply and demand for various categories of manpower is not available. However, existing shortages with respect to skilled manpower and professionals were probably higher than those for unskilled or semi-skilled workers. For one thing the increase in the supply of Lebanese skilled manpower was partly checked by emigration, and for another it was matched by an increasing demand, at least until the mid-1990s; and when, beginning in 1995, the rate of growth began to decline, accompanied by a slow-down in demand and in work opportunities, the level of emigration tended to rise. In contrast, the market for unskilled or semi-skilled manpower was flooded with non-Lebanese workers. In turn this helped keep the average wage relatively low by Lebanese standards, particularly in the construction and unskilled services sectors, to the benefit of employers in these sectors. For non-Lebanese workers, their monthly earnings in Lebanon were much higher than corresponding levels in their home countries, a good proportion being transferred abroad.[9] With non-strict controls of the in-flow of unskilled and semi-skilled labour, it is not surprising that the Lebanese market was attractive to them.

It has been argued that the substantial in-flow of Syrian workers did not lead to any major displacement of Lebanese workers, who would not only hesitate to work for relatively low wages but would also tend to shy away from the unskilled tasks that the Syrian and other foreign workers were willing to undertake.[10] On its own this argument is incomplete. What must also be investigated is the impact on the prevailing wage level for unskilled labour of hypothetically much stricter controls over the in-flow of non-Lebanese workers. If, with a given demand, a restricted in-flow leads to significantly higher wages in the construction and services sectors, then this might induce Lebanese workers to take up jobs they would not otherwise take at lower wage levels. This matter needs to be examined before any firm conclusions can be drawn concerning the question at hand. In any event, the in-flow of unskilled foreign labour probably influenced the evolving methods of production[11] (see section 2.2 below).

Regarding real wages in the formal sector, taking 1990 as base period, the real average wage is estimated to have fallen to 88 for 1994, rising to 131 for 1997 and falling back to 125–126 for 1998–2001. The evolution of the real minimum wage exhibited a roughly similar trend.[12] Despite the improvement in real wages after 1994, they remained substantially below their level in the mid-1980s (284) and a little less than four times below their 1974 level (448), with significant gender disparities continuing to prevail. It is estimated that for 1997 the average wage for males was more than 20 per cent higher than the average wage for females. And for specific sectors, such as agriculture, the disparity was more pronounced. Equally important, the proportion of wages in GDP is estimated to have declined over the period.[13] The major implication of these findings is that wages, along with salaries, bore the brunt of the burden of economic adjustment during both the war and post-civil-war periods.

2 Fundamental issues of development: political governance and the socio-economic dimension of development

There are a number of fundamental but interacting issues of development that Lebanon has been facing since the end of the civil war. I have chosen to classify them under two broad headings: (a) political governance and (b) the socio-economic dimension of development. I take them up in that order in recognition of the fact that the ability to adequately address basic socio-economic issues is intertwined with the prevailing quality of institutions and governance, which, in turn, is influenced by the nature of the existing political system.

2.1 Governance: the question of corruption

Governance has been broadly defined as including the traditions and institutions by which authority in a country is exercised. As such, it is multidimensional and, accordingly, various governance indicators have been developed to measure how institutions influence growth and the quality of development. They pertain to the processes by which the government is appointed, maintained and replaced; accountability; the degree of political stability or instability in the country; the ability to formulate and implement sound policies; regulatory quality; the degree to which the rule of law applies; and the amount of corruption that exists.[14] I do not intend here to detail how all these indicators stand in the Lebanese case: for one thing, available empirical data are fragmented. For another, and despite the plethora of analyses of the Lebanese political system and public administration, no systematic empirical investigation has been carried out of how governance in Lebanon has affected the process of development,[15] an area of research that deserves in-depth investigation. Rather, this section focuses on one major indicator, namely corruption, not only because it has attracted increasing attention in the postwar period and has been the subject of several investigations, but on account of its pervasive nature. Corruption takes various forms, including bribery to obtain governmental services or public procurement, but more important, as one source puts it, is the capture of the state when it is manifested in the illicit influence of the elite in shaping the laws, policies and regulations of the state.[16]

Before turning to the matter at hand, it should be observed that while the generally inadequate, not to say poor, performance of Lebanon's political governance is widely recognized, this should not obscure the fact that in a few areas progress has been made, specifically as regards regulatory quality and the maintenance of order, at least in comparison with the war period. Nevertheless it remains true that the persistence of what I referred to in

Chapter 1 as constrained democracy associated with the prevailing sectarian system; public sector inefficiencies; continued prevalence of nepotism and clientism; increased corruption; environmental degradation; and at times outright violation of existing rules and regulations on the part of the government itself point to major shortcomings in Lebanon's governance, which remains in need of fundamental reform (Chapter 5 below discusses the conditions for long-term reform).

Turning to corruption, both international and local reports point to its ascendancy during the post-civil-war period. To illustrate, indices constructed by Political Risk Services (PRS: a private New York-based firm) relating to institutional change in various countries (i.e. government repudiation of contracts, risk of expropriation, degree of corruption, law and order and bureaucratic quality) indicate that in the case of Lebanon for the period 1985–97 the rule of law, not surprisingly, improved after the civil war. Quality of bureaucracy remained low (with a score of 2 over 6, the latter number representing the highest level of quality) but corruption became worse with a score of 2 over 6 for 1992, declining to 1 over 6 for 1997.[17] The PRS corruption data measure the extent to which high government officials are likely to demand special payment as well as illegal payments that are expected in lower levels of government in the form of bribes. The more recent study cited above, which includes recent data up to 2000/1 for six indicators of governance, places Lebanon at a lower rank than the average for MENA countries for five of the six indicators, with the control of corruption indicator faring worst of all.[18]

At the domestic level, press reports on corruption abound, and so do public accusations against government officials, not only by opposition groups but also occasionally from within the circle of the responsible officials themselves.[19] Indeed, in the late 1990s corruption in public administration was considered to have become so widespread and endemic that public calls were made for the creation of an NGO to fight it.[20] When the time came for the presidential elections of November 1998, some political observers publicly called for the election of a president committed to fighting corruption as a matter of strategic choice.[21]

Equally significant are recent survey reports dealing with the issue of corruption. In March 2000, two reports commissioned by a local NGO concerned with corruption were completed.[22] A third report prepared for the United Nations CICP/UNICR was completed in early 2001.[23] The first two reports summarize the results of extensive public opinion poll surveys (conducted in October 1997) on perception of corruption in Lebanon by the population at large and business/professional groups respectively. For both groups the vast majority of those polled believed that corruption was all-pervasive in Lebanon and that the corruption of the political body was the main cause for this state of affairs.[24] The third and more recent and detailed report confirms the results of the earlier reports. Another survey of private sector firms pertaining to institutional obstacles facing the private sector concludes that corruption is regarded as the primary obstacle, followed by other factors such as constraining governmental bureaucratic procedures, taxes, informal competition, and the non-creditability of governmental policies. Together, all these, but especially corruption, had a negative impact on investments in Lebanon.[25] These findings corroborate similar conclusions regarding corruption arrived at by an earlier study on public sector accountability in Lebanon which singled out Lebanese political behaviour as the most important obstacle to administrative reform, pointing out that politicians have indulged in improper and/or corrupt practices without fear of punishment.[26]

The above outcome, documented, in part, by the state's own central control authorities (in particular, the Civil Service Council and Central Inspection), stands in sharp contrast with an ever growing number of plans and proposals on public sector reform in Lebanon, some of which were officially commissioned. It is as though these two factors, i.e. plans for reform and actual performance, were inversely related. While recognizing that the record of a few public entities (especially the monetary entities) was superior to the generally lower-level performance of the public sector, what matters is that all attempts at major administrative reform, intended to enhance its efficiency and accountability, have so far failed. The public sector has remained bloated, generally inefficient and subject to the influence of various forms of corruption.

As early as 1991 the Karami government formulated recommendations for administrative reform, but could not put them in place before it resigned.[27] The 1992 report of the Committee of Economic Experts explicitly recommended the overhauling of the tax administration along with public administration reform aiming, among other things, at eradicating disguised unemployment in the public sector and reducing its bloated size, in terms of personnel, by one fifth, so as to make it more manageable and efficient. In 1993 the first Hariri government attempted to deal with this issue selectively via the revitalization of central control agencies, but was unsuccessful.[28] In his report for 1997 the president of the Civil Service Council (CSC) points out that during the period 1993–97 successive governments ignored most, if not all, of the proposals the council had submitted pertaining to various aspects of administrative reform. Referring specifically to 1997, the report indicates that in most cases involving conflict of opinion between the Civil Service Council and individual ministries, the Council of Ministers chose to ignore the opinion of the CSC in favour of the ministry concerned, often consulting other bodies that are not entitled to give opinion on the matters at hand. In subsequent years, despite the work carried out by ministers of state charged with the task of proposing plans for long-term administrative reform, so far no steps in this direction have been implemented.

It can be argued that serious administrative reform cannot be divorced from political reform or the broader issue of governance. If the latter is collectively inadequate (the good performance of individual responsible officials notwithstanding), it is extremely difficult to bring about major reform, except perhaps under constant pressure from civil society. Public pressure for reform could also be exercised through parliamentary elections on the assumption that the citizenry can exercise fully and freely their right to choose members of parliament free from all types of influence (including the exercise by governmental agencies and/or officials of various direct and indirect forms of bribery), who will be accountable to the electorate. Post-civil-war Lebanon is yet to attain that stage in its political development which will allow, indeed require, full accountability of its political body and transparency of its public institutions. Indeed, the decision-making process in the post-civil-war period, at both the political and administrative levels, needs to be investigated in depth with a view to shedding light on possible avenues of administrative reform.

What matters, of course, is that poor governance has a negative effect not only on the rate of growth but also on the qualitative (socio-economic) aspects of development. It is not surprising, therefore, that in a number of areas within this domain (taken up in section 2.2 below) where the state is supposed to play an active role, major shortcomings have appeared, negatively influencing the quality of Lebanon's development.

2.2 The socio-economic dimension of post-civil-war development

Socio-economic development encompasses many areas: health, education, housing, the degree of prevailing poverty, the pattern of income distribution, unemployment levels, gender inequities and overall living conditions. The civil war caused socio-economic conditions to deteriorate across the board. And the inherited legacy (e.g. deteriorating health conditions, the reduced capacity and effectiveness of public sector institutions, environmental degradation) was expected to be countered in the post-civil-war period with the implementation of corrective policies and/or programmes that would gradually enhance the socio-economic aspects of Lebanon's post-civil-war development. While the public sector had a major role to play in this regard, Lebanon's private sector, which dominates the national economy, also bore responsibility for contributing to an improved socio-economic situation.

Unfortunately there are no systematic official or private surveys pertaining to the evolution of socio-economic conditions in Lebanon over the period under consideration. However, on the basis of ad hoc official and private studies that have been carried out during this period, it is possible to discern some major elements of the emerging socio-economic situation after the civil war and to compare it to that prevailing in the immediate pre-civil-war period.[29]

Based on the above studies and available data, we find that in specific areas some progress has been made, e.g. health and education – see below. But, in other areas, little if any improvement was accomplished, or else noticeable deterioration was witnessed. As a result the socio-economic dimension of development suffered. What concerns us here is the emerging overall socio-economic picture in the 1990s and early this decade. I shall briefly discuss five areas: (i) prevailing poverty levels and the skewedness of income distribution; (ii) the provision of social services; (iii) education; (iv) the level of unemployment; and (v) the environment.[30]

A preliminary observation is in order, namely that the levels of social attainment, as measured by the index of household satisfaction of basic needs, differed from one area to another. The statistical survey underlying the *Map of Living Conditions in Lebanon* carried out in the mid-1990s points out, for example, that, on average, households were relatively better off (or alternatively relatively less worse off) in terms of satisfying their housing needs and having access to water and water sanitation networks than in terms of satisfying their educational needs or as regards their overall situation as reflected in their income level.[31]

Poverty and income distribution

There are several estimates of the level of poverty in Lebanon that together indicate that it is substantial and was rising over the decade of the 1990s. The first study, carried out in 1994, revealed that 28 per cent of Lebanese urban households were poor (i.e. living at the lower level of poverty as measured by the required spending on food necessities), of whom 7.5 per cent were living at the upper level of poverty (absolute poverty), i.e. after including the expenses of other basic needs such as housing, clothing and health. Most of the poor households lived in the suburbs of Beirut and most of those facing abject poverty lived in rural areas. In fact, despite improvements in the infrastructural network and in social conditions in urban areas outside Beirut and the rural districts, the sharp unevenness in living conditions among the various regions of the country, noted for the pre-civil-war period, continued to prevail in the post-war period: Beirut and the neighbouring regions (the district of Kisirwan in particular) enjoyed substantially higher living standards than regions in the north, north-east and south.[32] With respect to income distribution, it was estimated that the category of households with low income made up more than one half of the total. This is comparable to the situation prevailing in the late 1950s but represents a substantial retrogression from that prevailing in the early 1970s.[33]

A second study, the 1997 official household survey, reveals that about 37 per cent of those surveyed considered that their income was insufficient to cover their basic needs, and that about 30 per cent were forced into debt in order to meet their basic living requirements.[34] And a more recent third study concludes that for the year 2000 about 42 per cent of the population was living below the upper poverty line, which covers basic nutritional and other needs.[35] One writer, comparing the results of the 1997 household survey (as regards Beirut) with a household survey carried out by the Directorate of Statistics for Beirut back in 1966, points out that in 1997 low-income households comprised a higher portion of the total than in 1966 (49 per cent against 42 per cent), and that the average real household income in 1997 was lower than in 1966.[36] It should be recalled that at the beginning of the 1990s real GDP is estimated to have stood at about one third its 1974 level and probably was not above its level in the mid-1960s.

In other words, real average income in Lebanon in the 1990s had not recovered its pre-civil-war level (although admittedly the statistical comparison is not necessarily totally reliable), and income distribution, after having improved over the pre-war period, became more skewed in the 1990s than in the 1960s. Two indirect indicators of the worsening income distribution during the 1990s are the fall in the average level of real wages and the decline in the share of wages in national income noted above. In principle, the latter decline could have been attributable to changing technology with a major substitution of capital for labour and/or of skilled for relatively unskilled manpower. But this was not the case. A supplementary indicator is worsening asset and hence income distribution as reflected in the evolving deposit concentration ratio. It is estimated that at the end of 1992 2.4 per cent of depositors owned 40 per cent of total deposits. By the end of 2002 the same percentage of depositors owned 60 per cent of total deposits.[37]

Whatever the adverse impact of the war on the socio-economic situation, post-civil-war policies during the decade of the 1990s did not pay serious attention to the issue of income distribution and more generally social equity.

Provision of social and health services

The increased skew in income distribution in the 1990s (in comparison with the immediate pre-war period) was only partly compensated for by an improved provision of social and health services, in other words the development of some of the required social safety networks. Efforts in this direction on the part of the public sector were successful only to a limited extent. Available studies indicate that little progress was made in reforming the public sector healthcare system, and the intended objectives of better-quality care at lower cost were not achieved.[38] It was not lack of studies which prevented serious efforts at reform. Rather, administrative bottlenecks combined with a lack of required political will prevented a serious move along this front. And, of course, there is always the fiscal side of any expansion in the provision of services to be taken into account.

Looking specifically at health coverage, it is estimated that for the period 1997–2000 40–50 per cent of households were covered by one of the existing health schemes.[39] Hence a sizeable proportion of households continues to have out-of-pocket health expenses. However, the Ministry of Health does support this segment of the population by covering part of their hospitalization expenses.[40] Present health coverage plans are included under: (i) the National Social Security Fund (NSSF), which covers employees in the formal private sector, contractual and public sector earners in the public sector, as well as students of the Lebanese University; as of the late 1990s, the NSSF had the highest coverage rate, although estimates vary; (ii) the Civil Servants Cooperative (CSC), which includes government employees, including teachers in public schools; (iii) the military medical coverage pertaining to the army and various security services; and (iv) private insurance schemes providing either partial or total coverage.[41] Nevertheless, it is estimated that by the late 1990s, nearly 40 per cent of the population did not have formal medical insurance and 23 per cent were totally uncovered.[42]

Governmental transfers for social services are supplemented by family remittances from abroad and family networks still play a role as social safety nets, while the private sector assumes the bigger role in the provision of social and health services at, of course, a higher cost than in the case of the public sector. Hence whereas progress in expanding the scope and quality of public sector provision of basic social and health services may have been limited, the overall health picture did improve thanks to the leading role of the private sector in this domain.[43] Available data indicate that the ratio of population to physicians declined from an estimated 1,200 for 1975 to 754 for 1990 and 430 for 1999, and probably less for subsequent years. This reflects the rapid increase in the number of practising doctors, albeit with qualitatively different training backgrounds.[44] Hospital bed capacity has been expanding, reaching in 1996 the ratio of about 4 per thousand inhabitants, which was higher than the corresponding ratios for the other countries of the region.[45] This has been accompanied by increased curative health services and increased awareness of the importance of preventive healthcare.

Education

Prior to the civil war, Lebanon enjoyed a significant regional comparative advantage in the domain of education. Its universities (and especially the American University of Beirut) and schools attracted a good number of students from the region and beyond. War conditions and the rapid expansion in educational institutions in neighbouring countries reduced this advantage. It remains to be seen whether post-civil-war Lebanon can significantly regain some of its lost attractions in the field of education. In Lebanon's favour is its traditional liberal environment, which permits the flourishing of liberal education along with a traditionally active role for the private sector in the field, especially in higher education. Historically, and until the 1950s, this was the preserve of private universities.[46] The national university, the Lebanese University, established in 1959, has since accounted for the greater proportion of student enrolment (about 60 per cent for 2000/1).[47] The post-war period has witnessed an increasing number of officially recognized private institutions of higher learning, reflecting the diversity of Lebanon's cultural climate. As of 2000 they totalled forty institutions (including fourteen universities), up from eighteen (of which eight were universities) at the beginning of the decade. While the academic standards may differ substantially from one private institution to another, the major private universities have on the whole probably been better situated to progress academically than has Lebanon's national university, despite its unfulfilled potential as an academic institution and its past impressive record in a number of disciplines. One major reason for this is that the Lebanese university has been increasingly encumbered with political interferences that affect its academic development adversely: the president and deans of the university, for instance, are appointed by the Council of Ministers along sectarian lines. It has also faced financial constraints resulting from budgetary considerations.[48]

In contrast with the relatively high tuition fees charged by private schools and universities, tuition fees at public schools are very low. At the pre-university levels, public schools accounted in 2000/1 for about 39 per cent of total student enrolment. To that extent, they provide an essential educational outlet for a large proportion of the population that comprises limited-income groups. Low-fee or free education, however, often comes at a cost. This includes overcrowded classes; relatively poor libraries; inadequately equipped laboratories; limited computer and Internet facilities; and, in general, a lower quality of education. Reform plans have been proposed, and recently initiatives have been taken to improve the level of public education in cooperation with international organizations. It is too early to assess their impact. Enrolment in vocational schools at the intermediate and secondary levels (both public and private) accounted in 2000/1 for about 8 per cent of total enrolment at that level.[49]

Steady progress has been made in the field of education. In addition to high enrolment numbers, the illiteracy rate dropped, according to official estimates, to 11.6 per cent for 1997 (12 per cent for 1987) compared to 31 per cent for 1970.[50] At the higher end of the scale, as noted earlier, the proportion of university graduates in the total workforce has been rising steadily, standing at about 16 per cent for 1997. Similarly, the number of professionals and those pursuing higher education has been rising at a rapid pace. What is significant is that the educational gap between the Lebanese communities (which was striking in the 1950s and the 1960s) has been steadily narrowed. At the same time, Lebanon's progress in education and in preparing ever increasing numbers of educated citizens and professionals seeking work opportunities has come face to face with the limitations of the domestic market and the circumstances of political instability. I shall briefly touch on this matter in the following section.

Unemployment

There are no employment series that can be used to portray the evolution of employment and unemployment for the period under review. The official household survey for 1997[51] reveals that the unemployment rate ranged from 8 to 9 per cent, and the recent study on the Lebanese labour market referred to earlier indicates that subsequently unemployment steadily increased, standing at 12.5 per cent for 2000. According to the 1997 official estimates, unemployment was relatively higher among the young seeking employment for the first time and the less educated than among the rest of the population. The 1997 unemployment rate estimate did not differ significantly from that prevailing during the war period.[52] Under prevailing circumstances, i.e. an economy recovering from a devastating war, the unemployment rate appears to have been relatively low, although in the subsequent three years (for which data are available) it increased in tandem with the slowing rate of growth. In assessing the domestic rate of unemployment, we should bear in mind that traditionally it has been tempered by emigration, whether of a permanent or temporary nature. As noted earlier, the trend of annual emigration tended to decline up to 1994 and rise subsequently, owing partly to the slowing down of the economy and hence diminishing work opportunities.[53] Unemployment was higher for males engaged in manual labour and for females engaged in office work. Finally, most of the unemployment was concentrated in three sectors: construction, trade and industry, which in recent years together accounted for over 40 per cent of GDP.

On the other hand the official survey does not include the majority of aliens working in Lebanon who have not set up households.[54] This omission has two implications: (i) the active resident population was larger than the survey revealed; in particular it excluded hundreds of thousands of Syrian workers who have been working in Lebanon since the end of the civil war, a large proportion of whom, if not most, did not obtain official work permits; and (ii) the actual rate of unemployment was different from the estimated one; if it is assumed that most alien workers were employed (otherwise they would not stay in the country), then the rate of unemployment was probably lower than indicated in the survey. This fact highlights an ongoing process of manpower substitution that has been taking place in the post-civil-war period: the emigration of Lebanese skilled manpower alongside an in-flow into Lebanon of relatively unskilled manpower that was able to seek employment, particularly in the construction and services sectors. In consequence, the move towards more capital-intensive methods of production, using skilled resources, which otherwise might have taken place, was slowed down, at least in those sectors where non-Lebanese workers have been substantially employed.

Lebanon, accordingly, has been facing an important manpower policy issue emanating from the continuously improved levels of education and specialization. To what extent can the internal market absorb the increasing number of fresh graduates, including those earning higher degrees abroad, who seek employment at home? In large measure, this will depend upon the rate and pattern of economic expansion of the domestic economy, which determine the extent and nature of available work opportunities. To absorb increasingly trained and specialized Lebanese manpower, Lebanon must maintain robust economic growth that allows for the absorption into the labour market of the growing pool of skills.

This brings to the fore two issues related to manpower planning that I shall touch on briefly. The first is the changing methods of production and management and the extent to which they are becoming skills-intensive or skills-oriented. This is partly influenced by emigration/immigration trends. Business enterprises seek to maximize their benefits or minimize their costs of production and adopt methods of production that reflect, by and large, relative factor prices: the more abundant the unskilled/semi-skilled manpower due, for example, to the in-flow of this type of labour force, the greater the incentive (methods of production permitting) not to substitute skilled for unskilled/semi-skilled manpower. The second issue concerns the type of specializations that are being sought by Lebanese students at university level and in vocational schools, and the extent to which they match evolving market demand. These issues need to be addressed by proper manpower policy planning. It would seem, however, that the government did not pay serious attention to this matter. With the exception of the six-year plan of the mid-1970s no employment policy has been promulgated either independently or as part of the overall economic and social plan.[55]

For Lebanon, the policy issue at hand goes beyond mere economic calculations by business enterprises. Its social dimension is clear. Can Lebanon resolve the issue of substantial emigration, particularly now that its economic costs in the form of lost human skills far outweigh benefits accruing from ever diminishing emigrant remittances? In addition to the pivotal role that the rate and pattern of economic expansion play in this regard, two other factors would seem to be relevant: (a) the degree of internal political stability and (b) the quality of governance. Both have a direct bearing on decisions to emigrate or not. In particular, globalization has greatly widened the scope of work opportunities for educated youth outside their home countries, especially for those who pursue their higher education abroad, along with ease of travel not experienced by older generations. Hence, other things being equal, the less stable the domestic political situation and the lower the quality of governance, the greater the inducement to establish footholds outside one's own country.[56] When the economic situation worsens, this becomes an added incentive to emigrate.

Environmental issues

The environmental dimension of development has become the focus of increasing attention since the end of the civil war. Many NGOs and other groups concerned with environmental issues have been established, calling for appropriate environmental planning. Towards the end of the war, a public outcry occurred when thousands of barrels of toxic waste, imported from Italy by unscrupulous businessmen, were found dumped along the coast and mountain range. As a result of this outcry, Lebanon passed one of the world's strictest laws dealing with the importation of hazardous waste. In the meantime, the issue brought to the public eye the relationship between the environment, the government and the business community. This relationship remains a troubling one, as for instance hazardous waste was shipped into Lebanon from Europe during the 1990s, and as at the time of writing no one has been prosecuted.[57]

In addition to the generally acknowledged vital importance of maintaining a healthy environment, for a small country such as Lebanon that is services-oriented and endowed with historic sites and geographic attributes rendering it highly attractive to tourists, proper urban/rural and environmental planning could greatly enhance national economic returns from activities associated with the country's natural endowments. Nevertheless, the creation of a Ministry for the Environment in 1991 and the existence of an urban planning authority, *al tanzim al muduni*, notwithstanding, the governmental record in this area has generally been dismal.[58] Privately concerned organizations have been active in drawing attention to the damage inflicted by public sector action in this area, and in certain instances have succeeded in halting potential damage.[59] Generally, the environmental degradation experienced during the war period continued with equal force in the post-civil-war period, as evidenced by a number of studies on environmental issues carried out in the past several years. In what follows, illustrations in the areas of urban/rural planning, pollution and deforestation are provided.

Important as the question of urban/rural planning is to Lebanon, the record in this area has been worse than poor. Uncontrolled and unplanned urban and rural growth has been accompanied by, among other things, gradual mutilation of natural and historic sites, deforestation, inadequate sanitation and water networks, and the illegal exploitation of quarries or, when licences are secured, non-compliance with their terms. It is not necessarily the absence of laws regulating urban/rural planning which explains this phenomenon, although some of them need to be revised. Rather it is the non-enforcement or at best inappropriate enforcement of existing laws and regulations which by and large has led to uncontrolled urban/rural expansion with major adverse environmental consequences.[60] Indeed, a government document prepared in mid-1999 and entitled 'Programme for Financial Reform' confirms the damage inflicted on the country's natural resources and the dangers they face.

Illustrations include the coastline dotted, as it is, with mostly illegal commercial operations (e.g. swimming areas, small ports, etc.), the unregulated spread of quarries in mountain areas and valleys, and deforestation.[61] Calls for the implementation of appropriate policies that govern the utilization of national space abound. Yet again the official response has, so far, been poor.

As to air pollution, there is growing evidence of a deteriorating situation, which the national authorities have not met with corrective policies. Two recent (1999) studies illustrate this matter. The first analyses the health impact of air pollution in Lebanon and the second air and noise pollution under different atmospheric/traffic conditions.[62] The first study points out that by the late 1990s Lebanon had among the highest per capita ownership of motor vehicles (comparable to the advanced industrial countries), over half of which were operating in Beirut and its suburbs. Motor vehicles were predominantly passenger cars that generally were relatively old and poorly maintained. At the same time, until 2002, when it was finally banned for private and small passenger cars, there was widespread use of leaded gasoline, the shift to unleaded fuel being very slow (14 per cent of the total in 1999). It is not surprising, therefore, that in recent years the major pollutants from motor vehicles have been lead and carbon monoxide, and the level of emission of various pollutants has either approached or exceeded WHO guidelines for health. One major consequence, as revealed by the second study, has been the emergence of a high concentration of lead in blood, with all its known adverse health effects. Similarly, diesel fuel, banned in the 1960s, was in 1994 permitted for use by buses and trucks (this takes no account of the ongoing illegal importation of diesel car engines).[63] In the absence of proper technical controls for vehicles, the widespread use of diesel has led to a drastic and visible deterioration in air quality.[64]

Conservative estimates of the social cost of air pollution (based on estimated mortality and morbidity values for Beirut and the annual impact of air pollution measured by 10 ug/m concentration of particulates) reach over $100 million annually, i.e. comprising the monetized national savings that would accrue (in the form of saved lives and reduced hospital admissions) were Lebanon to manage to reduce its level of air pollution to international standards.[65] Also, the second study found higher pollution levels in the vicinities of thermal power plants and cement factories. The above-mentioned environmental studies include specific recommendations for the control of pollution. But the responsible authorities are yet to begin taking the required action. As to noise pollution in Beirut, it was judged to be excessive in comparison with other cities. Among the contributing factors were improper vehicle maintenance and stand-by generators (used during electricity cuts) as well as the use of vehicle horns.[66]

Forests in Lebanon have been similarly neglected. According to a 1999 UNDP study,[67] deforestation has been steadily taking place as a result of urban expansion in the mountain areas, illegal tree cutting, unlawful grazing and over-grazing, forest fires, and poor management and harvesting policies. Deforestation has weakened the soil structure, accelerated soil erosion and led to the general degradation of soil quality.[68] On the other hand, some positive steps in this area should be recognized. A few forest areas have been designated by law as protected areas, e.g. the Barouk cedar forest (1991) and the Ehden forest (1992). Under the prodding of NGOs and outside organizations, the government has made some efforts to restore the forest cover. While legislation for this purpose has been introduced, the problem lies in its implementation.

Important as the preservation of the environment may be, in practice this has been an area of low priority for the Lebanese authorities. The rapidly increasing world concern with environment issues along with growing national civil society demands to deal properly with them are yet to influence the responsible authorities to address seriously the task of environmental preservation. Clearly, improper urban/rural planning and the environmental deterioration that Lebanon has been steadily experiencing are but two aspects of the country's governance issue. As already noted, where political patronage, conflict of interest and corruption prevail, the enhancement of the level of governance is a most difficult task, and so is the implementation of appropriate social/environmental policies. One way or another, the influence of the political actors responsible for this state of affairs has to be democratically curbed in favour of reform-minded political actors. Short of political reform from within, continuous and growing pressures from civil society groups in cooperation with reform-minded political actors may lead to the desired change in governance. Only then will environmental and other social issues be properly tackled. Whether this will happen remains to be seen.

3 Aspirations versus reality: lopsided development

Having endured the devastating effects of a sixteen-year civil war, it would be only reasonable to postulate that Lebanese citizens across the board, the educated and less educated, workers, salaried and professional classes, and the business class, had aspired to witness not only sustained economic recovery and the restoration of macroeconomic stability but the emergence of a new Lebanon characterized by enhanced governance and social organization, public sector reform, diminished sectarian influence over the political body and society, a greater degree of social equity and the strengthening of democratic practices. In short, drawing on the lessons of the war, the expectation that the policies of the national authorities would, first and foremost, be geared towards improving the quality of development and the public good was a legitimate national aspiration. The Lebanese paid a heavy national price for the devastating conflict (irrespective of who ultimately bears responsibility for it). With its conclusion national hopes for the emergence of a new and qualitatively better Lebanon were, to say the least, the natural outcome among those who shouldered its burdens and multi-faceted costs.

To what extent were these aspirations fulfilled? The foregoing analysis in this and the previous chapters leads to the conclusion that Lebanon's development since the end of the civil war has been seriously lopsided. On the one hand, the national authorities have been highly conscious of the urgent task of economic and financial recovery and have devoted considerable effort and resources to this end. The eventual economic/financial record, as we have seen, turned out to be mixed, reflecting some successes but also major failures. And when eventually the evolving fiscal/debt situation was judged to be unsustainable, the government sought outside assistance (the Paris II meeting) in an attempt to bring the debt dynamics under control.

On the other hand, the emphasis on economic and financial issues has been matched by relative neglect of the social, socio-economic, institutional and organizational dimensions of development. Whatever progress may have been achieved in these areas has been submerged by important failures stemming from Lebanon's inability to progress significantly, if at all, in enhancing its governance, institutional capacities and social organization. In this regard, incorporating the militias into the government may have served the purposes of internal peace but, in the context of the prevailing political set-up, at the very high cost of low-level institutional performance. The qualitative aspects of development suffered as a result. A corollary of this lopsided development is the continued coexistence of the traditional dynamism of Lebanon's private sector (with all its consequent positive and negative aspects under circumstances of inadequate social organization) with the traditional slowness and inefficiency of the public sector supported by a political set-up imbued with improper governance.

These failures, which prompt the characterization of Lebanon's post-civil-war development so far as lopsided, may be summarized under three headings: the first, as noted above, is the increased inequities in income and, by extension, asset distribution, environmental degradation, and increasingly more difficult living conditions for the majority of the Lebanese alongside the emergence of super-rich individuals. The second is the increasing concentration of political and economic power in the hands of the few, who, by and large, have not been held accountable for their actions irrespective of prevailing rules and regulations.[69] The third is the inadequate level of social organization which expresses itself not only in the lack of adequate urban and rural planning, environmental degradation, improper qualitative supervision, corruption in the public sector, and the survival of suburban slums, but also in such other lesser issues as inadequate traffic control and lack of proper or irregular road maintenance. Altogether, private interests often overwhelmed public interest. Indeed, one may go a step farther and question whether, on the whole, the political body and public sector were sufficiently conscious of, or sensitive to, issues of social organization and public interest to prompt them to take the required corrective action in both areas.

With the above in mind, Chapter 5 will take up, among other subjects, some of the fundamental issues facing Lebanon in any quest for national reform. It focuses on some major conditions required for long-term political stability, the improvement of governance, and sustainable development.

Lebanon, development and globalization: concluding reflections

§ WHAT lessons can we derive from Lebanon's developmental experience over the second half of the twentieth century? At the national level, what developmental challenges does Lebanon face in the context of globalization? At the beginning of the twenty-first century, whither Lebanon? What are the conditions for the fulfilment of the twin objectives of long-term political viability and sustained development?

In a wider context, how is the Lebanese experience instructive to other small open economies? How does it add to the discourse on the interlocking political and economic elements of national development of developing countries in the emerging global system?

This chapter offers concluding reflections on these questions by focusing on the following four major subjects: (i) the successes and flaws of Lebanon's development: a summary view; (ii) conditions for the long-term viability of Lebanon's development; (iii) the Lebanese economy in a global context; and (iv) the relevance of the Lebanese experience to other developing economies: issues of civil war, political economy and globalization.

1 Successes and failures of Lebanon's development

1.1 Aspects of success: pre-war economic expansion, resilience and liberalism

If one were to identify the most striking successes of Lebanon's economic development over the second half of the twentieth century, two stand out. The first is the broad-based economic expansion in the years that preceded the civil war, accompanied by relative financial and exchange rate stability. This was a noteworthy achievement, particularly since it took place under often turbulent domestic and regional political conditions. Few developing countries at the time could match this record. The second success is the resilience of the domestic economy, especially manifested during the long-lasting civil war. Despite the battering it received, it survived thanks in large measure to the private sector and civil society. As demonstrated in Chapter 2, even enfeebled successive governments attempted to cope with the deteriorating economic and financial situation, at times with a measure of success: macroeconomic policy often attained its targets in minimizing the impact of negative political developments on the national economy.

The post-war recovery record up to and including 2002 is at best mixed. Among its positive achievements are the restoration of relative price and exchange rate stability and the rebuilding and expansion of the damaged infrastructure. Lebanon has made great strides in improving its economic and regulatory environment, especially as regards the banking sector. The vitality of the private sector has remained strong, with certain sectors, notably banking and education, taking the lead in the process of recovery. While the rate of economic growth has tended to decline since 1995, Lebanon's estimated per capita GDP for 2001 ranked it first among the non-oil-producing Arab countries. And its Human Development Index (HDI) rank has climbed since 1990, standing at 65/162 for 1999 (with a value of 0.758).[1] But in the absence of concomitant progress in political and institutional performance, economic growth was eventually constrained, with a declining rate of growth and mounting public debt. Equally important was the fact that the quality of development suffered (see section 1.2 below).

The picture that emerges is that of a country that can achieve economic success when the right domestic and regional opportunities present themselves, and does not sink even when facing tremendous difficulties, such as civil war. This picture is linked to the dynamic private sector that since independence has greatly benefited from a market-oriented and open national economy and governmental policies that were generally supportive – or at least non-obstructionist – of private sector initiatives. There was, however, a substantial socio-economic cost to be paid in terms of social inequities and uneven development among the regions.

Given Lebanon's economic endowment, the liberal and outward-looking economic policies that were put in place after independence (e.g. a free foreign exchange market, a flexible exchange rate, conservative fiscal and monetary policy and limited state intervention) proved highly suitable for private sector initiatives. This was especially true at a time when neighbouring countries in the region chose to follow inward-looking and public-sector-oriented economic policies, maintaining various forms of exchange and trade controls. The socialist or statist ideology that at the time influenced these countries did not take hold in Lebanon. At the same time, the Arab petroleum-exporting countries had not yet begun their rapid process of economic development, made possible by the initial oil boom of the early 1970s.[2] The years following the end of the civil war witnessed an increasingly active monetary/fiscal policy linked in major ways to substantial deficit financing and rising public debt, which eventually influenced private sector initiatives negatively and contributed to the decline in the rate of growth. This, however, did not signal a change in the stance of the government *vis-à-vis* the private sector as much as it demonstrated the inappropriateness of the overall fiscal situation that had evolved, particularly after 1993, in conjunction with the overlapping of private and public interests.[3]

Regardless of the nature of the Lebanese state and what I have called the 'constrained democracy' which characterizes the political system, Lebanon's economic liberalism has been sustained by a relatively liberal political regime – strictly speaking a special brand of liberalism – with all its multi-faceted benefits. The liberal nature of the political regime is related to the dynamics of maintaining a balance of political, cultural and religious rights among the various sects. The right of self-expression at all these levels had to be mutually accepted and guaranteed if the sectarian system were to function at all. On the other hand, the absence of sectarianism would not on its own have led to a liberal economic and political regime, or, for that matter, to better government. To attain this objective, additional conditions would need to be satisfied (see below, section 2). After all, other countries that have not suffered from sectarian and/or ethnic problems have also suffered from low-quality governance and poor institutional performance.

Whatever Lebanon's economic successes, the state was clearly not 'developmental' in the sense it was in countries such as South Korea, Malaysia or, closer to home, Syria and Egypt, each with its own special developmental experience.[4] It did not directly undertake the management of economic enterprises other than certain public utilities or become actively engaged in the support of particular sectors. Indeed, as we have seen, some writers have described the Lebanese state as being 'neo-patrimonial' or 'familial/ clientist', within, of course, a sectarian political mould. This implies control by a coalition of parties or groups that cater to a combination of their own interests and those of the classes or groups they represent, and from whom they derive support, more than to 'national' interests or the public good. In the post-war period, with a few exceptions, the role of traditional political families generally declined. They were supplanted by the rising militia leadership, and a new super-rich business class that generally hailed from a different socio-economic background and tended to encourage rent-seeking activities. The above description of the Lebanese state will therefore need to be extended or redefined to include the new key political players. Whatever description of the Lebanese state one chooses, however, what matters is the quality of political governance that has come to prevail and its impact on national development, which I shall discuss below, in section 1.2.

With the downfall of the Soviet Union and the rising wave of privatization, the traditional developmental state model has either disappeared or is disappearing. Under the influence of Western countries and international monetary, financial and trade organizations, a new role for the state in developing countries is being advocated with a focus on regulatory and supervisory functions in otherwise totally market-oriented economies. This trend has been accompanied by the increasing participation in this domain of private sector or non-official organizations.[5] The regulatory and supervisory functions of the state, mainly in the banking and financial fields, have expanded since the end of the war, with no role yet for non-official organizations in this regard, and the economy, traditionally open, has moved farther in this direction. The Lebanese political set-up has not changed, however, and neither has the sectarian nature of the state and its institutions; nor, as emphasized above, has the performance of political institutions improved.[6]

It is worth noting that the impact of political developments on the country's economic performance seems to have changed from the pre-war to the post-war periods. Prior to 1975, negative political developments, manifested in the strained and often turbulent Lebanese–Palestinian relationship with all its domestic ramifications, did not seem to affect economic performance or the exchange rate significantly. It is as though private sector economic initiatives were relatively isolated from domestic political disturbances. The latter did not give rise to substantial fears on the part of the business community that they would have a lasting impact on the economic situation. In other words, they were generally regarded as containable. Or perhaps the political system was not considered to be as fragile as it came to be regarded after the civil war. In contrast, important political developments since 1990 – including, for instance, the domestic quarrels within the ruling 'Troika' – have had a direct and significant impact, particularly on the foreign exchange market and on the economic situation generally. The sensitivity of the private sector to the political situation increased tremendously. Perhaps this is partly attributable to the weaknesses that have appeared in the performance of the post-war political institutions, whereby the containment of negative domestic political development often required recourse to the Syrian leadership for resolution.

Also noteworthy is the fact that rapid economic expansion under conditions of relative financial stability can take place in the absence of a generally active economic policy with explicit targets and instruments, as demonstrated in the pre-civil-war period. An active policy does not necessarily ensure a sound economic expansion, as the experience of the post-conflict era clearly shows. On the contrary, if inappropriately designed and implemented, it could have major negative economic effects on the national economy.

1.2 Flaws: sectarianism, poor governance and the quality of development

Contrary to the general aspirations and expectations that accompanied the ending of the civil war, the expanding regulatory role of the government was not accompanied by institutional reform, i.e. increasing efficiency, greater transparency, decreasing corruption and nepotism, and enhanced independence of the judiciary. Had these been accomplished, they would have helped draw a clear distinction between public and private interests. All attempts at reform have met with failure. By the end of the 1990s and the beginning of this decade, the public sector was bloated,[7] generally inefficient, and afflicted with widespread corruption, while the judiciary was probably less independent than ever before.

The poor institutional performance eventually contributed to the major economic imbalances that Lebanon came to face. As demonstrated in Chapter 3, the target of relative financial stability has been achieved at major economic costs, such as a declining rate of growth after 1994, rising unemployment and mounting public debt. By 2002 the government had come under increasing pressure to implement corrective measures to address the difficult economic situation, including privatization of specific public utilities and a major reduction in the fiscal deficit. These measures on their own, however, were not deemed sufficient, and to avert a potential financial crisis the government had to seek substantial outside financial assistance (the Paris II meeting of 23 November 2002).

In the context of the post-war political system, the checks and balances that could have prevented the emergence of major macroeconomic imbalances seem to have been weakened at a time when, in contrast with the pre-war period, not only were regional economic conditions less favourable, but also an active economic and reconstruction policy was required to address the economic/financial consequences of the war. In addition, the government had to cope with the economic consequences of Israeli attacks on civilian infrastructure, and its occupation of the southern border area. To address all these issues, the implementation of coherent, transparent and efficient macroeconomic and reconstruction policies was required, hand in hand with a high degree of accountability of the public sector agencies entrusted with these tasks.

One major problem in this regard is that budgetary outcomes were not governed by built-in institutional restraints against financial indiscipline, but to a large extent were subject to a political and administrative decision-making process in a political environment that did not impose accountability in fiscal matters.[8] Furthermore, whenever corrective or belt-tightening policies were envisaged and put in place – irrespective of whether they succeeded or not – the burden of adjustment has in large measure been borne by the middle class and limited-income groups.

In the same vein, it is not surprising that the quality of development continued to suffer, and was characterized by various forms of social inequity, poor urban and rural planning, and persistent environmental degradation. Put differently, the various official economic and social plans notwithstanding, the promotion of the public good, whose benefits reach the population at large, being non-excludable and non-rival in consumption, was not an important priority of the political body, especially given that the distinction between the private interests of key political players and the public interest was blurred.

Some politicians and observers have tended to ascribe the persistent, if not deepening, qualitative shortcomings in the post-war era to the legacy of the war period. This is not a viable stand. Corruption, public sector inefficiency, illegal and/or inappropriate exploitation of natural resources, degradation of the environment, major shortcomings in urban and rural planning, inadequate official vision, and/or the absence of official willingness to deal with socio-economic issues are matters that cannot be blamed on the civil war and its corrupting influences. Nor for that matter can they be blamed on the continued and substantial Syrian influence in the political affairs of Lebanon after the war, or the continuing ramifications of the Arab–Israeli conflict. In large measure they have been endemic to the governance of the country since independence, and constitute a constant theme of Lebanon's development in the second half of the twentieth century. It would seem that governance, poor as it was before the war, grew even weaker after it. By contrast, with Syrian support the government grew stronger in maintaining security and forestalling what it perceived to be potential political conflicts from spilling over into domestic disturbances, sometimes at the cost of imposed restrictions on freedom of expression.[9]

The shortcomings in the quality of governance and development go hand in hand with the prevailing political set-up and the general political behaviour of the governing coalitions. In the Lebanese case, this is directly, but not solely, linked to the influences of sectarianism, which has become more pronounced after the civil war. It may be conjectured that the underlying reason for this is that the redefined formula for sectarian power-sharing that ended the war (the Taif Accord) allowed for, if it did not induce, whether intentionally or unintentionally, intensified jockeying for political, economic and administrative spoils among key political players whose power base generally derived from their respective religious communities. As already noted, however, the new phenomenon was the direct entry of a new moneyed class, the super-rich business people, into the political arena, albeit in the context of sectarian representation. They came to share power and influence, both within and outside parliament, with leaders of parties and militias that fought the civil war and, to a lesser extent, with traditional political groupings or personalities whose political stature had relatively diminished. Together, they represented a coalition of major sectarian and political interests that were not always in harmony with one another. The influence of secular political parties, never particularly strong, grew even weaker after the war. In these circumstances, the new formula for sectarian power-sharing implied the absence of a unified central authority. Instead it allowed for the emergence of the 'Troika' rule. One major consequence was that key governmental decisions frequently reflected compromises aimed at satisfying a combination of sectarian and vested interests, some of which could be arrived at only after recourse to Syrian arbitration.[10] Another important consequence of the new power-sharing formula was the absence of a coherent long-term national policy that focused on the public good.

Whatever its merits, the finely tuned sharing of political power among Lebanon's religious communities is inherently discriminatory: hence my reference to the country's political system as a 'constrained' democracy. It is a system that is imbued with potential instability. Conflicts among the various political and sectarian leaders have arisen – and can arise again in the future – over what they consider the rightful share of the religious community each represents in managing the affairs of the state. Conflicts can also occur because of the varying attitudes of the political and religious leadership towards specific national and regional issues. Such matters as the presence of Palestinian organizations, the role of Lebanon in the regional conflict, the distribution of governmental posts among the various sects, secularism, Syrian–Lebanese relationships, to mention only a few, could spill over, as they have done in the past, beyond the bounds of peaceful national dialogue, into major national conflicts. Instability has stemmed from the fact that emerging conflicts or shocks often could not be resolved within the institutional framework of the sectarian system itself, and therefore have required an outside steadying hand to help resolve them. (In the post-war period the steadying hand belongs to Syria.)[11]

In consequence, what may be described as an 'unstable political equilibrium' arose and, until its underlying reasons are properly addressed, it will continue to prevail.[12] Even if it is correct, the argument that Lebanese political instability in the post-Taif era is in large measure linked to the dominating Syrian military and political presence does not negate the existence of other elements of potential instability associated with the nature of the political system itself. After all, the Taif Accord did not bring about a major rupture in a system that embodied elements of instability, but only a necessary adjustment, which at the time was considered essential for ending the civil war. Sectarianism has continued to act as the mainstay of political behaviour and Lebanon's 'constrained democracy' has continued to flourish: the question of the 'unstable' domestic political equilibrium has not yet been laid to rest.

The combination of sectarianism, 'familialism', sustained 'clientism' and, after 1990, the growing direct influence of the super-rich businessmen and of 'political money' proved to be a major impediment to political and institutional reform, and therefore to a stable political system. It encouraged the persistence of poor governance that affected the quality of development negatively. Lebanon has yet to meet the challenge of resolving this problem, and it must. The country's sustained and long-term development cannot be rooted in a potentially unstable sectarian political system characterized by poor institutional performance.

2 Domestic conditions for viable long-term reform

As I see it, the major challenge facing Lebanon is to maintain the wealth of a multi-religious society while resolving the twin issues of 'unstable political equilibrium' and poor governance. More specifically, the objectives of reform should be to move towards a politically more mature state and a stable political system by eliminating discriminatory practices, improving democratic attributes, and in general arriving at a higher level of political governance.[13] Equally important, it should aim at creating the conditions for a modern economy in which the quality of development occupies a central position.

If, as is generally agreed, the attributes of a democratic system imply that equal political rights and opportunities among citizens are not only legislated for but also practised; fair representation and free parliamentary elections are assured; freedom of expression is guaranteed; the rule of law is invariably applied; public institutions are transparent and largely free of corruption, nepotism and discriminatory practices; and the judiciary is independent of political pressures, then, as amply demonstrated, the Lebanese political system has not measured up well to all these requirements. This is especially true of equal political rights. Even the advantages of Lebanon's relatively liberal political regime, including a substantial degree of freedom of expression, have been tarnished by political interferences, both overt and covert, in the work of governmental institutions, and frequently laxity in enforcing the law.[14]

Clearly, achieving the above goals will be difficult for at least two major reasons. First, sectarianism has proved to be firmly rooted in Lebanese political behaviour, as demonstrated by its survival despite sixteen years of civil war. Equally important and adding to the difficulty is the fact that sectarianism is as much a cultural as it is a political issue, if not more so. Breaking away from the sectarian mould would require political maturity based on a change in entrenched attitudes, perceptions and values that consider religious communities the cornerstones of the political system. Doing away with the sectarian nature of the system thus requires a gradual cultural and political break with past modes of behaviour.[15]

Second, sectarianism is not an issue that stands on its own. It is part of the larger question of governance. Eliminating sectarianism without reforming the management of government and its institutions, and thus essentially creating a new political culture, would not necessarily lead to improved governance. It might simply amount to a different political power structure and alliances that are outwardly non-sectarian, but effectively behave under sectarian influences, with no guarantee of improved political performance. In fact, the checks and balances of the Lebanese sectarian system that have allowed a good measure of political freedom and guaranteed the right of free religious expression may give way to the emergence of a political regime that, in practice, will be less democratic than the existing one. Reform has to go beyond the phenomenon of sectarianism to reach all aspects of political and civil life.

This brings me to the argument for 'consociational democracy' advocated by some writers and politicians across the sectarian divide. This idea is based on the notion that in a multi-religious society such as Lebanon's it is the most appropriate form of democracy. The reasoning is that mutually accepted political concessions among the various religious communities safeguard their respective identities and rights in power-sharing, while allowing for parliamentary elections and, in principle, the trappings of modern democracies. In the same vein, certain observers argue further that the elimination of the sectarian system could lead to the political – and possibly cultural – hegemony of a single religious community, or even to the emergence of a military dictatorship. In consequence, as noted above, Lebanon's cultural wealth, associated with the existence of various religious communities and the measure of freedom that the delicate sectarian balance has provided, will be greatly diminished. Thus, according to this argument, husbanding the sectarian system by addressing whatever elements of instability it might embody would be a preferable alternative to doing away with the existing sectarian balance altogether. The Taif Accord is seen as an attempt in this direction, although it has not been properly implemented.

The problem with this notion is that it assumes general acceptance over time of the agreed formula for mutual political concessions among the major sects, which, if need be, can be modified peacefully. The Lebanese experience, however, does not bear this out. The pre-war sectarian tensions embodying persistent calls for more equitable power-sharing eventually contributed to the outbreak of the civil war. There is no assurance that the Taif Accord, which amounted to a major – imposed – readjustment in the sectarian formula as a means of ending the conflict, has properly addressed the potential elements of instability. These elements, after all, have been linked in the first place to the discriminatory political practices of the system itself. They continue to prevail, with no guarantee of the system's general acceptance in the future. While the Taif Accord restored peace, the post-Taif era has not witnessed the creation of genuine political stability or, for that matter, better governance. As I said earlier, the reasons go beyond the question of sectarianism.

It is perhaps not surprising that no serious national initiatives have been undertaken to address the various dimensions of the sectarian problem. Key political players and groups have been reluctant to tackle it, one reason being their fear that doing away with sectarianism would be tantamount to losing the political position and advantages they derive from the present system. Another reason is that, to be successful, any fundamental changes would require a broad political consensus that is not readily attainable. However, open national dialogue on how to resolve major political and economic issues, whether carried out within or outside governmental institutions, which seeks broad political consensus, has not been a Lebanese tradition.[16] National political institutions have not been developed to serve this objective. On the contrary, over time, and particularly after 1990, they have come to suffer from increasing sectarian influences.

The inability to address the fundamental political question of what I have been calling 'unstable equilibrium' has been paralleled by the lack of a coherent national policy focusing on the quality of national development. There are, of course, various dimensions to this matter: among others, poverty, skewed income distribution, unbalanced provision of basic services, gender discrimination, environmental degradation, and inadequate management of natural resources.[17] Together they constitute major aspects of what has come to be referred to as sustainable development, defined as the process of creating, maintaining and managing wealth, whose components include environmental, social and human factors,[18] in addition to the more commonly measured variables.[19] By adding the environmental dimension to development, environmental degradation becomes an explicitly recognized cost of development. Basically, sustainable development requires the maintenance, if not the improvement, of the quality of life as reflected in the expanded measure of wealth defined above.

In Chapter 4 I pointed out failures in major socio-economic areas. While recognizing progress in certain sectors, such as health and education, it would not be an exaggeration to state that the Lebanese economy has been less than successful in becoming a modern economy, in which the quality of development occupies a central place. Indeed, if the present rate of environmental degradation continues, along with inefficient and hence costly institutional performance, one cannot but conclude that the Lebanese economy – irrespective of its purely macroeconomic outcome – will in fact be moving away from, instead of towards, a modern economy.[20] A basic condition for assuring that this will not be the case is a drastic improvement in Lebanese political and institutional performance.

Our emphasis on sustainable development and greater social equity is motivated by the fact that the dynamism of Lebanon's private sector has not as yet been properly matched by the requisite political, administrative and institutional performance, which would ensure, in case of conflict, the prevalence of the public interest over the private. Whereas in many advanced, and even in less advanced, economies the public good is to a large extent sought and sustained, this has not necessarily been the case here. Indeed, the public interest has often been sacrificed in favour of private interests, either with political protection or with the outright involvement of influential political actors. Environmental degradation, deforestation, illegal exploitation of other natural resources, inappropriate, not to say chaotic, urban and rural planning, inadequate implementation of rules and regulations are glaring illustrations of the disregard of the public interest in favour of the private. To the extent that the distinction between private and public interest is blurred and that the required guarantees to keep them separate are not in place, the public good will continue to suffer, and so will the quality of development.

The seriousness of this problem, especially for a small country with limited natural resources, is underscored by the fact that deterioration in the quality of development is not always reversible, at least in the foreseeable future, as in the case of, say, deforestation or damage to the country's bio-diversity. The harmful effects they bring in their wake will require a long time to contain, if they can be contained at all. In contrast, faulty macroeconomic policies are reversible and their adverse effects on the national economy can be countered in a much shorter period of time.[21]

Will Lebanon in the future be able to carry out the required political and economic reforms and thereby create the necessary conditions for its move towards the desired political system and economy as defined above? This remains to be seen. Its inability to undertake the required reforms, however, will not necessarily imply its demise but rather its evolution along paths that will diverge from the above-stated goals. First, at the domestic level the conditions for long-term political stability, or sustainable political equilibrium, will not be fulfilled. Lebanon will, in all likelihood, continue to oscillate between points of stability and instability, and the guarantor of domestic stability will continue to be exogenous to the system. Second, the inability to substantially improve the quality of Lebanese development will not only leave the socio-economic issues referred to above, with all their potential risks, inappropriately resolved but will also render Lebanon a less attractive place for its well-educated youth, many of whom will increasingly continue to seek work opportunities abroad, especially when the domestic economy is not robust.

Indeed, I submit that emigration from Lebanon has not been induced solely by slow-downs in economic activity and shrinking work opportunities, important though these factors may be, but also by the quality of governance, social organization and economic management. Other things being equal, the lower the level of national performance in these areas, the greater the incentive for the younger generation to emigrate. In the global economy, and with the increasing ease of communication and transportation, Lebanon, along with other developing countries, is facing a major challenge: to slow down the 'brain drain' of its educated youth, particularly those who have acquired advanced levels of specialization. No doubt the resolution of this issue, to the extent it can be resolved, is partly dependent on the evolving needs of the domestic market and its ability to absorb the ever increasing levels of university graduates. Even if a reasonable match between the demand and supply sides of the labour market is postulated, however, in the absence of perceived improvement in the quality of domestic development, including the creation of an attractive political and educational/cultural environment, the tendency to emigrate will continue to be strong.

How can the reforms outlined above be initiated, while bearing in mind the educational and cultural dimensions that form their essence, rather than simply focusing on their political and administrative aspects? How can a dialogue on the above issues be initiated at the national level, and what processes should govern it to assure its success? Both these questions in my opinion constitute basic elements of a future research and intellectual agenda for Lebanese reform. This reform, long overdue, will provide the opportunity to begin the process of bringing Lebanon into the fold of countries that aspire to establish forward-looking and politically and socially advanced societies.

3 Lebanon and the global economy

In today's global economy, the external and domestic challenges facing any single country are intricately intertwined. For developing countries, globalization, as the vast and growing literature on the subject points out, poses both opportunities and costs. Briefly, the opportunities arise from the drastic reduction in trade and other barriers and hence easier access to wider markets; the free flow of investments across countries; the much greater accessibility to technology and knowledge, with the Internet helping to globalize production and capital markets and promote efficiency across the board. The costs include the marginalization, and even, some argue, the end, of national sovereignty and loss of autonomy over economic policy;[22] the documented increasing income inequality in favour of high per capita income countries; rising levels of unemployment – unless the developing country is able to compete effectively on world markets; and generally the increasing dependence of the developing countries on the technologically advanced industrial economies that manage globalization through their control of international monetary, developmental and trade organizations.[23]

A major challenge facing Lebanon and other developing countries is how to maximize their welfare by ensuring that the benefits of integration in the world economy outweigh, to the greatest possible extent, its associated costs. This is not an easy task. Should these countries embrace full and rapid opening up, not only of the current but the capital account as well? This step is often advocated by the IMF and some academic writers. Or should liberalization be gradual or sequenced, taking into account the consequences of opening up particularly at the economic level, as argued by others?[24] What role should the state play in the process, and how does a country ensure that it will partake in whatever benefits globalization brings?

International monetary organizations, such as the IMF, and some academic writers have emphasized that to enjoy the benefits of globalization it is essential for developing countries to adopt a set of economic policies geared towards the maintenance of macroeconomic stability. These include openness to the outside world; improving the efficiency of the export sector; structural reforms;

greater spending on education; training; increased spending on research and development; and not least of all improving the level of governance and institutional performance, as well as putting in place required market regulations such as competitive laws.[25] The combination of well-implemented policies in all these areas, it has been argued, will strengthen the developing countries' competitiveness on the world market and offer them better opportunities to take advantage of the benefits of globalization.[26]

On the other hand, as noted above, other writers and policy-makers in developing countries point to the risks of full and rapid liberalization. They advocate a gradual approach to liberalization with the aim of benefiting from globalization while avoiding, to the extent possible, its negative effects, including marginalization, loss of policy autonomy[27] and the risks of capital volatility in the event of total capital account liberalization.[28] Still others stress that as political institutions in developing countries lag behind the globalization of technology, trade and investment, this tends to weaken their capacity to govern.[29] In this connection, it could be argued that had the countries of the world shared common political and other ideals and values, the cost of diminished national political sovereignty would be less intolerable than under conditions of heterogeneous, indeed divergent, political systems and values. Even then, however, diminished national sovereignty is a cost that developing countries have to bear in return for the presumed economic benefits of globalization. At best economic and political blocs that groups of countries seek to establish offer partial compensation for the loss of national sovereignty.[30]

More generally, the issue that developing countries face is that the interests of powerful industrial countries dominate the agenda of globalization. While the developing countries may not fully endorse the economic policy dicta of the international economic organizations that set and manage the rules of globalization, they have to account for them in designing their own national economic, developmental and social strategies. Some countries, it seems, have been more successful than others in this regard.[31]

The cost/benefit outcome of integration in the world economy may differ from one developing country to another. For some, especially those countries that have followed inward-looking policies and whose public sector has played a dominant role in the economy, the costs of adjusting to the new global economic environment might be greater than they are for countries that have followed more liberal policies and were already open to the outside world. For example, the transition from a highly protected to a liberal economy will entail adjusting domestic costs in line with prevailing international cost structures. During this transitional period, the loss of market share on the part of domestic firms in the liberalizing economy and a rising level of unemployment would not be surprising consequences. For economies that are already liberal, such costs of adjustment would be expected to be of a less severe nature.

Also, other attributes of individual economies, such as size, material and human factor endowment, geographic location and social systems, significantly affect the costs and benefits from integration in the world economy. For example, other things being equal, smaller economies are likely to be more vulnerable to the consequences of openness than would larger economies. Similarly, the more developed the infrastructure of a particular developing economy, and the more educated and skilled its human resources, the greater its potential readiness to meet the challenges of globalization, or the less the potential costs of the required adjustment.[32] Whatever the special characteristics of individual developing countries, the challenges of globalization call for a well-integrated and rational economic policy centred on maximizing national interest or the promotion of the public good. In turn, this assumes that national institutions are well placed to design and implement such a policy, which of course is not always the case.

Where does Lebanon stand at the beginning of the twenty-first century in its preparedness to meet the challenges of globalization? The country's liberal background in the years before 1975 permitted it to benefit immensely from its open interaction with the outside world at a time when globalization was not an issue and many economies in the region were public-sector-oriented and relatively inward-looking. It could count not only on its traditional economic and financial openness to the outside world, but on its cultural set-up as well. Its relatively well-advanced educational institutions; a general readiness of the private sector firms to update their methods of production and management by adopting available advances in areas of concern to them; and a generally liberal environment that welcomes foreign investments and initiatives, notwithstanding bureaucratic constraints – all of these were positive factors that contributed to robust growth and relative financial stability.

The environment at the beginning of the twenty-first century differs from that of the pre-war years, not only regionally but also domestically. Lebanon retains some of the positive features of its earlier domestic environment, specifically openness, liberalism and relatively advanced educational standards. The openness that has traditionally characterized its exchange system has taken on new meaning, and has gone beyond unrestricted current and capital movements and now includes the opening up of real estate, corporate and equity markets to non-nationals. As another aspect of the policy of opening up, reductions in Lebanon's tariff barriers, in conformity with the requirements of membership in the WTO, should not pose a major problem if they are phased in over time, as allowed under the WTO covenant.[33] This phasing will permit viable national industries to adapt to the conditions of open markets by becoming efficient and competitive, although some writers argue that this transitional period should be longer than what is allowed for.[34]

As to the regional economic environment, the economic and educational advances achieved by the neighbouring Arab countries since 1975 pose a major challenge to Lebanon's comparative advantages in the region. At the same time, the long-hoped-for Arab common market has so far failed to materialize despite various Arab multilateral decisions in this regard since the Arab League was established in 1945. In principle, the creation of such a market (if well designed and implemented) could have provided opportunities for Lebanon and other Arab countries to improve the competitiveness of their respective national economies, and to enhance their collective bargaining position *vis-à-vis* the outside world, thereby helping them become better situated to meet the challenges of globalization. In December 1997 an agreement was reached to create an Arab Free Trade Area to be gradually established over a ten-year period. In practice, its implementation has been slower than had been envisaged. While inter-Arab economic integration has not been seriously pursued,[35] Lebanon and other Arab countries have in recent years been individually seeking to conclude association agreements with the European Union (EU). Such cooperation can carry with it potential benefits to Lebanon, assuming that the required policies that will permit it to enjoy these benefits are put into effect, a matter that falls outside the purview of this chapter.[36]

We should bear in mind, however, that whatever their benefits, regional blocs and arrangements in the age of globalization may come to be less and less important. Perhaps they will amount to no more than transitional arrangements. In other words, if globalization implies complete and full elimination of all barriers between national economies, the significance of regional blocs, at least at the economic and financial levels, will greatly diminish, if not disappear altogether.

Regional considerations aside, the positive features of Lebanon's pre-1975 domestic environment that it has retained fall short, however, of the necessary conditions that will render it well prepared to meet the challenges of globalization. Foremost among these is a drastic improvement in political governance and therefore the quality of institutional performance, which affect all aspects of development, from the proper implementation of specific economic policies and regulations, including the planned privatization of public sector utilities, to the protection of the environment and the putting in place of an appropriate social safety net.

Unless this reform is put in place, Lebanon's position in a globalized world will weaken on at least three levels. To begin with, competitiveness of national production on open markets requires constant long-term investments in human skills, technology and the modernization of management. Such investments will not be forthcoming at the required pace unless investors are assured of both actual and potential economic and political stability, along with a conducive domestic working environment. Second, the benefits of globalization to Lebanon in relation to its costs will diminish. For example, with low-quality public sector performance (e.g. significant and multi-faceted bureaucratic hindrances, not to mention corruption), Beirut's potential competitive advantage as a regional financial and trading centre will be lessened. Similarly, with continued environmental degradation, poor urban and rural planning, and unwise exploitation of natural resources, Lebanon's comparative advantage as a tourist country will diminish over time. Third, with continued potential political instability accompanied by weak institutional performance, Lebanon's regional position will remain weak, and so will its negotiating stand within any regional bloc. It is true that Lebanon has had to bear a large share of the Arab–Israeli conflict, and could influence regional political developments only to a very limited extent. Nevertheless, a politically stable and institutionally better-performing country could have had – and can have in the future – a stronger voice in regional matters with which it is directly and vitally concerned.[37]

Other issues that the Lebanese authorities will need to address include potential macroeconomic instability underpinned in the latter part of the 1990s and early years of this decade by the persistence of large fiscal deficits and the rapid rise in the level of public debt. It remains to be seen whether and to what extent the Paris II meeting in November 2002 will provide the needed stimulus for the required corrective policy action. Additional issues are developing Beirut's nascent domestic financial market; adapting existing governmental regulations and procedures to the requirements of the rapidly developing information technology systems and communications networks (e.g. facilitating governmental services, let alone online government); and adapting public educational and training institutions to the changing economic and technological environments without losing sight of the fundamental cultural objective of the educational process.[38]

On the policy front, the loss of autonomy that globalization entails is probably not as crucial an issue for Lebanon as might be the case with larger and less open developing countries. In a small, open and, in large measure, dollarized economy the independence of macroeconomic policy action enjoyed by the Lebanese authorities has already been greatly constrained. Globalization, of course, accentuates this trend. But this should not imply inability to make policy decisions that address basic maladjustments. Constraints on interest rate, exchange rate or other policies associated with openness do not preclude, for example, taking measures to reduce the budget deficit or cope with the rising public debt. Similarly, openness on the world economy should not imply inability to implement fiscal and other policies intended to bring about greater social equity. These are policy concerns that continue to fall within the purview of the national authorities.[39]

Finally, Lebanon has to face challenges related to the potential instability of its political set-up, which is not conducive either to long-term sustainable development or to beneficial integration in the world economy. Dealing with this matter successfully could very well be at the heart of the corrective measures that Lebanon has to undertake in preparing itself to meet the challenges of globalization. In its favour is a tradition of peaceful transfer of power from one government to another and from one elected president of the republic to another. But this is not sufficient. The Lebanese experience teaches us that unless fundamental institutional reforms are implemented, the peaceful transition of power is only a veneer covering persistent poor governance.

4 Lebanon and small, open developing countries

Each country's development is influenced by its own set of special factors that span the economic, political, social, geographic and cultural domains. Nevertheless, the Lebanese experience may be instructive in at least three areas.

The first concerns the objectives of development and the interacting influences of the economic and political elements. The Lebanese case, not surprisingly, clearly demonstrates that a strict focus on macroeconomic issues to the neglect of the wider dimensions of development will entail major national costs embodied in the deterioration of the quality of development, including environmental degradation. This neglect is not only costly domestically but also weakens the developing country's position in increasingly open regional and global economies: its ability to compete on the open world market would diminish.

This, of course, brings to the fore the relationship between the economic and political elements, both domestically and externally. The Lebanese experience points to the negative impact on the quality of development of relatively poor governance and how this matter is linked to the existing political system and its institutions.[40] If, for whatever reason, the system is potentially unstable, the national economic performance will be adversely affected, and this in turn may (as in the Lebanese case) lead to major national conflicts, or even civil war. Hence addressing the twin issues of governance and political instability goes hand in hand with the resolution of economic issues and problems. This lies at the heart of the increasingly recognized multi-disciplinary dimension of development.

At the same time, domestic and external developments are closely intertwined, particularly as regards small countries that face external events over which they have no influence. Thus, in the Lebanese case, the booms and recessions of oil revenues exogenously affect the in-flow of investments from the Gulf region as well as the work opportunities for Lebanese citizens in the region. At the political level, the Arab–Israeli conflict, over which Lebanon has had no control, has weighed in heavily and negatively on domestic political and economic developments. While small countries have to face the impact of external influences over which they have no control, what matters is how they deal with them, and whether they try to maximize their potential benefit and minimize their negative impact. The ability to do so is directly related to the inherent economic and political stability of the country concerned. The Lebanese experience in this regard has generally not been encouraging. Lack of real national political unity alongside relatively low-level governmental performance has weakened Lebanon's ability to deal with the outside events with which it has been directly concerned. The process of globalization will further diminish the political and economic sovereignty of developing countries, especially small ones. If anything, this should act as an additional incentive for these countries to undertake the requisite national political and economic reforms that will enhance their opportunities to partake of any benefits globalization has to offer.

The second area of the Lebanese experience from which lessons can be drawn relates to the question of the civil wars that have plagued numerous countries, big and small, in Africa, Asia, South America and the Middle East. The Lebanese case highlights the issue of religious (as opposed to ethnic) fractionalization as one of the major causes of the civil conflict, the other being external intervention. For other countries that experienced civil conflict, the major causes may lie elsewhere, e.g. ethno-linguistic fractionalization, abundance of natural resources, geographic dispersion, a low level of per capita income, as well as external intervention. The point I wish to underscore is that while the Lebanese civil war is highly instructive as regards the role of religious fractionalization in the onset of a civil war, this element does not seem to have been given the attention it deserves in cross-country studies on the causes of the civil war, being considered in conjunction with other indices of social fractionalization.[41] In the Lebanese context, religious fractionalization assumes a great importance to the extent that the political system is based on sectarian power-sharing. The question that remains to be addressed is whether it would be an important risk element were the system non-sectarian or secular. In other words, does religious dominance by a single group play the same role as ethno-linguistic dominance? And to what extent would this depend on the level and quality of educational attainment? Addressing these questions would help define the nature of the requisite long-term policies that need to be implemented in order to forestall the reigniting, or the onset, of civil wars in countries where religious and other forms of social fractionalization prevail.

The third area of interest to other countries pertains to the more technical domain of economic policy. There are various aspects of Lebanese economic policy that may prove instructive to similarly situated developing open economies, not least of which is the policy of openness to the outside world. In particular, the relationship between openness, the exchange rate and financial stability is worth highlighting. The Lebanese exchange rate, even when independently floating, was relatively stable in the pre-war period mainly because the open national economy experienced financial stability and robust growth despite prevailing political tensions. In the post-war period the anchoring of the pound to the US dollar helped reduce the rate of inflation. However, in the absence of a healthy macroeconomic environment (exemplified by large fiscal deficits and rapidly mounting public debt), accompanied at times by occasional political disturbances, the pound was frequently subject to pressures sometimes of a sustained nature, leading to the depletion of the Central Bank's foreign exchange reserves. Clearly, a policy of anchoring has to be accompanied by policy measures that lead to macroeconomic stability; otherwise, pegging to a major currency such as the US dollar could turn out to be too costly in economic terms. By the same token, sustained macroeconomic stability has a significant positive impact on exchange rate behaviour whereby the need to anchor the national currency to the US dollar becomes less urgent. A more flexible exchange rate policy would then become more feasible. The fact that the Lebanese economy has become highly dollarized does not significantly affect the above conclusions, though the domestic impact of any exchange rate adjustment might be less than under conditions of limited dollarization.

On the other hand, Lebanon stands to learn a great deal from the experiences of other countries that have been able at once to achieve domestic political stability and robust economic growth while making significant progress in promoting sustainable development. The lessons that can be learned from the experiences of such countries will no doubt prove beneficial to the design of the political and socio-economic reforms that Lebanon is called upon to undertake. The major task for reform, however, remains rooted in an insightful reading of its past, sometimes painful, experience.

5 Final comment

The Lebanese had the national will to survive a long-lasting and devastating civil war. It is not beyond their ability to create the conditions that, in a fast-integrating world, will sustain progress towards the creation of a truly viable state and a modern national economy. A major prerequisite is willingness to engage in a constant open and free national dialogue that will address fundamental national political, economic and cultural issues by drawing on the lessons of the past without being burdened by it. In particular, this will have to be a dialogue among independent Lebanese intellectuals that can take various forms and which will pave the way for the required change in national political thinking and action. Breaking away from past modes of thinking and behaviour is difficult, but this is precisely where the responsibility of intellectuals lies. Despite the existence of a vigorous mercantile environment, this country is not short on intellectual talent.

It is my hope that this book will have made a contribution, however modest, in critically assessing certain basic dimensions of Lebanon's development over the second half of the twentieth century and, thereby, will have helped to articulate national issues that need to be addressed in order to attain the above goals.

Notes

Introduction

1. For example, one cross-country study on the impact of institutions on economic performance demonstrates that institutions that protect property rights are crucial to economic growth and investment (see S. Knack and P. Keefer, 'Institutional and Economic Performance: Cross-country Tests Using Alternative Institutional Measures', *Politics and Economics* 7, November 1985). In a subsequent cross-country study the authors conclude that 'trust' and 'civic cooperation' have a significant impact on growth and especially in countries with unreliable enforceability of contracts (see S. Knack and P. Keefer, 'Does Social Capital Have an Economic Payoff: a Cross-Country Investigation', *Quarterly Journal of Economics*, November 1997).

2. For a recent review of the literature on political economy see M. Castanheira and H. S. Esfahani, 'Political Economy of Growth: Lessons Learned and Challenges Ahead', an overview paper prepared for the Global Development Network (September 2001, unpublished), p. 4.

3. Ibid., pp. 6–12

4. See Clemens L. J. Siemen, *Politics, Institutions and the Economic Performance of Nations* (Edward Elgar, 1998), Chapter 6: 'Conclusion and Results'.

5. A large number of the analyses have so far focused on civil wars in Africa, but more recently case studies on civil wars in other regions of the world have also been undertaken (see papers presented at the 'Yale–World Bank Workshop: Case Studies on the Economics and Politics of Civil War', Yale University, 13–14 April 2002).

6. For a summary of and references to recent literature, see Chapter 2.

7. Although foreign troops did not depart until 1946.

8. Constitutional amendments were adopted by parliament on 21 August 1990 and signed into law by the president of the republic on 21 September 1990.

9. Article 95 of the constitution of the newly independent republic stated that for a temporary but unspecified period religious sects (currently eighteen are officially recognized) would be equitably represented in public employment and cabinet posts. The principle of equitable representation was not defined. However, an unwritten national accord reached among political leaders on the eve of independence specified that the post of the president of the republic was to be held by a Maronite Christian, that of the speaker of the House by a Shiite Muslim and the premiership by a Sunni Muslim. In practice a sectarian formula was applied to cabinet posts which were apportioned among the six largest religious communities in the country (normally along with representation of the Armenian community, considered an additional but a separate community) but frequently to the exclusion of other officially recognized religious communities. An overall balance between Christian and Muslims has been maintained in the cabinet to this day. Appointments to most, if not all, public

administrative positions have been subject to time-honoured sectarian considerations, particularly at the level of higher positions. The discriminatory aspects of the system also pertain to the personal status laws, which, among other things, deal with marriage/divorce and inheritance. These laws fall under the jurisdiction of the official bodies of the respective religious communities.

10. In analysing the role of the political system and its institutions, I do not focus explicitly on the decision-making process, the influence of various interest groups on this process and how it evolved over the period under study, although these questions are implicitly taken up in the discussion of the system's power-sharing formula among the major religious sects. The emphasis of the analysis is more on the nature of the political system, its stability, and how it influenced Lebanon's political environment and economic development, especially the quality of development.

11. Lebanon's political regime has been characterized by democratic practices such as the existence of multi-political confessional and secular parties, a relatively liberal environment with a high degree of freedom of expression, regular parliamentary elections (except during the war period), no matter how imperfect, and generally the peaceful transfer of power from one administration to another. Two elected presidents were assassinated shortly after their election: Bachir Gemayel in 1982 and Rene Mouawad in 1989. But in both cases they were immediately succeeded by constitutionally elected presidents, albeit not without substantial outside political influences.

12. During the war the private sector did come under the influence of the militias; rather it can be said that the militias became part of the private sector. See Chapter 2 for more details.

13. Investigating the relationship between political instability (measured by the number of irregular or non-constitutional governmental changes) and long-term growth, Siemen concludes that they are negatively related. Were the measure of political instability based on regular governmental change then, no matter how frequent the change, no correlation is established. Also, while repressive regimes are negatively related to growth, it does not follow that liberal democracies are necessarily conducive to high investment and growth (See Siemen, *Politics, Institutions*, pp. 203–4). In the Lebanese case, changes in governments have been regular and the political regime has been fairly liberal in its orientation.

14. By 2002 the government had come under increasing pressure to take corrective measures to address the debt problem. These have included the introduction of new taxes, plans to privatize certain public sector entities and attempts at reducing public spending. In addition, the government resorted successfully to outside financial support to avert a potential financial crisis.

15. Lobbying by NGOs and other civil society parties interested in the preservation of the environment has had very limited positive effects.

16. For a detailed analysis of the causes underlying the outbreak and duration of the civil war, see Chapter 2.

17. The choice of the year 1950 as the beginning of the first phase was due mainly to economic considerations. For one thing, some of the major statistical series, such as national income, begin with that year. For another the complete openness of the national economy was not consolidated until that time. Further, 1950 also happens to be the year when the Syro-Lebanese customs union was dissolved and the two countries chose to follow different economic policies. The alternative choice of say, 1946,

the year when foreign forces departed from Lebanon, as the starting point would be less appropriate. In any case, at the political level, going back four years would not significantly change the analysis pertaining to the political environment.

1. The period preceding the civil war

1. Certain urban areas – Beirut in particular – generally experienced a liberal way of life in contrast with the conservative environment that prevailed in other areas of the country.

2. A major crisis occurred in 1958, triggered, among other reasons, by the move of the then president of the republic, Camille Chamoun, to weaken the position of his political opponents and by fundamental disagreements between the government and its political allies on the one hand and opposition groups on the other over foreign policy issues and alliances. The possible amendment of the constitution, advocated by supporters of the president of the republic, to enable him to run for a second term was an additional factor of friction between the two groups. For several months, civil strife occurred between loyalist and opposition groups. The crisis had its external dimension, which was exacerbated by the creation of the United Arab Republic (comprising Egypt and Syria) in February 1958, and the overthrow of the Hashimite Kingdom in Iraq in July of the same year, followed immediately by the landing of US forces near Beirut. US and Egyptian intervention helped settle the conflict, which eventually led to the election of the commander of the army as president of the republic and the formation of a four-man cabinet that represented equally the loyalist and opposition groups. For an assessment of the 1958 crisis, see Michael Hudson, *The Precarious Republic, Political Modernization in Lebanon* (Random House, 1968, reprinted by Westview Press, 1985, pp. 105–6). A recent work in Arabic (with a sympathetic leaning towards the position of the then opposition groups) is Abbass Abu Saleh, *Al-'Azma al-Lubnânîya 'âm 1958* [The Lebanese Crisis of 1958], Beirut, 1998. For a detailed discussion of the US involvement in this crisis, see Irene L. Gendzier, *Notes from the Minefield. United States Intervention in Lebanon and the Middle East, 1945–1958*, part IV (Columbia University Press, 1997).

3. For a brief outline of attempts at administrative reforms prior to 1958, see Ralf E. Crow and Adnan Iskandar, 'Administrative Reform in Lebanon, 1958–1959', *International Review of Administrative Sciences*, 3, 1961.

4. For a review of the Chehabi reforms, see Hudson, *The Precarious Republic*, pp. 313–25.

5. On this point, see Kamal Salibi, *Cross Road to Civil War, Lebanon 1958–1976* (Caravan Books, Beirut, 1976, pp. 18–21) and Wade R. Goria, *Sovereignty and Leadership in Lebanon 1943–1976* (Ithaca Press, London, 1985, pp. 59–60).

6. Military confrontations took place between the Palestinian military organizations and the Lebanese army in 1968 and 1969. One major cause of the confrontations was that the Palestinians wished to have freedom of action against Israel from Lebanon's southern borders while the Lebanese government (at least the faction which supported the president) was reluctant to grant them this freedom for fear of Israeli reprisals. The then prime minister favoured a policy of coordination with the Palestinian organizations that were supported by certain Lebanese political groups. With the help of Egyptian mediation, this matter was eventually settled under the so-called Cairo

Agreement (November 1969) between the two parties. While nominally Lebanese sovereignty was to be respected by the PLO, in practice the agreement sanctioned a measure of freedom for Palestinian political and military action against Israel from Lebanese soil. For an analysis of the circumstances which led to the Cairo Agreement and its subsequent implications, see Farid el-Khazen, *The Breakdown of the State in Lebanon, 1975–76* (I.B. Tauris, 2000, part IV, pp. 83–112) and Salibi, *Cross Roads to Civil War*, pp. 40–6. With their expulsion from Jordan in 1970–71, the Palestinian military organizations became increasingly active in Lebanon. Their activity often led to clashes with Lebanese security forces and Christian political parties.

7. On 18 August 1975 (a few months after the outbreak of the civil war), the National Lebanese Movement, which grouped leftist and other groups opposed to the government, issued its Transitional Programme for Democratic Reforms of the Political System in Lebanon. Among other proposals, it called for the abolition of political confessionalism.

8. There are numerous writings on the pre-1975 Lebanese political system and political divisions among the Lebanese. See, for example, el-Khazen, *The Breakdown of the State*; Elizabeth Picard, *Lebanon, a Shattered Country* (Holmes and Meier, 1996); Ghassan Salameh, 'The Lebanese Crisis: Interpretations and Solutions', N. Shehadi and B. Harney (eds), *Politics and the Economy in Lebanon* (Centre for Lebanese Studies, Oxford, 1989); Hussein Sirriyeh, *Lebanon: Dimensions of Conflict* (IISS, 1989); Halim Barakat, *Lebanon in Strife* (University of Texas Press, 1977); Hudson, *The Precarious Republic*; and Michael Johnson, 'The New Patrimonial State Before 1975', paper presented at a workshop on 'The Developmental State Model and the Challenges to Lebanon' organized by the Lebanese Centre for Policy Studies, Beirut, 15–16 February 2002.

9. As might be expected, explanations of the major causes of the civil war differ from one source to another. Two contrasting views are those of Farid el-Khazen and Halim Barakat. Khazen, in his book *The Breakdown of the State* referred to above, argues, in opposition to certain authors he cites, that the confessional system was sufficiently adaptable to the required changes. The breakdown that occurred in 1975–76 was due to rising Palestinian militarism (especially after 1967) and outside intervention, and much less to any inherent contradictions in the system itself. In contrast Halim Barakat, in his book *Lebanon in Strife*, also cited above, describes Lebanese society as being 'mosaic' rather than 'pluralistic'. The latter, according to Barakat, encompasses harmonious relationships among several diverse interests, religious and ethnic groups. The former consists of diverse groups, which interact without consensus on fundamentals (in the Lebanese context, e.g., national identity and confessionalism). Generally there is unbalanced distribution of rewards and power. (This was partly taken care of by the Taif Accord.) Barakat concludes that the civil war that broke out in 1975 was caused, among other domestic factors, by the prevailing social mosaic structure.

10. One study points out that the state failed to implement adequately its economic and/or regulatory measures, and especially in the period 1970–75 was not able to adapt to evolving economic conditions. (See Albert Dagher, *L'état et l'economie au Liban, action gouvernementale et finances publiques de l'indépendance à 1975* (Les Cahiers du CERMOC no. 12, Beirut, 1995.)

11. For further discussion, see Picard, *Lebanon, a Shattered Country*, chapter 5, and especially pp. 60–1, and Hudson, *The Precarious Republic*, pp. 252–7.

12. For a detailed analysis of Lebanon's pre-1975 economic and financial perform-ance and the role of financial policies in economic growth: see Samir Makdisi, *Financial Policy and Economic Growth, the Lebanese Experience* (Columbia University Press, 1979). This section draws on it.

13. Major exceptions included the short-lived 1958 crisis and the later occasional clashes between the Lebanese army and the Palestinian military organizations. These events did not, however, seem to unduly affect the expectations of the private sector.

14. See Albert Badr, 'Economic Development of Lebanon', in C. A. Cooper and S. A. Alexander (eds), *Economic Development and Population Growth in the Middle East*, American Elsevier, 1972.

15. See S. Makdisi, 'Flexible Exchange Rate Policy in an Open Economy, the Lebanese Experience, 1950–74', *World Development*, vol. 6, no. 7, July 1978.

16. The analysis in this section draws on Makdisi, *Financial Policy and Economic Growth*, chapters 6–7.

17. The Intra Bank was one of the largest commercial banks in Lebanon with assets at the end of 1965 estimated at about 17 per cent of total bank assets. The bank was forced to suspend payments on 14 October 1966 as a result of a run on it. To forestall the spread of the crisis to other banks, the Central Bank made available to them special credit facilities. The crisis was soon afterwards resolved, leading to banking reforms. See Makdisi, *Financial Policy and Economic Growth*, p. 53.

18. For a detailed analysis of exchange rate movements based on the record of daily quotations available at the Beirut Bourse, see ibid., chapter 4.

19. For details, see ibid., pp. 95–7.

20. For the academic year 1972/3, non-Lebanese students in pre-university levels of education comprised about 7 per cent of the corresponding student population (*Receuil statistiques libanais* 9, 1973, pp. 330–7).

21. Refer, for example, to T. Benhabib and M. Spiegel, 'The Role of Human Capital in Economics Development: Evidence from Cross-Country Data', *Journal of Monetary Economics* 34 (1994), and N. G. Mankiw, D. Romer and D. N. Weil, 'A Contribution to the Empirics of Economic Growth', *Quarterly Journal of Economics*, vol. 5, no. 107, May 1992. The authors augmented the Solow growth model by including accumulation of human as well as physical capital. By adding human capital, the augmented model accounted – according to the authors – for 80 per cent of cross-country variation in income.

22. The data are taken from various *UNESCO Statistical Yearbooks*.

23. Indeed, even in the 1990s enrolment in vocational schools was judged to be deficient and the relative shortage of trained technicians was considered a major prob-lem faced by industry. See Youssef El-Khalil, *Les facteurs de développement industriel dans une petite economie ouverte en voi de développement: les secteurs des beins capitaux au Liban* (1997), unpublished doctoral thesis, Université d'Auvergne, January 1996, p. 77.

24. Data derived from a major statistical survey carried out in 1970 by the Directorate of Statistics, *L'enquête par sondage sur la population active au Liban, Novembre 1970* 2 (Beirut, 1972).

25. Ibid., p. 107.

26. See, for example, Salim Nasr, 'The Crisis of Lebanese Capitalism', in *MERIP Reports* 73, where it is mentioned that the level of unemployment reached 10–13 per cent of the workforce in 1969 rising to 15–20 per cent in 1974 (p. 11).

27. See Kamal Hamdan and Samir Makdisi, 'Lebanon: Labour Force', unpublished paper submitted to Dar Al Handassah Consultants (August 1991).

28. See Nasr, 'The Crisis of Lebanese Capitalism', p. 12.

29. See Riad Tabbarah, 'Population, Human Resources, and Development in the Arab World', *Population Bulletin of ESCWA*, 20 November 1981, p. 28.

30. Nasr, 'The Crisis of Lebanese Capitalism', p. 11.

31. On the role and organizational structure of Lebanese labour unions up to 1967 see Samir Khalaf, 'Lebanese Labour Unions: Some Comparative Structural Features', *Middle East Economic Papers 1968* (American University of Beirut). For details of labour action over the pre-war period, as recorded by a leftist labour leader, see Elias Al Bouari, *Târîkh al-Ḥaraka al-'ummâlîya wa al-Niqâbîya fi Lubnân* [History of the Labour and Union Movement in Lebanon], vols II and III, Dar al Farabi, 1987.

32. Up until then, the use of monetary instruments was limited to the imposition of a 5 per cent reserve requirement in May 1969, raised to 7 per cent effective 1 September 1972. Also, in May 1972, the Central Bank issued a regulation whereby a bank's lending to any individual or group of individuals became subject to a limit of 30 per cent of the equity of the bank.

33. For a review of the above measures and discussion of economic policy trends see Makdisi, *Financial Policy and Economic Growth*, pp. 27–31 and 48–59.

34. See Makdisi, ibid., pp. 27–32. Prior to 1972 attempts were made to set up public investment programmes covering specified periods. The closest attempt at economic and social planning was the drawing up of a Five Year Plan (1965–69). This was based on earlier studies carried out by the Institut International de Recherche et de Formation en Vue de Développement (IRFED) at the request of the Lebanese government. The study covered various economic and social sectors. The Five Year Plan, however, lacked well-defined objectives and consistent means to attain them. It was essentially reduced to a collection of investment projects.

35. An analogy is provided by the principle of comparative advantage. Free trade provides an opportunity to raise the level of welfare, i.e. to push outward the consumption possibility curve. To realize this objective the parties concerned must act to take advantage of such an opportunity.

36. Illustrations of political upheavals include: the 1948, 1967 and 1973 Arab–Israeli wars; the revolutions or *coups d'état* in Egypt (1952), Iraq (1958) and Syria (1970); the Jordanian–Palestinian military confrontation of September 1970; the creation and dissolution of the United Arab Republic (1958–61); and the October 1973 war between Egypt and Syria, on the one hand, and Israel on the other.

37. See Kamal Hamdan, 'Siyâsat al-'Ujûr wa al-Madâkhîl' [Policy on Wages and Remunerations], *Abaad* 2, November 1994, p. 144.

38. For example, the economic programme of the Progressive Socialist Party (founded by the Druze leader Kamal Joumblatt), while calling for the adoption of planning, endorsed private initiative and competition within the overall economic objectives of the state.

39. See Ministry of Health *Annual Reports*, 1959 and 1971.

40. For a review of this code, see Paul Klat, 'Labour Legislation in Lebanon', *Middle East Economic Papers, 1959*, American University of Beirut.

41. See his paper, 'La redistribution des revenues au Liban', in *Semaines sociales du Liban, l'économie libanaise et le progrès social, du 19 avril au mai 1955* (Editions Les Lettres

Orientales, Beirut, 1955). According to the author, the working-class family earned an income of less than LL2,000 per annum ($578). The rich family earned upward of LL10,000 ($2,890). The translation of these figures into 1998 dollar equivalents is constrained by the non-availability of reliable inflation and real exchange rate series. With this caution in mind, available data seem to indicate that the average wage of a worker in 1955 translates, in 1998 dollars, into an average annual wage of less than $3,500, or about $290 per month. This compares with a 1998 average monthly income for workers of about $500. Family earnings are, on average, higher than that. In 1998, family monthly earnings of about $850 were considered as being equivalent to a subsistence level. In all probability, the 1955 average earnings of a working-class family were also equivalent to a subsistence level, bearing in mind that the definition of 'subsistence level' may differ for each of the two years.

42. See Institut de Recherche et de Formation en Vue du Développement, *Besoins et possibilités du développement du Liban* (Mission IRFED, 1960–61), p. 93.

43. See Central Statistical Office, Ministry of Planning, *Mizânîyat al-'Usra li-'âm 1966* [Household Survey for 1966], pp. 34, 54–8. The survey includes results relating to household earnings but points out that they are less reliable than the expenditure estimates, as those surveyed were more cautious in revealing their earned income.

44. The study was carried out by Yves Schmeil, *Sociologie du système politique libanais*, Editions Universitaires de Grenoble, 1976, and is referred to in Boutros Labaki and Khalil Abou Rjeily, *Bilan des guerres du Liban, 1975–1990*, Editions L'Harmattan, 1993, p. 182. The authors adjusted the 1973–74 results in terms of 1960 prices.

45. See, for example, Kamal Hamdan, *Al-'Azma al-Lubnânîya, al-Tawâ'if al-Dînîya, al-Tabaqât al-Ijtimâ'îya wa al-Huwîya al-Wataniya* [The Lebanese Crisis, Religious Communities, Social Classes and National Identity], Dar Al Farabi, Beirut, 1998. The author emphasizes (pp. 116–18, 133–7) that the pre-1975 economic and political developments brought in their wake social/class changes, which have not been properly recognized. Over the period, oligopolies became more pronounced and a progressive concentration of economic/financial power in the hands of the merchant/industrialist class (largely Christian) took place. Disparities among social classes widened but did not strictly conform to a sectarian division. While the Christian community was generally better off than the Muslim community, there were poor Christians just as there were rich Muslims. According to the author, while the familial/sectarian nature of the political system was deeply embedded in it, socio-economic developments up to the mid-1970s resulted in the emergence of social classes that over time became politically active, as demonstrated by the political events of the early 1970s. The civil war thwarted this social trend.

46. See Iliya Harik, 'The Economic and Social Factors in the Lebanese Crisis', in S. Ibrahim and N. Hopkins (eds), *Arab Society, Social Science Perspectives* (American University in Cairo Press, 1985, p. 418).

47. See Harik, ibid., p. 417. The author points out that based on the IRFED mission report the Gini coefficient for Lebanon in the early 1960s was 0.53, a little above the range of 0.40 to 0.50 for most countries. According to Harik the 'notoriety acquired by the IRFED report is due to the fact that the top ten percent of the population were shown as earning an unduly high percentage of income' (p. 417).

48. See el-Khazen, *The Breakdown of the State*, pp. 251–62, and Harik, ibid., pp. 421 and 428–9.

49. On this point see, for example, Farhan Saleh, *Lubnân al-Junûbî, wâqi'uha wa Qadâyâhû* [Southern Lebanon, Its Reality and the Issues It Faces], Dar Al Talia' Publishing House, Beirut, 1973.

50. This phenomenon should not obscure the fact that the wide cultural and professional gap between the Christian and Muslim communities at the beginning of independence, in favour of the former, was progressively reduced over the period under consideration. See, for example, Labaki and Abou Rjeily, *Bilans des guerres du liban*, p. 185.

51. See Hamdan, *Al-'Azma al-Lubnânîya*, pp. 111–13.

52. See Charles Churchill, 'Village Life of the Central Beqa'', *Middle East Economic Papers, 1959*, American University of Beirut, pp. 5–6.

53. We cannot, of course, ignore the prevailing unstable security situation in southern Lebanon at that time, which might partly account for the lack of a reduction in this ratio.

54. See IRFED Report, vol. II.

55. See Central Bureau of Statistics, *Dirâsat al-Quwa al-'Âmila fi Lubnân, Mash bi-l-'Ayyina* [The Working Force in Lebanon, a Statistical Sample Survey], November 1970, vols 1 and 2, Beirut, July 1972.

56. Summarized in Samir Makdisi, 'Al-Jawânib al-Iqtisâdîya li-l-'Azma al-Lubnânîya' [The Economic Aspects of the Lebanese Crisis], in *Al-'Azma al-Lubnânîya* [The Lebanese Crisis], Arab Organization for Education, Culture and Sciences, 1977.

57. One source mentions that in 1970 the walls of 60 per cent of all buildings in the Beqa' were made of mud with wooden roofs. Most comprised three rooms altogether. See Ibrâhîm Rizq, 'Al-Tanmiya al-'Ijtima'îya' [Social Development], in *Tanmiyat Muhâfazat al-Biqâ'* [Development of Muhafazat al Biqa'], Centre for Development Studies, Beirut, 1970. Lebanon is administratively divided into five provinces called 'Muhafazat'.

58. See ibid., pp. 70–4.

59. See Makdisi, 'The Economic Aspects of the Lebanese Crisis'.

60. See el-Khazen, *The Breakdown of the State in Lebanon*, pp. 230–5.

61. See Makdisi, *Financial Policy and Economic Growth*, chapter 5.

62. For a critical assessment see ibid., part two, and especially chapter 8.

63. On that day the leader of the Kataeb Party was scheduled to participate in the consecration of a new church in Ayn al-Rammaneh, a suburb of Beirut. As a security measure, the area surrounding the church was closed to traffic. On the morning of that day an unidentified car attempted to break through the security checkpoint. The resulting shoot-out left four people dead, including two Kataeb Party members. Armed men from the Kataeb and National Liberal parties took to the street. In the afternoon of that day a bus carrying thirty passengers (some armed) belonging to various Palestinian organizations passed through Ayn al-Rammaneh. Shooting broke out, leaving twenty-seven of the passengers dead.

64. For details of political/military developments in the period 1970–75, see el-Khazen, *The Breakdown of the State in Lebanon*, pp. 158–64, and Salibi, *Cross Roads to Civil War*, pp. 54–98.

2. The war period, 1975–90

1. Some writers, in drawing attention to the external, as opposed to the internal, dimension of this long-lasting conflict have termed it the 'wars of others', or 'proxy wars' in Lebanon. See, in particular, Ghassan Teuni, *Une guerre pour les autres* (Jclattes, 1985).

2. The main Christian parties were the Kataeb (Phalange–Maronite) and the National Liberal Party (Maronite). The main parties supporting the PLO were Amal (Shia), the Progressive Socialist Party (PSP–Druze), the Syrian National Party (secular) and the Communist Party (secular). On both sides of the conflict there was a host of other minor militias. Hezbollah came into prominence only after 1982.

3. In 1970–72, the average annual exchange rate ranged from LL3.0 to 3.2 per US dollar. The pound appreciated in 1973–75, averaging annually LL2.3–2.5 per US dollar. In 1976 and 1977 it depreciated: the annual average exchange rate stood at LL2.9 and 3.0 per US dollar respectively.

4. For 1977 the coefficient of variation (COV) was 1 per cent, where COV is defined as the standard deviation for the monthly average rate quotation as a percentage of the annual average exchange rate. No monthly quotations for 1976 are available. An alternative measure of exchange rate volatility is the difference between the monthly minimum and maximum rate as a percentage of the average monthly rate. We find that for 1977 it remained relatively limited, ranging from 0.9 to 3.7 per cent.

5. See Council for Development and Reconstruction, *The Reconstruction Project* (April 1983), p. I.5.

6. For an insider's account of the negotiations, see Elie Salem, *Violence and Diplomacy in Lebanon. The Troubled Years: 1982–1988* (I.B.Tauris, 1995).

7. See the report on civil war casualties published in the daily *Annahar* on 5 March 1992.

8. For a vivid portrayal of the survival of civil society amid the horrors of the civil war, see Jean Said Makdisi, *Beirut Fragments, a War Memoir* (Persea Press, New York, 1990, reissued 1999).

9. This section draws, in part, on S. Makdisi and R. Sadaka, 'The Lebanese Civil War: Background, Causes, Duration and Post-conflict Trends', paper presented at a Yale/World Bank workshop on 'Case Studies of Civil War', held at Yale University, 13–14 April 2002.

10. It should be mentioned that different operational definitions of civil war have been used. The first estimate is that of Pat Regan, 'Data on Third Party Interventions in Intrastate Conflicts', paper presented at a workshop on 'Identifying Wars: Systematic Conflict Research and Its Utility in Conflict Resolution and Prevention', held at Uppsala University, 8–9 June 2001. His adopted definition of a civil war is that of an armed conflict that has resulted in at least a total of 200 related battle deaths. The second estimate is that of P. Collier and A. Hoeffler, 'On Economic Causes of Civil War', *Oxford Economic Papers* 50 (1998), which considers a sample of 98 countries of which 27 had civil wars. Counted as civil wars are domestic armed conflicts that resulted in at least 1,000 battle-related deaths per year and in which the stronger force sustained at least 5 per cent of the number of fatalities suffered by the weaker forces. The Conflict Data Project at Uppsala University recorded 225 armed conflicts during the period 1946–2001. This total includes three types of conflicts: (1) minor armed

conflicts, i.e. at least 25 battle-related deaths per year but fewer than 1,000 battle-related deaths during the course of the conflict; (2) intermediate armed conflicts, i.e. at least 25 battle-related deaths per year and an accumulated total of at least 1,000 battle-related deaths but fewer than 1,000 in any given year; and (3) large conflicts, i.e. at least 1,000 battle-related deaths per year. Of the total number, 163 were intra-state conflicts (civil wars) and of these thirty-two witnessed external interventions. See N. P. Gleditsch et al., 'Armed Conflict: A New Dataset', *Journal of Peace Research*, vol. 39, no. 5, September 2002.

11. As part of a research project on the 'Economics of Political and Common Violence', organized by the World Bank's Economic Research Group, a number of working papers have been prepared that examine civil war cases in various regions of the world (see papers presented to the Yale/World Bank workshop on 'Case Studies of Civil War', held at Yale University, 12–13 April 2003). Two recent books each comprising a collection of papers on the economics of civil wars are M. Berdal and D. M. Malone (eds), *Greed and Grievance, Economic Agendas in Civil Wars* (Lynne Rienner Publishers, 2000), and F. Stewart and V. FitzGerald and associates, *War and Underdevelopment*, vol. 1, 'The Economic and Social Consequences of Conflict', and vol. 2, 'Country Experiences' (Oxford University Press, 2001).

12. See P. Collier and A. Hoeffler, 'Greed and Grievance in Civil War', Working Paper Series, Centre for the Study of African Economies, Oxford, 2003. Collier and Hoeffler find that most of the variables, which they use to represent grievance, drop out of their base-line regression. With the incidence of civil war as the dependent variable, different indices measuring, for example, land ownership inequality, income inequality and the level of democracy prove to be statistically insignificant as explanatory variables.

13. This hypothesis or model is elaborated in P. Collier, 'On the Economic Causes of Civil War', *Oxford Economic Papers* 50, 1998; P. Collier and A. Hoeffler, 'Economic Causes of Civil Conflicts and Their Implication for Peace', World Bank unpublished paper (15 June 2001); and P. Collier and A. Hoeffler, 'Greed and Grievance in Civil War'. In the first cited the investigation of the causes of civil wars is based on utility theory. Distributional considerations apart, it concludes that (a) the higher the per capita income (on an internationally comparable measure), the lower the risk of civil war, i.e. the opportunity cost of rebellion increases; (b) the effect of natural resource endowment is non-monotic; (c) the larger the population, the greater the risk of war; (d) more fractionalized societies (i.e. into ethno-linguistic groups) are not more prone to civil wars than highly homogeneous societies; and (e) the danger of civil war arises when the society is polarized into two groups.

14. D. Keen, 'Incentives and Disincentives for Violence', in M. Berdal and D. M. Malone (eds), *Greed and Grievance: Economic Agendas in Civil Wars* (Lynne Rienner Publishers, 2000).

15. See N. Sambanis, 'Ethnic War: a Theoretical and Empirical Inquiry into Its Causes', DECRG World Bank paper, 2000, and M. Reynal-Querol, 'Ethnicity, Political Systems and Civil Wars', unpublished paper, 2001. See also J. Mueller, 'The Remnants of War: Thugs as Residual Combatants', unpublished, 2001.

16. See P. Collier and A. Hoeffler, 'Greed and Grievance in Civil Wars', and I. de Soya, 'The Resource Curse: Are Civil Wars Driven by Rapacity or Paucity', in M. Berdal and D. M. Malone (eds), *Greed and Grievance: Economic Agendas in Civil Wars*, Lynne Rienner Publishers, 2000.

17. See M. Ross, 'How Does Natural Resource Wealth Influence Civil War?' unpublished paper, 6 December 2001.

18. See de Soya, 'The Resource Curse', pp. 123–4. The study finds little evidence that ethnicity causes conflicts.

19. See P. Collier, A. Hoeffler and M. Soderbom, 'On the Duration of Civil War', Centre for the Study of African Economies, Oxford, 2003. The authors point out that forecasting errors on the part of the warring parties can contribute to the prolongation of the war. Further, once a civil war goes beyond its first year, the probability of peace becomes radically lower (pp. 15–16).

20. See I. El Badawi and N. Sambanis, 'External Interventions and the Duration of Civil Wars', paper presented at the World Bank conference on the 'Economics and Politics of Civil Conflicts', Princeton University, 18–19 March 2000. The paper points out that the mean duration of civil wars that experienced external interventions was nine years, while wars that did not had a mean duration of 1.5 years.

21. See, for example, Keen, 'Incentives and Disincentives for Violence', pp. 31–2.

22. The relatively small Armenian community (about 7 per cent of the population) has fully integrated into Lebanese political life while maintaining its cultural heritage.

23. Each of these communities probably constituted between 20 and 30 per cent of the total population.

24. The last population census was conducted in 1932. Hence no official estimates of the religious composition of the population have since been available.

25. In the post-conflict era the sensitivity to sectarian power among the main religious communities has become more accentuated.

26. At the level of the private sector, Christian dominance of economic and financial activities would over time relatively decline as the Muslim communities grew in political and educational stature.

27. For 1973–74, the two years preceding the outbreak of the civil war, estimates of real per capita GDP range from the equivalent of $1,000 to $1,300.

28. In Makdisi and Sadaka, 'The Lebanese Civil War', it is estimated that on the basis of data available for 1970, the Collier–Hoeffler model predicts a very low probability (2.6 per cent) for a civil war breaking out in Lebanon. This is less than the probability for countries that did not experience a civil war (5.8 per cent). For countries that experienced a civil war the average probability was 21.6 per cent. The paper points out that the probability on the eve of the war in 1974 could not be calculated as the model uses data at five-year intervals. But if it could be calculated for that year, it would probably be lower than that for 1970, considering the recorded rise in per capita real income from 1970 to 1974.

29. See S. Makdisi, 'Al-Jawânib'.

30. In the personal memoir of a high-ranking Kataeb official who was close to both the founder of the party, Pierre Gemayel, and his son Bashir Gemayel (the leader of the Lebanese Forces, assassinated in 1982 as president elect), the author laments how greed manifested in the seeking of power and financial wealth by party / militia officers in the camp to which he belonged was one of the factors that contributed to the prolongation of the civil war. See Joseph Abou Khalil, *Qiṣṣat al-Mawârina fi al-Ḥarb, Sîra Khâṣṣa* [The Story of the Maronites in the War, a Personal Memoir], Beirut, 2000, p. 143.

31. See G. Corm, 'The War System: Militia Hegemony and the Reestablishment

of the State', in D. Collings (ed.), *Peace for Lebanon? From War to Reconstruction*, Lynne Rienner Publishers, 1994, pp. 216–18.

32. 15 October 1990, p. 8.

33. See Hamdan, *Al-'Azma*, pp. 154 and 172 respectively.

34. F. Tarabulsi, 'Identités et solidarités croisées dans les conflits du Liban contemporain', unpublished doctoral dissertation, University of Paris VIII, 1993.

35. E. Picard, 'Liban: La Matice Historique', in F. Jean and J. C. Ruffin (eds), *Economie des guerres civiles*, Hachette, Paris, 1996.

36. Corm, 'The War System', p. 218.

37. *Annahar*, 15 October 1990, p. 8.

38. See Salim Nasr, 'The Political Economy of the Lebanese Conflict', in N. Shehadi and B. Harmy (eds), *Politics and the Economy in Lebanon*, Centre for Lebanese Studies, Oxford, 1989.

39. This section draws on S. Makdisi, 'Political Conflict and Economic Performance in Lebanon, 1975–1987', Centre for Contemporary Arab Studies, Georgetown University, Occasional Paper series (September 1987), republished (with minor revisions) in Banque du Liban, *Bulletin trimestriel* (second and third quarters, 1987).

40. This may not have applied to certain other minor political groups in the country.

41. IMF, *Lebanon – Economic Recovery, Stabilization and Macroeconomic Stability*, 8 August 1994.

42. It should be mentioned that there have been no reliable GDP series since 1975. The outbreak of the war disrupted the work of the Central Directorate of Statistics, which had been engaged in the preparation of Lebanon's national income estimates since 1964. In 1975 the official national income series was discontinued. In later years, several international and regional agencies attempted to provide estimates of GNP and related aggregates utilizing extrapolation methods and other available indicators. They were based, however, on outdated base year information, and a variety of indicators were used which measured the growth of GNP in different ways. In 1977 the Council for Development and Reconstruction prepared a study on national income accounts largely based on trade data. Further, certain individual attempts have been made to measure GDP for selected years. However, they were not comparable and their degree of reliability could not be ascertained, particularly as they did not rely on any significant sample surveys. In 1989 the UNDP sponsored a study to estimate Lebanon's GNP and GDP for the year 1988. To a large extent, the estimates relied on field surveys of major activities. Reasoned choice sampling was adopted as an alternative to random sampling, which for budgetary and other reasons could not be carried out. It made up for the non-randomness of the sector samples by choosing representative observations to the fullest extent possible (see UNDP/LEB/89/001, *Lebanon, the Gross Domestic Product and Gross National Product for 1988*, Department of Technical Cooperation for Development, United Nations, 1991 – the team members who carried out the study included S. Makdisi, I. Chatila, K. Hamdan and M. Sader). GDP extrapolations for 1989 and 1990 were also carried out. An estimate for the 1987 GDP was made by T. Gaspard (see his article 'The Gross Domestic Product of Lebanon in 1987', Banque du Liban, *Bulletin trimestrielle*, fourth quarter, 1989). After the war the Central Directorate of Statistics began gradually to resume its work. In 1997 it published official estimates of national income for 1994–95 based primarily on foreign

trade data, the industrial census of 1994 and estimates of the Ministry of Agriculture concerning agriculture production. The directorate has been engaged in a number of surveys related to various economic sectors. In 2002 the government engaged a French institute (Institut National de la Statistique et des Etudes Economiques) to carry out a study of national income for the years 1997–2002.

43. It should be re-emphasized that estimates of real GDP are not reliable on two counts. The first is the non-reliability of the extrapolations of GDP in nominal terms and the second the non-reliability of the constructed price indices for the period under consideration.

44. See IMF, *Lebanon – Economic Recovery, Stabilization and Macroeconomic Policies*, SM/91/207, p. 6. For a study of the loss of output over the war period up to the Israeli invasion of 1982, see N. Saidi, 'The Effects of the War on Economic Activity in Lebanon: Quantitative Estimates', Bank of Lebanon *Quarterly Bulletin* 20, 1984. It is estimated that by 1982 production was more than 30 per cent below its pre-war 1974 level.

45. Some industrial enterprises tried to protect themselves from the havoc of war by relocating to 'safer' areas and thus were able to export in response to increased demand.

46. The rise in the share of public administration is explained by the changed composition of a lower GDP in consequence of declining industrial output.

47. This section draws on K. Hamdan and S. Makdisi, 'Lebanon: the Evolving Labour Market', unpublished report prepared for the World Bank (1995).

48. See respectively K. Hamdan, 'Emigration Policies, Trends and Mechanisms', ILO/UNDP Lebanon Project, Cairo, May 1992, and Labaki and Abou Rjeily, *Bilan des guerres*, p. 94.

49. See Anîs Abî Farah, 'Les émigrés libanais, 1975–1996', *Al-Chu'ûn al-'Iqtişâdîya* [Economic Affairs], Bulletin of the Chamber of Commerce, Industry and Agriculture for Saida and Southern Lebanon, November 1997.

50. See N. Issa, 'Unemployment and the Reconstruction of Lebanon', *Unemployment in the ESCWA Countries*, ESCWA, February 1994.

51. See Hamdan and Makdisi, 'Lebanon: the Evolving Labour Market'.

52. This refers to a study carried out by the University of St Joseph on the population movement during the period 1975–87 in Lebanon, cited in ibid., p. 11.

53. Ibid., p. 12.

54. The repeated Israeli attacks on regions in southern Lebanon, especially during the first half of the 1970s, constituted an additional factor in inducing migration from these regions northwards.

55. Study of the University of St Joseph, cited in Hamdan and Makdisi, 'Lebanon: the Evolving Labour Market'.

56. In practice, wage adjustment for both the public and private sectors was generally similar. Given the difficult budgetary situation of the government, the latter always attempted to minimize wage adjustments for the public sector and in consequence the private sector. To overcome this constraint, some of the successful private enterprises resorted to concealed methods of adjusting wages of their own employees, such as partial payment in dollars at accounting rates that were below the prevailing rate and/or improving fringe benefits.

57. See S. Sena and T. Helbing (eds), *Back to the Future, Postwar Reconstruction and Stabilization in Lebanon*, Occasional Paper 176, IMF, Washington, DC, 1999, p. 86.

58. To the knowledge of the author, there are no quantitative studies pertaining to the impact of the militias on the labour market and specifically the market for unskilled labour. In particular, no investigations have been carried out as to whether unskilled militia members tended to receive a wage premium in comparison with other unskilled workers. This would throw light on the ability of the militias to retain a regular fighting force.

59. Balance of payments surpluses or deficits are defined as changes in the net foreign assets of the banking system as a whole.

60. Source of data: Bank of Lebanon.

61. The index of nominal effective exchange rate (with 1989 as a base) fell from 19,103 for 1975 to 11,614 for 1981 rising to 13,240 for 1982. Available data pertaining to Lebanon's real exchange rate index (also with 1989 as a base) show that it rose from 122 for 1975 to 127 for 1981 and 142 for 1982 (i.e. an appreciation of the pound in real terms). Real exchange rate movements reflect changes in the competitiveness of exports and are not directly related to the balance of payments surpluses or deficits.

62. The ratio of foreign currency denominated deposits to total deposits rose from about 25 per cent at the end of 1975 to about 40 per cent at the end of 1981. It tended to fall in 1982 and 1983 but rose sharply thereafter.

63. See IMF, *Lebanon – Staff Report for the 1990 Article IV Consultation* (SM/91/21), pp. 7 and 10. It should be remembered that customs receipts, which traditionally accounted for an important portion of governmental tax revenue, fell significantly after 1984. A number of important factors account for the fall in customs revenue, e.g. militia control of ports and smuggling. In addition, on 14 December 1985 the government introduced the 'accounting dollar' on the basis of which customs duties were levied. The accounting dollar was substantially below the actual dollar rate prevailing in the market. Hence, while its introduction amounted to an import subsidy benefiting consumers, in practice it led to a fall in the effective rate of customs duties and hence revenues. The first accounting rate was initially set at LL6 per US dollar. It was raised to LL100 per US dollar on 15 May 1991, to LL200 at the end of July 1991 and to LL800 on 14 August 1992, and finally eliminated in July 1995.

64. The ratio of foreign currency denominated deposits to total deposits rose from about 26 per cent at the end of 1983 to a peak of 90 per cent at the end of 1987, falling back to about 68 per cent at the end of 1990. An attempt was made to quantify the increased use of the dollar as a means of exchange by estimating a currency demand function for the pre-dollarization period; the difference between the predicted and actual local currency holdings in the post-dollarization period was taken as the postulated change in the stock of foreign currency held by residents. The exercise (its shortcomings being duly acknowledged) showed that the use of the dollar as a means of exchange rose substantially after 1983 in tandem with the trend of holding dollar denominated assets. The ratio of actual Lebanese currency to the estimated demand for total currency declined from about 114 per cent for 1983 to as low as 7.4 per cent for 1987, rising to 19.4 per cent for 1990. See IMF, *Lebanon: Economic Recovery, Stabilization and Macroeconomic Stability* (background paper to the 1994 Article IV Consultation), 8 August 1994, pp. 29–30.

65. The index of nominal effective exchange rate (1989 as base year) fell from 11,614 for 1982 to about 66.6 for 1990. The index of real effective exchange rate (the same

base year) fell from about 143 for 1982 to 71.6 for 1986, but then rose to about 107 for 1990.

66. One study, applying co-integration tests, investigated the long-run relationship between the exchange rate and inflation in Lebanon for the period prior to the civil war (1951–74) and after (1975–93). It arrived at the following conclusions: (a) for the pre-war period the relationship was positive but not statistically significant, (b) for the period since 1975 it was both positive and strongly significant and (c) for the entire period, 1951–93, the relationship proved to be positive and significant. Tests were also made for the periods January 1989 until the end of 1992 and 1993 up to March 1994, when the nominal exchange rate took on a gradually appreciating trend. (Actually the pound began to gradually appreciate immediately after the end of national elections in September 1992 and accelerated with the announcement in late October that Rafic Hariri, the Lebanese billionaire/businessman/politician, was to form the government – see Chapter 3 below.) The tests, according to the study, seemed to indicate a close relationship between the exchange rate movements and inflation in 1989–92 but not subsequently when the pound began to appreciate, though the period covered by the study (1993–March 1994) is relatively short. This, it was observed, could reflect the fact that an appreciation of the pound is not passed through to prices as fully as a depreciation (see IMF, *Lebanon – Economic Recovery, Stabilization and Macroeconomic Policies*, pp. 59–76). However, the same study also examines the short-term dynamics of inflation and the exchange rate and the two-way relationship between them. A significant impact of the exchange rate movement on inflation is indicated. It finally notes that the possibility of a feedback from the price level to the exchange rate could not be rejected, indicating that the exchange rate and the price level are determined simultaneously in Lebanon (pp. 76–80). Limitations of the statistical analysis apart (the study advises cautious interpretation of the results – p. 72), it would seem appropriate to hypothesize that a significant relationship between the exchange rate and inflation existed at all times, including periods of relative exchange rate stability or a gradually appreciating pound, i.e. the pre-1975 and 1993–98 years. Indeed, the stability of the price level in the pre-war years was to a large extent influenced by the relative stability of the exchange rate (see Makdisi, *Financial Policy and Economic Growth*, pp. 95–7. For the 1993–99 period, the gradual appreciation of the nominal pound contributed to the deceleration of the inflation rate. This question is discussed in Chapter 3 below (section 3.2).

67. According to data from the Beirut Stock Exchange (BSE), at the end of that year the market capitalization of the Beirut stock market amounted to about $1.4. billion, or less than 1 per cent of the combined Arab market capitalization; the Saudi capital market ranked first with a share of about 43 per cent. The BSE data on capitalization differ from those published by the Bank of Lebanon. The former include the capitalization of the shares actually listed and traded while the latter include the capitalization of both listed and unlisted shares of the same company.

68. For a detailed analysis of banking developments during the period 1975–92, see S. Makdisi, K. Hamdan and H. Bsat, 'Lebanon: the Structure and Evolution of the Financial Services Sector and Its Role in the Recovery Phase', report submitted to Dar Al Handassah engineering group (October 1993) as part of its commission by the CDR to prepare plans for sectoral reconstruction. This section draws on it.

69. Most of the new banks were of Lebanese nationality. A few banks changed their

nationality, with an increase in Lebanese and Lebanese–Arab banks, and a reduction in Lebanese–foreign banks.

70. During the conflict of 1975–76, almost fifty bank branches, located in the commercial centre, were destroyed or seriously damaged.

71. The biggest concentration of Lebanese banking presence was in Europe (Paris and London), followed by the Arab region, especially the UAE, and finally Cyprus, which became a passageway for travelling Lebanese during the periods of crises and the closure of Beirut airport.

72. During the period the ratio changed. It declined to less than 20 per cent at end 1978 and then rose to about 40 per cent at end 1981, falling back to about 29 per cent at end of both 1982 and 1983. Total assets of the banking sector increased in nominal terms: from LL12.3 billion ($5.3 billion) at the end of 1974 to LL61.7 billion ($16.2 billion) at the end of 1982. In constant prices this amounted to an increase of about LL15.2 billion. Total deposits increased from LL9.4 billion ($4.1 billion) to LL45.5 billion ($12.0 billion) respectively or an increase in constant prices of about LL 11.2 billion. Domestic credit rose from LL6.7 billion ($2.9 billion) to LL27.3 billion ($7.2 billion) respectively, remaining constant in real terms. During this period, the share of Lebanese pound denominated deposits of total deposits declined to a low 55 per cent at the end of 1981, recovering to 79 per cent at the end of 1982.

73. Capital and reserves rose from LL496 million ($215 million) at the end of 1974 to LL2,162 million ($569 million) at the end of 1982.

74. See Fadi Osseiran, 'Banking Performance in Lebanon, 1928–1987', Association des Banques du Liban, *Rapport du Conseil, 1989–1990*, p. 54.

75. The number of Lebanese-owned banks increased from thirty-one on the eve of the war to fifty-four banks at the end of 1989, and foreign-owned banks declined from twelve to seven banks respectively. Lebanese banks with Arab capital control doubled to eight banks during the same period, whereas the number of wholly owned Arab banks remained the same.

76. For similar indicators of negative growth rates and more generally the deteriorating performance of Lebanese banks during the period 1982–87, see Osseiran, 'Banking Performance', pp. 54–6; Institute of Money and Banking, *Al-Damj al-Maṣrifî fî Lubnân* [Bank Mergers in Lebanon] (American University of Beirut, 1990, p. 83); and Saʿd Andary, 'Taṭwîr sûq Bayrût al-Naqdî' [Developing Beirut's Money Market], paper submitted to a seminar organized by the Institute of Money and Banking at the American University of Beirut, 22 February 1992.

77. Osseiran, 'Banking Performance', p. 61.

78. For a brief review of the positions of the Bankers Association and the Central Bank respectively on the issue of implementing circular 435 and the ensuing discussions between the two parties, see H. Bast, 'Malâat al-Jihâz al Maṣrifî, 1982–1989, Asbâb al-ʿAzma wa Dûrûs al-Tajruba' [Capital Adequacy of the Lebanese Banking System, 1982–1989: Causes of the Crisis and Lessons of Experience], Association des Banques du Liban, *Rapport du conseil, 1989–1990*.

79. On 15 July 1991 the Beirut Bankruptcy Court took a decision to liquidate the bank and appointed a committee to oversee this process (*Annahar*, 16 July 1991).

80. See Makdisi, Hamdan and Bsat, 'Lebanon: the Structure and Evolution', pp. 12–13.

81. Internal report submitted to the Prime Minister, May 1990.

82. Four banks were declared in cessation of payment. Two banks were bought by other operating banks in Lebanon. Two banks chose the solution of auto-liquidation. The remaining banks were subjected to various flotation attempts. In case of failure, this was to lead to their auto-liquidation, or transfer of their control to the Central Bank after the competent courts declared that the banks were in cessation of payments.

83. Lebanese bankers estimated that by the late 1980s between $15 and $20 billion were held abroad by Lebanese citizens (residents and non-residents). *International Financial Statistics* (November 1993) reports $12.4 billion (at year-end 1990) as the value of cross-border bank deposits held by Lebanese residents, compared with $5.02 billion at year-end 1983 and $4.27 billion at year-end 1981.

84. One such grouping was the so-called United Front of Ras-Beirut. The Ras-Beirut district, where the American University of Beirut is situated, has historically been and remains a multi-religious community.

85. The bureau included the minister of finance, the president of the CDR, the governor of the Bank of Lebanon, and a policy coordinator. Its meetings were held regularly (generally twice a month, its deliberations being based on an agenda specifically prepared for each meeting). For an assessment of policy coordination in Lebanon, see Wael Hamdan, 'Policy Co-ordination with Reference to Lebanon' (MMB thesis, Institute of Money and Banking, American University of Beirut, 1986), and Report of the Governor of the Bank of Lebanon, 'Al-taṭ aûrât al-'Iqtisâdîya wa al-Mâlîya fi Lubnân, 1977–1981' [Economic and Financial Developments in Lebanon, 1977–1981] (Bank of Lebanon, *Bulletin trimestriel*, November/December 1981).

86. Legislative decrees nos 47/47 and 130/77, and law 8/81.

87. Legislative decree no. 131/77. During the period June 1978–June 1985, total loans of LL904 million were approved. Loan contracts amounted to LL605 million, and actual disbursements were LL576 million. Credit was extended via specialized credit institutions (source: CDR).

88. Legislative decree no. 9/83.

89. As mentioned above, in November 1976 an Arab deterrent force was dispatched to Lebanon to help the government maintain law and order in the capital. In subsequent months, all the Arab forces were withdrawn except for the Syrians, who, at the time of writing, have maintained a military presence in coordination with the Lebanese authorities.

90. See CDR, *The Reconstruction Project*, April 1983, p. I.2. The privilege of contracting loans without prior parliamentary approval was in conflict with constitutional stipulations in this regard. However, the extraordinary situation facing Lebanon at the time was considered an overriding justification for such a step.

91. See address of CDR president to the seminar on 'Development in the Arab World: Planning vs. Implementation', held in Kuwait, 25–29 October 1987.

92. See CDR, *Progress Report on Reconstruction, 1983–87*, p. 40.

93. Ibid., p. 33. A new project was added to the reconstruction programme, pertaining to national waste management.

94. Ibid., p. 41.

95. See Arab Fund for Economic and Social Development (in association with Team International and Coopers and Lybrand Deloitte), 'Dirasatun 'Hawl Majlis al'Inma' wa al 'I'mar' [Study of the Council for Development and Reconstruction], prepared at the

request of the then prime minister, July 1990, p. 13 (unpublished). In the preparation of the study, the author and Dr Ahmed Sbeity represented the prime minister and the AFESD respectively.

96. Based on data provided by the CDR.

97. During the period in which the bureau functioned, the minister of finance was first Adel Hamieh followed by Ali el-Khalil; the President of CDR was the late Mohammad Atallah; the governor of the Central Bank was Sheikh Michel el-Khoury; the author served as the policy coordinator. Information concerning the work of the bureau is, in large measure, based on the minutes of the bureau meetings. For some details pertaining to the functions and work of the bureau, see Wael Hamdan, 'Policy Co-ordination'.

98. A reclassification of the budget was carried out for 1980. It showed that estimated capital expenditure represented only 16 per cent of total expenditure. In contrast, under the then existing official classification, expenditures under chapters 11 and 111 represented 32 per cent of the total (see W. Hamdan, 'Policy Co-ordination', p. 155). Thus the proposed classification conveyed a more accurate picture concerning the amount of capital expenditure included in the governmental budget. This would have allowed for better investment planning by the authorities. The bureau even discussed the possibility of having the Ministry of Finance plan for current budgetary expenditure and the CDR (in coordination with the ministry) for investment expenditure. However, no formal decision was taken in this regard. It should be mentioned that IMF missions had at the time carried out studies on the consolidation of the Lebanese budget, but none of their recommendations was carried out.

99. Circular no. 514, 10 October 1984. This measure was opposed by the Bankers Association, which claimed it would not lessen the pressure on the pound. Lebanese banks operating in Europe began to attract Lebanese currency deposits that were not subject to the 100 per cent requirement. They were used for speculative purposes on the foreign exchange market.

100. Circular no. 537, 2 February 1985.

101. Circular no. 689, 5 January 1986. The aim of this and similar measures was to control the banks' ability to speculate on the so-called europound market, primarily in Paris. An earlier measure taken in late 1984 reduced the foreign exchange position that a bank could maintain from 50 to 15 per cent of paid-up capital.

102. See respectively circular no. 508, 4 October 1984, circular no. 541, 2 February 1985, and circular no. 625, 12 February 1986.

103. At one point, the Central Bank required commercial banks to ensure compliance with the reserve requirements on a daily basis (circular no. 621, 28 January 1986).

104. Circular no. 688, 5 December 1986.

105. One source quotes a total of $1.9 billion of governmental foreign exchange obligations that the Central Bank had to accommodate during the period 1986–90. Of this total, fuel imports represented 61 per cent and wheat imports 15 per cent (see Ghassân Ayyâch, 'Azmat al-Mâlîya al-'Âmma fi Lubnân: Qiṣṣat al-'Inhiyâr al-'Iqtiṣâdî, 1982–1992' [The Crisis of Public Finance in Lebanon, the Story of Monetary Collapse, 1982–1992], Annahar Publishing House, 1997, p. 123.

106. The Bank of Lebanon imposed minimum ratios of TBs to deposits while modifying the applicable reserve ratios (circular no. 635 mentioned in the text). Effective 17 March 1987, however, the bank netted new subscriptions to TBs from

deposits subject to reserve requirements (circular no. 636, 26 March 1986). The Bankers Association strongly opposed the imposition of minimum ratios. The two sides attempted to resolve pending issues throughout the year with occasional interventions made by the prime minister and the minister of finance. On 10 June 1986, the bank issued circular no. 657 which set the reserve ratio at 10 per cent and modified the minimum ratios of the TBs to deposits as follows: for banks with outstanding deposits of less than 1 billion pounds, the ratio was set at 15 per cent; for banks with deposits of 1 billion pounds or more, the ratio was set at 30 per cent. After protracted delays in implementing its announced policies, the Bank of Lebanon, as noted in the text, issued on 5 December 1986 circular no. 688, which increased the minimum ratio of TBs to deposits to 30 per cent for banks with outstanding deposits of less than 1 billion pounds, and to 45 per cent for banks with outstanding deposits of 1 billion pounds or more. The attainment of these ratios was set in accordance with a weekly schedule over the period 8 January to 19 February 1987. Effective 4 January 1987, new deposits were made subject to a ratio of 60 per cent. Reserve requirements were raised to 13 per cent effective 5 January 1987. As also noted, other measures introduced by the Bank of Lebanon pertained to the establishment of solvency ratios, which had already been decided upon in 1983, and the imposition of restrictions on loans in Lebanese pounds to, or the opening of Lebanese pound accounts for, non-residents (circulars nos 691 and 689 of 5 December 1986). On 10 January 1987, the Bank of Lebanon issued circular no. 700, which extended the periods of implementation for new ratios as follows: the reserve ratio was to be increased to 11, 12 and 13 per cent effective 5 January, 5 February and 5 March 1987 respectively. These increases could be held in the form of special treasury bills. Increases in the TB/deposit ratios were to be effected during the period 8 January–30 April 1987. Subsequently, on 7 July 1987, the Bank of Lebanon issued circular no. 739, which raised the reserve ratio to 16 per cent, of which 4 per cent could be held in the form of special treasury bills. Also as of 7 July 1987, 15 per cent of the new deposits denominated in LL were to be held in the form of treasury bills. Opposition by the Bankers Association eventually led on 21 October 1987 to an agreement with the Bank of Lebanon whereby circular no. 739 was cancelled and effectively the provisions of circular no. 700 were maintained.

107. This 'profit' represented the difference, in Lebanese pound counterparts, between the value of the bank's foreign assets at the initial exchange rate at which they were purchased and their value at the time of their revaluation on the basis of the prevailing exchange rate. Thus, as the Lebanese pound depreciated, the revaluation 'profit' increased. In effect, with the rapid depreciation of the pound beginning in 1984, these revaluations represented substantial amounts. The problem arose because the Law on Money and Credit specified that the government had the right to transfer up to 80 per cent of any such 'profits' to its account at the Central Bank.

108. For a detailed account of the respective positions of the government and the Central Bank on this matter, and the ensuing controversy between them, see Ayyach, *The Crisis of Public Finance*, pp. 131–49.

109. It is reported that during the period 1976–83 revaluation 'profits' transferred to the government amounted to about $1.5 billion (see ibid., p. 134). And this was a period of relatively moderate depreciation of the pound.

110. For the period 1983–85 it is estimated that salaries and wages accounted for 23 per cent of total fiscal expenditure, transfers for 15 per cent, fuel subsidies for 17

per cent, and interest payments for 22 per cent, amounting to a total of 77 per cent (sources: Ministry of Finance and Bank of Lebanon).

111. See J. Mailat, *The Document of National Understanding, a Commentary*, Centre for Lebanese Studies, May 1992.

112. For a comparative reading of the pre- and post-Taif constitutions, see *Beirut Review*, vol. 1, no. 1, spring 1991, under 'Documents', with an introduction by Paul E. Salem.

113. For a critical assessment of the Taif Accord, see Mailat, *The Document of National Understanding*, especially pp. 53–8.

3. The post-war period 1

1. In May 1991 a 'Treaty of Brotherhood, Cooperation and Coordination' between Syria and Lebanon came into effect. It called for close cooperation in various areas (e.g. foreign affairs, security, military, economic) and set up a Higher Council headed by the presidents of the two countries and a general secretariat to oversee the implementation of the treaty. In practice it formalized prevailing relationships between the two countries, notably in the areas of foreign affairs and security.

2. One writer describes the post-civil-war order as an enlarged reproduction of the pre-war political and economic system. See F. Trabulsi, 'The Role of War in State and Society Transformation: The Lebanese Case', unpublished paper, November 1994, p. 14.

3. Albert Mansour (a deputy in the parliament that ended in 1992) accuses the then political leadership of the country, in particular the President of the Republic, of a deliberately inadequate implementation of the accord, indeed its contravention. See Albert Mansour, *Al-'Inqilâb 'ala al-Tâ'if* [The Turn against the Taif], Beirut, 1993.

4. See, for example, Farid el-Khazen, 'Tâ'if mâ ba'da al-Harb, Chajara Judhûruhâ 'Aghsânuhâ' [The Post-war Taif: a Tree Whose Roots Constitute Its Branches], *An-nahar*, 31 December 1997.

5. Hoss was the premier designate at the time Rene Mouawad, the newly elected president, was assassinated in November 1989, after the Taif Accord. With the election of Elias Hrawi as the new president immediately afterwards, he was again called upon to head the government.

6. See *Annahar*, 20 December 1990. Additional reasons may have related to disagreements on administrative and other appointments.

7. For public accusations of deliberate instigation on the part of high officials, and specifically the President of the Republic, see the interview with former prime minister Omar Karami, *Assafir*, 5 May 1995, and Mansour, 'The Turn against the Taif', pp. 167–70.

8. A word on the involvement of the four post-war prime ministers in parliamentary elections is in order. Karami has been a member of parliament representing Tripoli in the north since 1991. Salim al Hoss ran for elections and won in the district of Beirut in both 1992 and 1996. The coalition he headed was much less successful in the latter than in the former elections. He ran again in the 2000 elections but lost. Rashid Solh was a member of parliament representing Beirut from 1964 to 1968, and then from 1972 till 1996, when he decided not to run again. Rafic Hariri first ran for elections in 1996 in Beirut at the head of a coalition that won the majority of the

parliamentary seats in that district. In 2000 he ran again and his coalition won all the Beirut seats. Regarding the last two elections, in particular, public accusations were made concerning the illegitimate use of political money to influence the elections. Prior to the elections of 2000 an unsuccessful attempt was made to pass a law to regulate the use of campaign funds and monitor its uses (see Salim Hoss, *Li-l-Ḥaqîqa wa al-Tarîkh; Tajarûb al-Ḥûkm ma baîna 1998 wa 2000* [For Truth and History, Experiences in Governing, 1998–2000], Beirut, 2001, pp. 300–1.

9. The formation of cabinets in post-war Lebanon is usually a complex process. Under the existing sectarian system it is difficult for any single political party or group to gain a majority of seats in parliament. By necessity cabinets are made up of coalitions of political groups and actors whose representation in the cabinet is subject not only to the time-honoured sectarian formula but so far also to consultation with the Syrian leadership.

10. For the period under review, but in particular 1993–98, the local press (including daily newspapers not necessarily opposed to the government) abounds with reports on the sharp disagreements (certainly not over political ideology) among the three principal officials and/or critical comments on the 'Troika' rule. By way of illustration, see *Al Safir*, 15 and 24 December 1992, 22 January 1993; *Annahar*, 27 January 1993, 18 February 1993, and 8, 10 and 17 August 1998; and *Al Diyar*, 2 January 1994 and 10 October 1997. In a particularly bitter attack on the prime minister prior to the 1998 presidential elections, the speaker of the House accused him of propagating economic chaos and exploiting nominal economic revival to consolidate his control over the state apparatus and exploit the private sector. The response of the office of the prime minister was equally strong in rejecting the accusations of the speaker, alluding to the responsibility that the former militias bear in blocking institutional reform (see *Al Diyar*, 10 August 1998).

11. Under the Taif Accord agreement was reached to carry out administrative decentralization and the drawing up of electoral districts. The former has not yet been implemented while the electoral laws put in place have not been in conformity with the stipulations of the accord. Also, whereas it stipulated the creation of an Economic and Social Council, this was not established until 1995 (law no. 389, 12 January 1995) and did not become operational until 9 December 1999, when the Council of Ministers finally appointed its members.

12. Syria's role as an influential arbiter of many of Lebanon's domestic political quarrels was (is) publicly acknowledged and often referred to in the local press. On 18 August 1998, *Annahar*, a leading daily newspaper, headlined its commentary on the local situation 'Syria is no longer embarrassed in declaring its choice of the new president'. In Lebanese diplomatic jargon Syria's accepted role as an arbiter and dispenser of friendly advice to Lebanese politicians and officials is subsumed under close cooperation and coordination between the two countries, particularly when invoked in the context of Israeli plans to destabilize the Lebanese domestic situation.

13. To some the term 'steadying hand' may sound benign or even beneficial and many prefer the term 'steadying fist' to denote the authoritarian nature of Syrian involvement in Lebanese affairs.

14. As noted above, Israeli troops withdrew from southern Lebanon in the latter part of May 2000.

15. Two major Israeli aerial attacks were the bombing of (a) the village of Qana

(near Tyre) in April 1996, which resulted in over 100 civilian deaths, and (b) electric installations outside Beirut, which for a period of several months, led to severe rationing of electric power (June 1999).

16. From 1984 to 1997 the US State Department imposed a ban on the travel of US citizens to Lebanon.

17. Again we caution about the reliability of GDP estimates. In the absence of official national accounting series, they are anchored on the GDP estimate for 1988 arrived at by the UNDP study referred to in Chapter 2 (note 42). Other indicators of economic activity confirm this trend – see, for example, the Coincident Indicator compiled by the Bank of Lebanon. The indicator is a weighted average of eight series: four measured in volume (e.g. electricity production and imports of petroleum derivatives) and four in US dollars (e.g. imports c.i.f. and broad liquidity).

18. One writer points out that were a proper GDP deflator used, instead of the price index relied upon to arrive at estimates of real GDP, the annual rate of growth in real terms would be much less. For the period 1993–98 he estimates the average annual growth rate at about 1.6 per cent, in contrast with the official estimate of about 5 per cent. See Charbel Nahhas, 'Quel modèle de croissance économique pour la prochaine décennie?', UNDP 'Conference on Linking Economic Growth and Social Development in Lebanon' (11–13 January 2000, Beirut, p. 56). This issue apart, Lebanese national income estimates do not take into account the cost of environmental degradation.

19. Effective 12 October 1991, this ratio was set at 55 per cent (decision no. 4539). As of 12 February 1998 it was raised to 70 per cent (decision no. 6893), only to be replaced, effective 18 March 1999, by a net liquid assets to deposit ratio of 30 per cent intended to ensure a tighter control of liquidity risk in foreign exchange than was the case previously. The 70 per cent net loans to deposit ratio did not specify that the remaining 30 per cent must be invested in liquid assets. Thus part of the available resources could be invested in foreign currency denominated participations that were not classified as loans.

20. For the period 1991–2002 the ratio of foreign currency to total deposits ranged from a low of 56.6 per cent at the end of 1996 to a high of 72.5 per cent at the end of 2001 (69.4 per cent at end 2002) for a period average of 65.7 per cent (see Figure 3.3 and Table 3.4). For the period 1992–2000 the average ratio of net liquid assets to deposits in foreign currency ranged from roughly 50 to 60 per cent, with some banks observing the set limit while others managed to contravene it, but generally to a limited extent. For the alpha group (the biggest banks), the ratio declined from 63.48 per cent at the end of 1992 to 51.86 at the end of 1996, rising to 61.08 at the end of 1997, declining to 54.97 at the end of 1999, and rising again to 61.12 at the end of 2000. For the beta and delta group (the smaller banks) the ratio was almost consistently below the specified limit. For the gamma group the record was mixed. Obviously the record of individual banks varied (source: Bilanbanques [1993–2002]).

21. Oil export revenues (at constant 1995 prices) declined from a peak of $296.8 billion for 1980 to $93.7 billion for 1995, rising to $106.9 billion for 1996, falling again to $73.4 billion for 1998 and then rising to an estimated $163.5 billion for 2000, but falling back to $137.0 billion for 2001 and an estimated $119.5 billion for 2002 (source: OAPEC databank). As for the Asian financial crisis of 1997, it did not have a significant negative impact on Arab capital flows to the Lebanese economy: Arab Gulf investments in Asian financial markets were relatively limited.

22. See Republic of Lebanon, *Global Medium Term Note Programme, Offering Circular*, 2 August 2001 and 23 December 2002.

23. Based on data published in ESCWA, *National Accounts Studies of the ESCWA Region* (United Nations, 2000). Again we caution about the non-reliability of Lebanon's GDP series.

24. Central Directorate of Statistics, *L'Etat des comptes economiques, 1994–1995* (October 1997) – in Arabic.

25. See, for example, *Annahar*: 30 July 1992, 4 August 1992 and 30 July 1992; *Assafir*: 7 August 1992, 18 July 1992, 23 July 1992 and 25 July 1992; and *Al Diyar*: 21 July 1992; see also Albert Dagher, 'Siyâsat Si'r Ṣarf al-'Imla, al Tajriba al-Lubnânîya wa al-Dawr al-Maṭlûb min hâdhihi al-siyâsa' [Exchange Rate Policy: the Lebanese Experience], *National Defence Journal* (Beirut, October 2002), pp. 31–2.

26. To my knowledge no attempt has been made to quantify for Lebanon the relationship between the real exchange rate and export competitiveness. A recent cross-country econometric study of selected MENA countries confirms the negative impact of exchange rate misalignment (overvaluation of the national currency) on both total and manufactured export performance. See M. K. Nabli and M.-A. Veganzones-Varoudakis, 'Exchange Rate Regime and Competitiveness of Manufactured Exports: the Case of MENA Countries', World Bank Discussion Paper (August 2002).

27. See IMF, *Lebanon – Staff Report for the 2002 Article IV Consultation*, 6 December 2002, p. 13.

28. See S. Makdisi and S. Neiame, 'Exchange Rate and Inflation under Conditions of Volatility and Relative Stability: the Experience of a Small Open Economy', unpublished paper (Institute of Financial Economics, AUB), 2001.

Earlier econometric investigations of the long-term relationship between the exchange rate and inflation have been carried out for both the pre-civil-war period and subsequent periods up to 1993 (see, for example, Makdisi, *Financial Policy*, Chapter 7; and S. Eken et al., *Economic Dislocation and Recovery in Lebanon*, IMF Occasional Paper no. 120 [1995], section VI). In particular, the IMF paper, which investigates periods of stability and volatility, concludes that the relationship between the Lebanese–US inflation differential and exchange rate movements was positive but not statistically significant before the civil war but was both positive and strongly significant from 1975 up to 1993. A related conclusion is that in the period from late 1992 until 1993, when the authorities were able to maintain relative exchange rate stability, the earlier close relationship between inflation and exchange rate movements had not been present. This latter period of investigation was relatively short and hence its results cannot be taken as conclusive. Makdisi's 1979 investigation points to a significant relationship between the exchange rate and inflation in the pre-civil-war period. It should be borne in mind that co-integration and other econometric tests developed subsequently were not used.

29. Concurrently, total foreign currency deposits held by Lebanese residents abroad, as reported in the *International Financial Statistics* (August 1994) under 'Cross Border Deposits of Nonbanks by Residence of Depositor', increased from $1.95 billion at the end of 1981 to $9.46 billion at the end of 1990, declining to $6.32 billion at the end of June 1994. Reporting by the IFS on this data was discontinued after June 1994. Data from the Bank of International Settlements indicate that external deposits of reporting banks for Lebanon stood at $6.04 billion at the end of 2001 and $6.89 billion at the end of June 2002.

30. For a discussion of dollarization in Lebanon and the 'ratchet effect', see Johannes Mueller, 'Dollarization in Lebanon', IMF Working Paper (WP/94/129), October 1994; and Eken et al., *Economic Dislocation*, section IV. Mueller's (econometric) study examines the period 1982–93 and concludes that currency substitution (from pounds to dollars) is mainly driven by the expected depreciation of the rate and that voluntary de-dollarization is slowed down by the presence of a strong ratchet effect which lasts for at least 4½ to 4¾ years.

31. In practice, this risk was really important for debtors whose income was generated in Lebanese pounds. As the pound depreciated, increasingly incomes came to be generated in dollars.

32. The greater the use of foreign money, the stronger the inflationary impact of the monetization of any given fiscal deficit. See Eken et al., *Economic Dislocation*, p. 23.

It may be pointed out in this connection that there is a growing literature on the advantages and disadvantages of a fully dollarized national economy. Its main advantage is that it leads to the convergence of Lebanese interest and inflation rates towards their respective US levels. With lower US interest rates, this would help reduce the cost of financing reconstruction and of public debt. Further, full dollarization, it has been pointed out, reduces the frequency and scale of currency crises. On the other hand, dollarization is associated with several major costs, including loss of national autonomy over monetary policy, of seignorage revenues and the lender of last resort function of the Central Bank. It is obvious that the arguments for or against full dollarization are not conclusive. For a brief review of this subject see A. Berg and E. Bornszstein, 'The Dollarization Debate', *Finance and Development*, vol. 37, no. 1, March 2000.

33. The fall in the 1998 proportion in comparison with 1997 is partly due to the exceptional bulge in the recorded expenditures for December 1997 (more than twice the monthly average for the year) to the benefit of the 1998 budget. In this connection, it may be noted that the cost of swap operations between short-term and longer-term treasury bills conducted by the Central Bank have been borne by the bank as part of its open market operations and not debited to the Ministry of Finance.

34. Throughout, opposition groups accused successive governments of wasteful spending, which took the form of padded contracts, outright bribes and unaccounted-for public expenditure, in particular as regards certain public sector bodies such as the Council for the South and the Central Fund for the Return of the Refugees. Specific aspects of fiscal mismanagement were publicly exposed by the Minister for Administrative Reform in the first government that was formed following the presidential elections of 1998. This government proceeded to investigate a number of cases related to the misuse of public funds. Later the process was effectively halted (see Chapter 4, section 2.1).

35. See IMF, *Lebanon – Staff Report for the 2001 Article IV Consultation*, p. 24. In his book *For Truth and History*, Hoss mentions (p. 299) that the government he headed in 1998 was faced with accumulated governmental arrears amounting to LL1,200 billion or about $796 million.

36. In May 2002 the government decided to resolve the issue of outstanding arrears (up to April of that year) due to contractors and other private sector parties by making them hold government eurobonds issued in settlement of these obligations.

To secure needed liquidity, holders of these bonds could only discount them with the commercial banks at a high discount rate.

37. In November 2002 the government and Central Bank agreed that profits accruing to the government from the rise in the price of gold (purely accounting profits amounting to about LL18 billion) would be used to retire TBs held by the Central Bank.

38. In particular, the occasional surfacing of political disputes among the ruling 'Troika' tended to give rise to pressures on the pound. During 1997 the Central Bank intervened heavily on the foreign exchange market in support of the pound at a cost of about $1.5 billion from its foreign exchange reserves. The consistent pressure on the pound prompted the government (in particular the prime minister) to seek the assistance of Saudi Arabia and Kuwait. This assistance took the form of $500 and $100 million deposits respectively with the Bank of Lebanon in December 1997 for a period of three years, both being renewed in January 2001, with the Kuwaiti deposit raised to $200 million. The result was that the bank's gross but not net reserves rose by these amounts. As a result of the Central Bank intervention at the end of 1997 its net foreign exchange reserves had declined by about 1 billion US dollars in comparison with the end of 1996 (see IMF, *Lebanon – Staff Report for the 1999 Article IV Consultation*, appendix, table 4). Similarly, during 2001 and the first half of 2002 the bank incurred huge losses in foreign exchange, estimated at about $2.8 billion, in defence of the pound. The net foreign exchange position of the Central Bank (excluding gold) declined to minus $3 billion at the end of June 2002 (see IMF, *Lebanon – Staff Report for the 2002 Article IV Consultation*, p. 33). Subsequently, and especially after the Paris II meeting held in November 2002 in support of Lebanon, the market trend was reversed, at least until early 2003.

39. See D. Gressani and J. Page, 'Reconstruction in Lebanon, Challenges for Macroeconomic Management', MENA Working Paper Series no. 16, World Bank, April 1999.

40. Frequently, the government resorted to borrowing in excess of the budgetary deficit requirements, the intention being to sterilize part of the existing bank liquidity. This policy gave rise to an additional interest burden. One study calculates that for the period 1993–2001 the cumulative additional financing, i.e. over and above budgetary needs, amounted to $4 billion or 12 per cent of outstanding public debt at the end of that year (see R. Hijazi, *The Costs of Monetary Stabilization in Post-Conflict Lebanon: a Political Economy Approach*, Appendix B). For an earlier critique of governmental policies, including exchange rate policy, see Elias Saba, *Hiwâr Hawla al-'Iqtisâd fi Jumhûriyat al Tâif: Al Mashrû' al Badîl* [Dialogue about Economics in the Taif Republic: the Alternative Project].

41. Many Lebanese economic observers (not to mention the IMF) had early on repeatedly warned about the explosive nature of the fiscal policies. But the government did not pay serious attention to these warnings until 2001/2, when it acknowledged that the debt dynamics were spiralling out of control and potentially threatening the political position of major political actors.

42. In February 2001 the French president had called for a meeting of donor countries and international financial institutions in Paris (referred to as the Paris I meeting) to consider assistance to Lebanon. It did not lead to any significant results as the economic/financial policies of the government were not considered adequate for controlling the deteriorating fiscal situation.

43. See the report submitted by the Lebanese government to the Paris II meeting of 23 November 2002, convened by President Chirac, dated 13 November 2002.

44. Effective 11 February 1993 nominal interest rates on the shorter-term TBs were substantially raised: for the three-month TB to 19.96 per cent (effective yield 21.01 per cent) from the 12.59 per cent (13.0 per cent) that had prevailed since 26 November 1992 and for the six-month TBs to 19.83 per cent (22.1 per cent) from 13. 96 per cent (15.0 per cent). At the same time, the interest rate on the one-year TB was raised slightly to 18.05 per cent (22.01 per cent) from 17.36 per cent (20.99 per cent), while that on the two-year TB remained unchanged at 24.5 per cent (26.0 per cent). In effect the gap between the short-term and two-year interest rates was narrowed but the average interest rate level was raised substantially. (At the end of 1992, three-month, six-month and one-year TBs comprised about 70 per cent of the total.) The 11 February 1993 increase in interest rates came in the wake of temporary pressure on the pound in late January/early February of that year which was also countered by Central Bank intervention on the foreign exchange market. Press reports at the time attributed this pressure mainly to political disagreements between the President of the Republic and prime minister, related, among other things, to pending administrative appointments (see *Assafir*, 30 January 1993). Although in the following months pressures on the pound subsided and it tended to appreciate gradually, interest rates were not changed. For a review of the evolution of effective yields on TBs with shorter- and longer-term maturities, see Table 3.6a.

45. It should be noted that a large part of the foreign debt was also held indirectly by resident banks via their branches or subsidiaries abroad.

46. This level of reserve requirements had been set effective 5 March 1987. Decision no. 6894 of 14 February 1998 specified that required reserves above 10 per cent should be held in special TBs carrying an interest rate to be set by the Ministry of Finance.

47. In accordance with legislation promulgated in 1977 which created a free banking zone.

48. At the end of 1991 1 million Lebanese pounds were equivalent to $1,137. Had the exchange rate remained stable instead of depreciating, 5 million pounds would have been equivalent to $5,600 as at the end of 1993.

49. Banks with deposits of over $1 billion. At the time they numbered thirteen.

50. Based on data published in the Bank of Lebanon Quarterly Bulletins.

51. The number of financial institutions stood at twenty-eight but their activities were still in their infancy.

52. For the period 1991–2002 the ratio of deposits to GDP averaged about 174 per cent and that of bank claims on the private sector about 66 per cent.

53. In the post-war period, especially after 1992, Lebanese banks generated large profits (some call it a profit bonanza), thanks in large measure to the high yields on TBs in Lebanese pounds. To illustrate, for 1998 interest income totalled $3.8 billion, of which about one half accrued from TBs and bonds held by the banks. For the subsequent three years the share of TBs averaged a little less than one half owing to some decline in interest rates, with interest income reaching $4,252 and $4,039 billion for 2000 and 2001 respectively. It has been observed that the large difference between the cost of external borrowing (the eurodollar rate) and internal borrowing (linked to high-yielding TBs) has helped many banks survive without a viable business base. See

S. Hakim and S. Andary, 'The Lebanese Central Bank and the Treasury Bills Market', *Middle East Journal*, vol. 5, no. 2 (1997), p. 234.

54. For a review of Lebanese banking operations and policies in the 1990s see B. Akkad, *The Lebanese Banking System and the Effects of Globalization*, Institute of Money and Banking project, February 2000, AUB.

55. For capital adequacy ratios, see circular no. 1114 (dated 12 August 1992), circular no. 1612 (dated 20 March 1998) and circular no. 212 (dated 20 May 1999). For limits on foreign currency exposure, see circular no. 1596 (dated 2 February 1998), circular no. 1709 (dated 18 March 1999) and circular no. 213 (dated 27 May 1999, issued by the BCC). For credit risk management, see the BCC circular of 23 October 2002. Further, effective 21 August 1996 the Ministry of Finance required adherence to International Accounting Standards by business entities and banks operating in Lebanon.

56. See IMF, *Lebanon – Staff Report for the 1999 Article VI Consultation*, pp. 26–7.

57. For limits on foreign exchange positions, see circular no. 1516 of 24 April 1997. According to this circular, the net foreign exchange trading position in assets or liabilities of a bank may not exceed 5 per cent of the total components of tier-one capital. Similarly the global position (total debtor or creditor position, whichever is higher) may not exceed 40 per cent of total tier-one capital.

58. A major Lebanese bank carried out simulations in early 2001 to determine how a hypothetical depreciation of the pound would affect its level of profits. The result was that in comparison with 2000 a 100 per cent depreciation would have led to a cumulative loss of about 60 per cent in net profits for 2001 and 2002, after which the process of recovery would begin. Had a 50 per cent depreciation been assumed, the loss in 2001 would have amounted to 55 per cent with recovery beginning in the following year.

59. The annual reports of many banks lacked sufficient detail and were published late in the year concerned.

60. See N. Hantas, *The Role of the Banking Control Commission in Controlling Bank Risks*, Institute of Money and Banking project, 2000, AUB.

61. For a review see ibid., pp. 76–89.

62. See IMF, *Lebanon – Staff Report for the 1999 Article IV Consultation*, p. 29.

63. With 1996 = 100, the Central Bank's Financial Market Value Weighted Index stood at 89.35 at end 1998, declining to 16.62 at end 2001 and rising slightly to 18.43 at end 2002. The trading system is computerized and so far based on a price-fixing system that takes place once a day for all the stocks except Solidere's (see note 70), which is priced twice a day with a limit up/down of 5 per cent. On 25 September 1996 a regional cross-listing agreement was signed (effective 1 January 1997) with the Egyptian and Kuwaiti stock exchanges. Furthermore, little progress has so far been made in developing the Beirut secondary market, opened on 21 June 1994, to deal with securities, notably TBs.

64. The Beirut stock exchange, originally established in 1920, has traditionally not attracted a significant share of domestic savings.

65. For recent analyses of the role of the financial sector in economic growth, see N. Hermes and R. Lensink (eds), *Financial Development and Economic Growth* (Routledge, 1996); also P. Demetriades, 'Financial Markets and Economic Development', M. El-Rian and M. Mohieldin (eds), *Financial Development in Emerging Markets: The Egyptian Experience* (Egyptian Centre for Economic Studies, 1998).

66. The circulars in question are respectively: circular no. 1448 relating to decision no. 6219 of 4 July 1996, circular no. 1475 of 24 October 1996 relating to law no. 520 of 6 June 1996, circular no. 1581 relating to decision no. 6856 of 19 December 1997, circular no. 1653 relating to decision no. 7074 of 5 September 1998 and circular no. 1707 relating to decision no. 7224 of 11 February 1999.

67. See IMF Staff Team, *Macroprudential Indicators of Financial System Soundness* (IMF, April 2000). These indicators comprise both aggregate micro-prudential indicators of the health of individual financial institutions and macroeconomic variables associated with financial systems. Identified micro-prudential indicators include capital adequacy, asset quality, management soundness, earnings and profitability, liquidity, sensitivity to market risk and market-based indicators. Identified macroeconomic indicators comprise economic growth, balance of payments, inflation, interest and exchange rates, lending and asset price booms, contagion effects and other factors (e.g. arrears in the economy).

68. A number of private consulting organizations (International Bechtel and Dar al-Handasah Consultants) as well as the World Bank and other UN agencies were involved in the initial preparation of reconstruction plans.

69. World Bank, *Lebanon, Stabilization and Reconstruction* (1 March 1993), pp. 36–8.

70. The reconstruction of downtown Beirut falls outside the official reconstruction programmes as it has been undertaken by a privately funded real estate company, the so-called Lebanese Company for the Development and Reconstruction of Beirut Central District (better known as Solidere), formally established in May 1994. Its share capital is made up of two types of common stock (A and B) totalling $1.82 billion. By a special law passed by parliament in 1991, it has been allowed to purchase the real estate of the destroyed central district against issuance of stock (type A shares) to property holders. Type B shares have been issued to investors against cash subscriptions in the amount of $650 million.

The proposed creation of Solidere engendered a host of critical assessments of its economic, social, architectural and legal obligations, and indeed the objectives, other than reconstruction, behind its creation. For critical readings by a number of writers, see *'I'mâr Bayrût wa al-Fûrsa al-Dâ'î'a, Wasat Bayrût al-Tijârî wa al-Sharika al-'Qârîya* [The Reconstruction of Beirut and the Missed Opportunity: the Beirut Central District and the Real Estate Company], Beirut, 1992, and *Beirut construire l'avenir, reconstruire le passé?*, Dossiers de l'Urban Research Institute, Beirut, 1992. For a subsequent critical reading of how Solidere came into existence and the manipulation of financial power that brought it about, see H. Edde, *Al Mâlu In Hakam* [Money, Were It to Govern], Beirut, 1999.

71. CDR, *Progress Report* (January 1994), pp. 7–8.

72. CDR, *Progress Report* (August 1995), p. 1.

73. CDR, *Progress Report* (March 1966), pp. 1–2, and *Progress Report* (October 1996), p. 2.

74. CDR, *Progress Report* (January 1998).

75. The announced plans were not sufficiently detailed for purposes of investment planning by the private sector.

76. Data taken from IMF, *Lebanon – Staff Report for the Article IV Consultation* (various years), and the Ministry of Finance. Expenditure data were revised to include expenditure financed through the accumulation of arrears to the private sector.

77. CDR, *Progress Report*, May 2002.

78. Ibid.

79. In a memo dated 19 April 1999, submitted to the prime minister, the president of CDR warns about past and current delays in utilizing available foreign financing concomitant with delays in the preparation and execution of specific projects that rely on such financing.

80. During the period 1993–2002, total capital expenditure (inclusive of projects financed through CDR) is estimated at about $13.7 billion, of which about 75 per cent was domestically financed (data provided by the Ministry of Finance). For CDR projects, about 60 per cent of the total cost was covered by domestic financing. It is worth noting that although annual public capital expenditure continued to rise until 1997, the annual rate of growth declined after 1994. One explanation is that the flow of private investment tended to decline after 1995, being influenced, among other factors, by the crowding-out effect.

81. We cannot go into this matter here. For those interested in an analysis of the post-Taif Lebanese political situation, which sheds light on the factors influencing the parliamentary elections, see Farid El Khazen, *'Intikhâbât Lubnân mâ ba'da al-Ḥarb, 1992, 1996 wa 2000: Dîmuqrâtîya bilâ Khayâr* [Post-war Lebanese Elections, 1992, 1996 and 2000: Democracy without a Choice], Dar Annahar, 2000, and LCPS, *Al-'Intikhâbât al-Niyâbîya fi Lubnân 2002: bayna al-'I'âda wa al-Taqhyîr* [Parliamentary Elections in Lebanon, 2000: between Repetition and Change] (Beirut, 2002).

82. See decree no. 13/91 issued by the prime minister concerning the formation of this committee (Beirut, 19 March 1991).

83. Information based on minutes of the committee's meetings, which were circulated to the committee members.

84. In this connection ways were considered to address absenteeism in the finance ministry as a result of the destruction, during the fighting of 1989–90, of buildings that housed certain departments of the ministry.

85. The committee members included (names listed as per the cabinet decision) Samir Makdisi, Hicham Bsat, Elie Yashoui, Kamal Hamdan, Elie Assaf, Hasan Awada, Marwan Iskandar and Amin Alame. The committee held twenty working sessions to complete its report. As the domestic political atmosphere was tense and the local press wished to report on the deliberations of the committee, it was decided to keep the place and dates of its meetings confidential.

86. One member of the committee, Amin Alame, chose not to sign the report but to submit his own separate report to the Council of Ministers.

87. As noted in Chapter 2, this was an accounting rate used during the period 1985–95 for the valuation of imports for the purpose of levying tariff duties. Throughout it was substantially below the prevailing market rate. It is not surprising that the Association of Industrialists constantly demanded that it be abolished.

88. Data for interest rate on dollar deposits in Lebanon are available only from 1995, when the dollar rate in Lebanon began to diverge from the eurodollar rate. Prior to that year the three-month LIBOR rate, which governed the interest rate on three-month dollar deposits in Lebanon, is used to calculate the interest rate differential.

89. See A. Dah, G. Dibeh and W. Shahin, *The Distributional Impact of Taxes in Lebanon*, Lebanese Centre for Policy Studies, 1999, chapter 4, and G. Dibeh, *'Al-'Asar al-Ijtimâ'î Li-L Siyâsât al-Mâlîya wa al-Naqdîya fi Lubnân ma Ba'da al-Ḥarb'* [The Social Effect of

Financial and Monetary Policies in Post-war Lebanon], unpublished paper, 2003. In his paper Dibeh observes that the Lebanese income tax system is mildly progressive but that if the flat corporate tax is also included the system may very well be regressive.

90. Source of data: Ministry of Finance.

91. See S. Atallah, 'Reducing the Budget Deficit: a First Reading', a working paper prepared by the Lebanese Centre for Policy Studies in collaboration with the Commission of the European Community (1999, unpublished).

92. The study cited in the previous note, examining taxes on gasoline as a case study, concludes that indirect taxation in Lebanon is regressive (chapter 5). Dibeh, 'The Social Effect', corroborates this result. As a result of all the tax measures, the ratio of revenue to GDP rose from about 25 per cent for 1993 to 28 per cent for 2001.

93. For a discussion of Lebanese public debt management during the period 1993–98 see T. Hebling, 'Issues of Public Debt Management', in S. Eken and T. Hebling (eds), *Back to the Future, Postwar Reconstruction and Stabilization in Lebanon*, IMF Occasional Paper 176, Washington, DC, 1999.

94. Foreign currency borrowing for debt financing requires parliamentary approval, which the government was able to secure subject to specified ceilings.

95. See 'Work Programme of the Lebanese Government for Financial Reform', (June 1999). For a critical assessment of the background conditions leading to this programme and why it was not implemented, see C. Nahhas, *Ḥuzûz 'Ijtnâb Al-'Azma wa shurût Takhatîha: Sîrat Tajruba fi Al-'Islâh; Muqadimat Li Wasîkhat Barnâmj al 'Amal li-l Tashîh al Malî Hzairân 1999* [The Prospects for Averting the Crisis and the Conditions for Overcoming It: the Record of an Attempted Reform; an Introduction to the Work Programme for Financial Adjustment, June 1999], Dar Annahar, Beirut, 2003.

96. See Lebanese government document presented to the Paris II meeting.

97. They include the cell phone system, fixed line communications and the water sector. Strictly speaking, the cell phone system was already managed and operated by two private companies. The government decided to void existing contracts and solicit new bids for operating the system with a view to enlarging its share of the revenue.

98. See C. M. Henry and R. Springborg, *Globalization and the Politics of Development in the Middle East*, Cambridge University Press, 2001, p. 201. Referring to the period 1992–98, the authors assert that the attempt of Rafic Hariri to construct a Saudi-type rentier state ultimately collapsed for various economic as well as domestic and regional political reasons.

99. The reference to Paris II indicates a follow-up meeting to one that had also been called by the French president in Paris in 2001 (hence Paris I) to consider assistance to Lebanon. This first meeting had not led to any significant assistance.

100. Eleven countries and six international and regional organizations pledged assistance. It is noteworthy that of the $3 billion pledged to ease the debt problem, Saudi Arabia and France, the two strongest supporters of Lebanon and its government, contributed a total of $1.2 billion or 40 per cent of the total. Some of the countries that attended the meeting withheld support pending further progress of the part of Lebanon.

101. The conditions for bilateral assistance were not immediately known after the meeting. It remains to be seen to what extent the Lebanese government will succeed in meeting its pledges to the Paris II meeting. (For the first nine months of 2003 the

budget deficit was running at an annualized rate of 40 per cent instead of the planned 25 per cent of public expenditure.)

102. Divergence of opinion between the IMF and the government had arisen in the past over exchange rate policy, more specifically as regards the need to introduce a greater degree of rate flexibility, favoured by the IMF, albeit in the context of fiscal/ monetary reform (see *Lebanon – Staff Report for the 2001 Article IV Consultation*).

4. The post-war period 2

1. See Economic Research Forum for the Arab Countries, Iran and Turkey, and Consultation and Research Institute (Beirut), *Preliminary Report on Micro and Small Enterprises* (2000).

2. The active population is defined as including the working population plus unemployed workers looking for work and those looking for work for the first time.

3. See Central Directorate of Statistics, *Mîzânîyat al-'usra li-'Âm, 1997* [Household Survey for 1997].

4. See the study by St Joseph University, 'L'entrée des jeunes libanais dans la vie active et l'emigration', preliminary results, June 2002.

5. For 1997 the largest concentrations of the female labour force were in the educational sector (24 per cent), household services (15 per cent) and the health/social fields (8 per cent). For the male labour force they were in commercial activities (24 per cent), construction (14 per cent) and industry (14 per cent).

6. See the study by St Joseph University cited above. This estimate is close to the one arrived at in a survey conducted by Information International (Beirut) in late 2001, which, for the period 1991–2001, puts the total at 100,000 of which half were married – a grand total of 150,000 or 15,000 annually (see *Annahar*, 26 and 27 November 2001). Clearly, the total number of emigrants is much higher. Certain sources put it as high as 1.28 million for the period 1991–2000, with the rhythm of annual emigration picking up substantially, beginning in 1995. See B. Labaki, 'Lebanese Emigration after the Taif Agreement, 1990–2000', a paper presented to a conference on 'The Lebanese Presence in the World', organized by the Lebanese–American University, 29 June 2001. No estimates are available regarding net emigration, i.e. after allowing for returning Lebanese nationals who decided to take up residence at home.

7. See A. Dagher, 'Al Quuâ al-'Âmila fi Lubnân: al Waq'i wa al Afâk al Mustak-balîya' [Manpower and Development in Lebanon: Reality and Future Prospects], *Linking Economic Growth and Social Development in Lebanon* (UNDP conference, 11–13 January 2000, Beirut), p. 87.

8. See Consultation and Research Institute (Beirut), *al Quuâ al-'Âmila fi Lubnân: al Fajwa Bâyna al 'Ârd wa al Ṭalab* [The Lebanese Labour Market: the Gap between Supply and Demand], a study prepared for the Ministry of Industry, 2002. The data exclude Syrian and other foreign workers, especially those who did not hold work permits.

9. One estimate put the transfers of Syrian workers for 1995 at $0.7–1 billion, equivalent to 6–9 per cent of that year's GDP (see Dagher, 'Manpower and Development', p. 89.) For later years such transfers are likely to have declined.

10. See ibid., p. 89.

11. Despite the greatly significant multi-dimensional impact of foreign manpower on the domestic economy, no in-depth studies on this subject have been attempted.

12. Source of data: Research and Consultation Institute.

13. Based on data provided by the Consultation and Research Institute.

14. See D. Kaufmann and A. Kraay, *Growth without Governance* (unpublished World Bank paper, 2002).

15. In the literature on governance, empirical findings confirm that it matters significantly for long-run growth.

16. See ibid.

17. See Economic Research Forum, Indicators, *Economic Trends in the MENA Region, 1998*, pp. 53–4.

18. See Kaufmann and Kraay, *Growth without Governance*. The indicators refer to the country's percentile rank with higher values implying better governance ratings. For the control of corruption indicator, Lebanon's percentile rank was 31.4 compared to an average of 51.6 for the MENA region and a slightly lower world average. The one indicator on which Lebanon fared better than the MENA average was 'regulatory quality'. The study notes that the governance indicators reflect the statistical compilation of perceptions of the quality of governance of a large number of survey respondents in industrial and developing countries as well as non-governmental organizations, commercial risk-rating agencies and think tanks during 1997–98 and 2000 to mid-2001. It further notes that the reported relative positions are subject to a wide margin of error.

19. For illustrations of public accusations of corruption, see *Assafir*'s editorials of 1 and 11 January 1993 (i.e. shortly after the formation of the first Hariri government), which claimed that the government included the worst offenders in matters of corruption and conflict of interest (implicitly the prime minister and a few other ministers). In early 1994 one of the deputies, in a written statement submitted to the Al Niyâba al-Mâlîya al-'Amma (General Prosecutor), accused the prime minister of bribing members of parliament to approve the passage of a law pertaining to the creation of Solidere.

In 1998 Najah Wakim (then a deputy in parliament) published a book, *Al-'Ayâdî al-Sawdâ'* [The Black Hands], which, he claimed, chronicled the acts of corruption and nepotism of certain cabinet members. Those concerned, in turn, accused the deputy of falsifications and unfounded charges. While he was threatened with libel and court action, investigations were not concluded and, in any case, at the time he benefited from immunity from prosecution extended to members of parliament. For additional examples of public accusations of corruption, see *Al Anwar*, 13 December 1994. See also *Annahar* of 28 and 29 January 1999, *Al Anwar* of 30 January 1999 and AFP report of 21 November 1999.

Clearly, in political battles all sorts of accusations and counter-accusations are laid by the protagonists. What seems to distinguish the Lebanese case is that public accusations of corruption were usually not dealt with judiciously by the authorities concerned, a number of them not being resolved one way or another. The prevailing political wisdom was often to let things fade away, or put them on hold, rather than stir up political embarrassments.

The new administration that took over in late 1998 quickly endeavoured to deal with corruption in public office by investigating certain past officials suspected of having been involved in cases of corruption and/or misuse of public office. A major criticism of the manner in which this matter proceeded is the selectivity in the choice of officials to be investigated. With one exception, all those who have been investigated did not hold high political office. As of mid-2002, of sixteen cases that had been prosecuted, nine were referred to the courts and seven were shelved. Of the cases referred to the courts, four resulted in indictments and four in acquittal; one case remains pending. Despite good intentions, early attempts at serious administrative reform have so far failed to materialize.

20. See *Annahar*, 20 August 1998.

21. See *Annahar*, 7 July 1998.

22. They are entitled *Lebanon Anti-corruption Initiative Report 1999* and *Benchmark Polls on Corruption in Lebanon 1999*, prepared by the Information International SAL Research Consultants.

23. The report was prepared for the 'Expert Meeting on National Action for Fighting Corruption in Lebanon', which was held on 21 January 2001 in Beirut. It was undertaken as part of an agreement between the government of Salim Hoss and the UNICR to formulate plans to fight corruption in Lebanon. Not surprisingly, the circulation of the report led to official protests.

24. See *Benchmark Polls*, p. 78.

25. See S. Atallah, 'Roadblocks to Recovery, Institutional Obstacles Facing the Private Sector in Lebanon', unpublished paper, Lebanese Centre for Policy Studies, 1999.

26. See *Public Service Accountability in Lebanon* (an unpublished study prepared jointly by a team of AUB faculty members and senior government officials, in collaboration with the John Kennedy School of Government at Harvard, 1996 – A. Iskandar, principal author), pp. 9, 50 and 88.

27. For a detailed review of the proposed measures, see Iskandar Bachir, *Al-Tanmiya fi Lubnân* [Development in Lebanon], Beirut, 1994, pp. 105–11.

28. The government did dismiss many government employees suspected of corruption through a special procedure approved by parliament. Its action was overruled by the Council of State for lack of sufficient evidence, and the dismissed employees were returned to office.

29. Refer, in particular, to: (1) Republic of Lebanon, Ministry of Social Affairs/UNDP, *Khâritqt Ahwâl al-Ma'îcha fi Lubnân* [Map of Living Conditions in Lebanon], Beirut, 1998; (2) Central Directorate of Statistics, *La population active en 1997*, August 1998; (3) Lebanon, Directorate of Statistics, *Mîzânîyat al-'usra li-'Âm, 1997* [Household Survey for 1997], February 1998; (4) A. Haddad, *Al Faqr fi Lubnân* [Poverty in Lebanon], United Nations, ESCWA, 1996; (5) Consultation and Research Institute, *Community Development Fund Project: Rapid Needs and Capacity Assessment Study, Phase I* (unpublished report prepared for the High Relief Committee), April 1995.

30. Though it constitutes an important dimension of socio-economic development, the question of gender inequities is not taken up here. For analyses of gender issues in Lebanon, see ESCWA, *Al-Nâû' al-'Ijima'î wa al-Mûatna wa Dawr al-Mûnazamat Ghaîr al-Hûkûmîya fi Bûldan al-Escwa al Mût'sra bi-l-Niza'ât: Dirâsat Hâlat Lubnân* [Gender, Citizenship and the Role of NGOs in the ESCWA Countries Influenced by Conflict: The Case of Lebanon], Beirut, December 2000; National Committee for Lebanese Women, *Al-Taqrîr al-Rasmî al-'Âwal Hawl 'Itifaqîat 'Ilgh'â al-Tamîz Dd al-Mar'â* [First Official Report on the Convention on the Elimination of All Forms of Discrimination

against Women], Beirut, 2000; UN, *Women and Men in Lebanon: a Statistical Portrait*, Beirut, 2000; and Comité Nationale de la Femme, *La femme libanaise, 1970–1995, chiffres et sens, banque des données*, Beirut, 1997, two vols.

Briefly it may be noted that while women won the right to vote in 1953, since then their representation in national political institutions has been minimal. On the other hand, women have been active in the educational and to a lesser extent the economic life of the country, bearing in mind, as noted above, the increasing proportion of the female active population. While in universities female teachers and professors represent a good percentage of the total faculty (about 27 per cent for 1999/2000, compared with 24 per cent for 1992/3 – source of data: Educational Centre for Research and Development), this is not reflected in the decision-making ranks of university administrations. An active women's movement has been fighting against various forms of gender discrimination and has had a degree of success in amending some though by no means all of the discriminatory labour and criminal laws. One of their unaccomplished and principal targets remains the divisive personal status laws (Lebanon approved the Convention on the Elimination of Discrimination against Women with reservations concerning the articles on the right to choose a family, marriage and family, and arbitration of disputes – see UNDP, *Globalization: towards a Lebanese Agenda*, Beirut, July 2002, p. 135). Another important goal is a more equitable citizenship law. As things stand now a Lebanese man who marries a foreign woman can pass his citizenship on to her and to their children, while a Lebanese woman married to a foreigner cannot pass on her citizenship to her husband or children.

31. See Lebanon, Ministry of Social Affairs/UNDP, *Khâriṭat Aḥwâl al-Maʿîcha fî Lubnân* [Map of Living Conditions in Lebanon], Beirut, 1998, pp. 18–19.

32. See ibid., section 2. The study is based on a statistical survey comprising eleven indicators of living conditions grouped under four headings: housing, the water and sanitation network, education and income level. A scale of 0–2 is adopted, representing respectively the highest level of unsatisfied needs and highest level of satisfied needs; 1 is the threshold level: scores below 1 indicate that basic needs are not being satisfied. A composite index of living conditions is finally constructed and used to classify households into five categories in accordance with the degree that basic needs are being satisfied: very low, low, medium, high and very high.

The study points out that individual indicators of 'unsatisfied basic needs for housing, water/sanitation and education outscored the indicator for income. The reason is that income levels are subject to change over the short run, being influenced by evolving political and economic conditions: the rate of growth began to decline after 1995. In contrast, the other variables are less amenable to change in the short run as they embody results of past policies and actions or services made available by the public sector (p. 59).

33. See ibid., pp. 41–2.

34. Ibid, p. 43.

35. Study carried out in 2002 by the Consultation and Research Institute for the Ministry of Industry.

36. See Anis Abi Farah, '*Ḥawla al-ʾAwḍâʿ al-Maʿîchîya al-Lubnânîya*' [On the Living Conditions of Households], *Annahar*, 18 August 1999. It should be remembered that at best these are rough estimates, which may contain an important margin of error.

To compare the results of the two years, the writer uses available price indices, which suffer from major limitations.

37. Data provided by the Bank of Lebanon.

38. See UNDP, *Development Cooperation Report for Lebanon*, 1999, p. 18.

39. See 'The Impact of Health Costs on the Right to Health Care in Lebanon', report prepared by the United Nations Children's Fund (UNCF) in cooperation with the Consultation and Research Institute, Beirut, March 1999, and UNDP, *Development Cooperation Report for Lebanon*, 2000, p. 13.

40. Over recent years the government had often not reimbursed private hospitals for the amounts due to them on account of admitting government-sponsored patients, or only after a long delay. These unpaid obligations were part of its accumulating arrears to the private sector referred to in Chapter 3, section 3.2.

41. For analyses of the health sector in Lebanon, see UNDP, *Human Development Report for Lebanon, 1997* (chapter 3), UNDP, National Human Development Report – Lebanon 2001–2002, *Globalization: towards a Lebanese Agenda*, Beirut, July 2002, and UNCF, 'The Impact of Health Costs'.

42. See UNDP, *Globalization: towards a Lebanese Agenda*, p. 123.

43. For 1997, there were 165 private and sixteen governmental hospitals, a total of 181. Private hospital beds accounted for close to 90 per cent of the total. (Source: *Statistical Abstract of the ESCWA Region*, 1999.)

44. According to UNDP, *Human Development Report for Lebanon, 1997* (chapter 3), the number of doctors rose from 4,837 in 1992 to 7,900–9,500 in 1996. The majority (over 60 per cent) are graduates of medical schools abroad, mainly Arab and eastern European countries. The report mentions that eastern European-trained medical graduates are not offered any structured orientation courses upon their return. As a result many of the doctors are not equipped to meet the country's health needs. On the other hand graduates of the established medical schools in Lebanon are well trained.

45. See ibid., chapter 3.

46. The two oldest private universities in Lebanon are the American University of Beirut, established in 1866 as the Syrian Protestant College, and the St Joseph University, established in 1875.

47. Source of data on student enrolment: Centre for Educational Research and Development (Beirut).

48. For an assessment of the Lebanese University, see A. Amin et al., *Qaḍâya al-jâmi'a al-Lubnânîya wa-Iṣlâḥuhâ* [Problems of the Lebanese University and Its Reform], Dar Annahar, November 1999.

49. Had we considered vocational training of all types and at all levels, its proportion of total enrolment at corresponding levels would be roughly the same.

50. As at the end of the 1990s, Lebanon had the lowest illiteracy rate among the Arab countries. One source puts the illiteracy rate at 6 per cent for 2000 (see *Statistical Abstract of the ESCWA Region for 2001*).

51. Central Directorate of Statistics, *La population active en 1997*, August 1998, no. 12.

52. Unemployment is defined as including: (a) those seeking employment for the first time who have not as yet found a job and (b) those who have lost their jobs and are in the process of seeking new employment.

53. To the extent that there was also a return flow of Lebanese living abroad, net emigration was of a lesser magnitude, but only to a limited extent.

54. It includes, though, Palestine refugees inside and outside the refugee camps.

55. For a discussion of this matter, see Najib Issa, *Al-Quwâ al 'Âmila wa siyâsat al-'Âmâla fi Lubnân* [Manpower and the Policy of Employment in Lebanon], Lebanese Centre for Policy Studies, 1996.

56. According to the survey carried out by Information International cited above about one third of those emigrating were motivated by non-economic reasons.

57. For a detailed account of the hazardous waste issue see K. Makdisi, *Trapped between Sovereignty and Globalization: Implementing International Environmental Treaties in Developing Countries*, unpublished doctoral dissertation, Fletcher School of Law and Diplomacy, Tufts University, 2001, chapter 4.

58. It should be recognized that some public officials and even one or two of the ministers who held the environment portfolio attempted to address environmental issues. Their individual efforts, however, could not stem the overall trend of environmental degradation.

59. *Annahar*, Lebanon's leading daily newspaper, often carries a special section on 'environment and heritage'. Its coverage has frequently exposed serious abuses in both areas.

60. For a discussion of these issues, see respectively papers by Mohammad Fawwaz (former head of urban planning) on 'Fâ'lîyat 'Idârat al-'ûmrân al-Tanzîmîya wa Hudûdiha' [Efficacy and Limits of Urban Regulatory Management] and Charbel Nahhas on "Idârat al-'Umrân fi Lubnân Wâq'an wa-Hâjâtn, 'Adwâtn wa 'Islâhât' [The Management of Urban Urbanization in Lebanon: Reality, Needs, Instruments and Reforms]. Both papers were presented at a conference organized by the Ministry of Public Works and the Order of Engineers on 29–30 June and 1 July 2000. The first author states that instead of standing as exceptions, violations of building permits have become the rule (p. 18). He calls for the revision of article 17 of the existing building code which permits an excessively high exploitation ratio of 80 per cent by the urban planning authority in yet unclassified areas that comprise a large portion of the total; this has resulted in the eradication of natural resources and the conversion of agricultural and forest land into unplanned built-up areas (p. 9).

61. See 'Barnâmaj al-Hukûma al-Lubnâniya li-l-'Islah al-mâlî [Work Programme of the Lebanese Government for Financial Reform], 23 June 1999, p. 35.

62. See S. Djoundourian, I. Nuwayhid and F. Chaaban, *The Economic and Social Impacts of Mobile Source Pollution on Public Health in the Greater Beirut Area*, a country case study for METAP III, MedPolicies Initiative, submitted to the Harvard Institute for International Development, January 1999, and F. Chaaban and G. Ayyoub, *Database of Air and Noise Pollution in Lebanon*, final report submitted to the Lebanese National Council for Scientific Research, 19 February 1999. METAP stands for the Mediterranean Environmental Technical Assistance Programme.

63. The use of diesel fuel engines results in twenty times more emissions than from the equivalent petrol engines.

64. As noted, in 2002 the cabinet decided to ban the use of diesel by small passenger buses but allowed larger vehicles to continue using it. METAP estimates that for 2000 the cost of environmental degradation in Lebanon was about $665 million or close to 4 per cent of estimated 2000 GDP.

65. See Djoundourian et al., *The Economic and Social Impacts*, Chapter 5.

66. See Ayoub and Chaaban, *Database of Air and Noise Pollution*. A further illustration of environmental deterioration derives from improper waste management. A recent paper points out that in Lebanon, as in the case of other countries in the region, untreated municipal and industrial sewage is released into the environment either into the sea or the beds of small rivers. Untreated sewage is, in some cases, reused for irrigation in an uncontrolled manner entailing substantial health risks. See J. Saghir, 'Urban Water and Sanitation in the Middle East and North Africa Region: the Way Forward', paper presented at the Third Mediterranean Development Forum, 5–8 March 2000, Cairo, p. 6.

67. Republic of Lebanon, Ministry of Environment, *Lebanon's First National Communication under the United Nations Framework Convention on Climate Change: Final Report* (UNDP, Global Environment Facility, June 1999).

68. Ibid., pp. 2–59.

69. Prior to the civil war, the political scene was characterized by a plethora of active political parties and groupings (Palestinian resistance organizations apart), representing a wide spectrum of traditional and various shades of progressive political ideologies. In practice, despite the important constitutional prerogatives enjoyed by the president of the republic in the pre-Taif era, political power was then more diffuse than was the case after the end of the war. In the post-civil-war period, strong Syrian influence over the political process diluted the effective role of political parties and groupings. Political power was in large measure imbued in the Syrian-supported Troika, comprising the President of the Republic, the prime minister and the speaker of the House, all of whom have been enthusiastic advocates of very close cooperation and coordination with Syria. Another distinguishing trait of the post-Taif political scene is the greatly increased power of super-rich businessmen, albeit subject to the prevailing conditions of Syro-Lebanese political coordination. It is reported that the parliament elected in 1992 included twelve very rich/super-rich deputies (9.4 per cent of membership). After the parliamentary elections of 2000, this number rose to twenty-four (18.7 per cent of membership) – see LCPS, *Al-Intikhabât al-Niyâbîya fi Lubnân 2002: bayna al-'I'âda wa al-Taqhyîr* [Parliamentary Elections in Lebanon, 2000], Beirut, 2002, p. 73.

5. Lebanon, development and globalization

1. The HDI value rose from 0.565 for 1990 (102/173) to 0.794 for 1994 (65/175), declining to 0.735 for 1998 (82/174).

2. With the oil boom, the Lebanese banking system played a conduit role for surplus oil funds in search of investment outlets abroad.

3. It should be recalled that during the period 1991–93 the authorities managed to implement policies that reduced the fiscal deficit as a ratio of both expenditure and GDP. This trend was not maintained in subsequent years up to 2001. Limited progress in reducing the fiscal deficit was made in 2002. Under pressure from international organizations, and in preparation for the Paris II meeting, a further significant reduction in the fiscal deficit was planned for 2003.

4. For a discussion of this question, see papers presented at the workshop organized by the Lebanese Centre for Policy Studies on 'The Developmental State Model and the Challenges to Lebanon', Beirut, 15–16 February 2002.

5. On this point see J. A. Scholte, *Globalization, a Critical Introduction* (St Martin's Press, 2000), pp. 151–2.

6. For a discussion on how political institutions have lagged behind in the rapid process of economic globalization, see B. Amoroso, *On Globalization: Capitalism in the Twenty-first Century* (Macmillan Press, 1998).

7. For a recent inquiry into surplus manpower in one major public sector (public education), see *Al-Infâq fî Qiṭâ'ât mukhtâra* [Expenditure on Selected Sectors], prepared for the Ministry of Administrative Reform by the Consultation and Research Institute and Marwan Iskandar and Partners (December 2002). One public enterprise that underwent (in 2002) a restructuring of its manpower was Middle East Airlines.

8. On this point, see Sami Atallah, 'Âl-mu'assasât al-Ḥukûmîya wa 'Âlîyât Taḥḍîr al-muwâzana' [Governmental Institutions and the Budget Preparation Process], in *Al-Muwâzana wa al-Tanmiya al-'Ijtimâ'iya fi Lubnân* [The Budget and Social Development in Lebanon], Lebanese Centre for Policy Studies, 2000.

9. Some observers argue that Syrian political influence has contributed to weak institutional performance. Assuming it has, it would constitute only one element among those responsible for this state of affairs.

10. Disagreements over administrative appointments and/or domestic political issues among the three principal officials (the President of the Republic, the speaker of the House and the prime minister) and the role of the Syrian leadership in helping or dictating their resolution are well illustrated in the recently published memoirs of former president Elias Hrawi (as narrated to Camile Menassa), *'Awdat al-Jumhûrîya, nim al Duwaylât ilâ al-Dawla* [The Return of the Republic from Mini-states to One State], Dar Annahar, 2002, e.g. pp. 293, 295, 389, 402–5, 422, 488, 585 and 587.

11. As noted before, Syrian influence over Lebanon's sovereignty is publicly recognized and widely acknowledged. The Lebanese press regularly refers to and/or carries commentaries on this issue. For a recent critical commentary see Mohamad El Hojeiry, 'Siyadatun fi 'uhdat al Ghayb' [Sovereignty in Absentia], *Annahar*, 22 September 2002. Certain political groups, such as the followers of General Aoun, would maintain that the Syrian role in Lebanon has helped promote instability in order to justify the need for the continued presence of Syrian troops in the country.

12. Using an economic analogy, an equilibrium is considered stable when shocks/disturbances produce only a temporary divergence from the point of equilibrium.

A relatively minor civil war in the late 1950s, a subsequent devastating long-lasting civil war (1975–90), and frequent recourse in the post-Taif era to the (sometimes subtle and at other times unsubtle) steadying hand of Syria to resolve domestic political conflicts (frequently of a personal rather than a national character) are, to say the least, clear symptoms of potential disequilibrium.

13. It is tempting to use the alternative term a 'modern' state. This terminology, however, may give rise to a misunderstanding as to what modernity in the Lebanese context implies, as indeed it may for other developing countries as well. For many writers it is associated with existing Western liberal democracies, with all their embodied political notions and values; but for others to be modern does not necessarily imply the wholesale adoption of modern Western political systems and values.

14. Many Lebanese and other writers point out that, compared to the Arab and other developing countries, Lebanon has fared well in terms of political, economic and

cultural freedoms. Admirable as this may be, it does not constitute a viable argument, as some have tried to demonstrate, in defence of the status quo.

15. A recent study of nineteenth-century Ottoman Lebanon emphasizes that sectarianism is a modern construct. While the cultural roots of sectarianism have their origin in Ottoman modernization and European colonial influences, 'it was only in the twentieth century, specially with the creation of the nation state, that the term sectarianism was coined ... Sectarianism ... marked a rupture, a birth of a new culture that singled out religious affiliation as the defining public and political characteristic of modern subject and citizen. To overcome it, if at all possible, requires yet another rupture, a break as radical for the body politic as the advent of sectarianism was for the old regime. It requires another vision of modernity.' See Ussama Makdisi, *The Culture of Sectarianism, Community, History and Violence in Nineteenth-century Ottoman Lebanon*, University of California Press, 2000, Epilogue.

16. Occasionally, motivated by specific domestic political developments, elected officials or members of parliament call for the establishment of the National Body for the Elimination of Political Sectarianism, but so far no steps have been taken in this direction. Also, a number of private bodies have been formed, some with close links to political and/or religious leaderships, with the objective of promoting national dialogue on key issues of national concern. Their influence, if any, has been negligible.

17. See ESCWA, *World Summit on Sustainable Development, Assessment Report for the ESCWA Region* (United Nations, 2002).

18. That is to say raw labour, human capital and social capital. Social capital is taken to include social relationships that affect economic outcomes and are affected by them. See P. Dasgulpta and I. Serageldin, *Social Capital, a Multifaceted Perspective* (World Bank, 1999).

19. Hence the integration of economic and environmental accounting – loosely dubbed green national accounting. For an analysis of these concepts, see World Bank, *Expanding the Measure of Wealth, Indicators of Environmentally Sustainable Development* (Washington, DC, 1997).

20. In 2002 parliament passed the 'Environmental Code'. However, it needs to be translated into effective environmental legislation that is properly implemented.

21. To illustrate this point, the authorities, if need be, can readily change the interest rate to serve the objective of macroeconomic stability. But hundred-year-old trees that are felled cannot be replaced, certainly in the foreseeable future.

22. For a discussion of the end of sovereignty see Scholte, *Globalization*, pp. 135–43.

23. Free trade and capital mobility that are associated with globalization have generally not led, so far, to convergence between the advanced and less advanced economies in terms of per capita income. The one striking exception is East Asia, whose economic policy performance, it is sometimes argued, should guide (despite the crisis the region experienced beginning in late 1997) other developing regions, with regard, for example, to openness, outward-oriented industrialization, and greater spending on education and technology. On the other hand, certain studies indicate that were the Human Development Index (HDI) taken as an alternative measure, then, unlike GDP trends, it would show convergence at the level of large regional

blocs. The reason is that, in addition to income, HDI includes education and life expectancy at birth (proxy for health measures) and in both areas developing countries have made notable strides. See, for example, *World Economic Outlook*, chapter V, 'The World Economy in the Twentieth Century: Striking Developments and Policy Lessons' (May 2000).

24. No less an authority than Joseph Stiglitz (who served as senior vice-president and chief economist of the World Bank from February 1997 to February 2000) has critiqued the IMF's stand on capital liberalization. He points out that, in many ways, it amounted to stripping away the regulations intended to control the flow of hot money and considers that capital account liberalization was the most important factor leading to the East Asia crisis of 1997. See his book *Globalization and Its Discontents* (Norton, 2002), pp. 65 and 95 respectively.

25. See, for example, N. Crafts, 'Globalization and Growth in the Twentieth Century', IMF Working Paper (WP/00/44, March 2000); *World Development Report, 1997*; E. Grundlach and P. Nunnenkamp, 'Some Consequences of Globalization for Developing Countries', in J. H. Dunning (ed.), *Globalization, Trade and Foreign Direct Investment* (1998); K. Nashashibi et al., 'Al Jawânib al'-Iqtisâdîya al-Kulîya li-l-Tadafuqât al Ra'smâlîya fi al-'Âlam al 'Arabi' [Macroeconomic Aspects of Capital Inflows to the Arab World], in S. Makdisi (ed.), *Dawr al Qitâ' al Khâs fi al-'Iqtisâdât al-'Arabîya* [The Role of the Private Sector in the Arab Economies], Arab Fund for Economic and Social Development and the Arab Monetary Fund, 2000.

26. The issue of openness has led to controversy, fuelled by the 1997 Asian crisis, regarding capital account liberalization. The prevailing view of the IMF continued to be that reimposition of controls on capital outflows was not an effective policy instrument in a crisis. But at the same time, capital account liberalization must be fully supported by consistent macroeconomic policies and an adequate institutional set-up to strengthen the ability of financial intermediaries to manage risk and support monetary and exchange rate policies (see IMF, *Annual Report 1999*, pp. 46–7). On the other hand, in line with Stiglitz's stand on this matter, a World Bank discussion note points to an emerging consensus that for countries with relatively closed capital accounts and underdeveloped financial systems, sequencing capital account liberalization is the appropriate policy to follow. For financially integrated countries that may not have in place a sound regulatory system during a period of rapid capital in-flows, re-establishing selective capital controls may temporarily help reduce vulnerabilities. In any case it is suggested that countries should develop their own financial integration strategies based on their own characteristics. See Sara Calvo et al., 'Stabilizing Capital Flows, with Special Reference to the Debate on Capital Account Liberalization', World Bank, Managing Volatility Thematic Group Discussion Notes, May 2000.

27. To illustrate, as a consequence of globalization, domestic interest rates in developing countries become increasingly linked to international interest rates, tax policies and structures are made to conform to those prevailing abroad, and exchange rates become anchored to major currencies, in particular the US dollar (with some countries adopting outright the US dollar), for the purpose of achieving relative price stability. In addition to exchange rate targeting, anchors include monetary and inflation targeting. The diminished freedom of policy action in developing economies accentuates their growing involuntary dependence on policy decisions taken in the major industrial countries.

28. These writers warn that rich international institutions such as the IMF, the World Bank and the WTO represent the interests of the developed countries in contrast with the United Nations and its organizations, which tend to promote the interests of the developing countries as reflected in the concept of sustainable development. Hence they call for strengthening the role of the UN and greater South–South cooperation. For a discussion of these issues, see, for example, M. Khor, 'Globalization and the South: Some Critical Issues', UNCTAD/OSG/DP/147, April 2000. With this in mind, industrial countries have been accused of bearing the primary responsibility for environmental degradation (e.g. logging of natural forests or an inadequate regulatory response to the rapid development of genetic engineering). The free market approach, it is pointed out, represents a development paradigm that submerges concerns for equity or protection of the environment to the free play of market forces and the interests of large corporations that dominate the market. In contrast, the approach adopted at the United Nations Conference on Development and the Environment (the Rio Declaration of 1992 and the Johannesburg Declaration of 2002) represents a development paradigm based on consensus-seeking and partnership among countries, large and small. See M. Khor, 'Effects of Globalization on Sustainable Development after UNCED', *Third World Resurgence*, no. 81/82, May/June 1997.

29. See Amoroso, *On Globalization*.

30. The fear of losing political sovereignty in a globalized world is of course one major consideration behind the drive for establishing economic/political blocs among countries that share geographic proximity, in addition to common values and concerns. While such blocs, it is expected, would enhance the collective bargaining power of the countries concerned *vis-à-vis* the rest of the world, this is accomplished at the expense of the reduced sovereignty of individual countries within the bloc. Nevertheless, whether they join a particular bloc or not, globalization implies, particularly for the smaller developing countries, a further diminishing of political sovereignty.

31. Stiglitz has sharply criticized the IMF's policy model based on 'market fundamentalism'. As he points out, among other implications of this model is that it assumes well-functioning markets, which especially for developing countries is not the case. Hence, in contrast with the policy prescriptions of the 'Washington Consensus' (a consensus between the IMF, the World Bank and the US Treasury) that underlies this model, there is a role for governmental policies in correcting market failures. See his book *Globalization and Its Discontents*, pp. 14–15, 35, 76–8, 219–21.

32. Trade liberalization could well affect the demand for particular categories of labour and hence their earnings. It has been observed that affected workers should be assisted to acquire new skills that fit the evolving pattern of demand. Workers need to be empowered to adapt to constant economic change and to succeed in multiple career paths.

33. Effective 29 November 2000, the Lebanese government substantially reduced tariff barriers across a wide range of imported goods. The maximum tariff was reduced from 105 to 76 per cent and the minimum tariff was set at 0 per cent. The import-weighted average tariff was reduced from about 16 to 7 per cent.

34. Unlike those of several other small open developing economies, Lebanese exports are not concentrated on a few products and hence domestic income is not vulnerable to outside shocks, or as vulnerable as in the case of, say, the Arab oil or Central American economies. For 1999, Lebanon's export diversification index (the

Herfindahl Index of Concentration) was less than 0.2 per cent. This was comparable to Turkey, but much lower than the average for the other Arab countries. See ESCWA, *WTO Issues for Ascending Countries: the Cases of Lebanon and Saudi Arabia*, United Nations, 2001, p. 14.

35. There are various economic and political reasons for the failure to create a common Arab market. A great deal has been written on this matter.

36. There is a growing literature on the conditions that ought to be satisfied if the countries seeking association agreements with the EU are to fully benefit from such an association or, put differently, to maximize their benefits and minimize their costs. See, for example, S. Dessus et al. (eds), Development Centre Seminars, *Towards Arab and Euro-Med Regional Integration*, OECD, ERF and the World Bank, 2001.

37. This question raises the controversial issue of Lebanon's political sovereignty in the context of continued Syrian influence and its impact on stability, whether positive or negative. I shall not take up this matter here. Whatever the case, as noted earlier, the Syrian presence in Lebanon could not, on its own, have prevented improvement in institutional performance. Domestic political factors bear the primary responsibility.

38. For a brief review of selected issues facing the educational system in Lebanon, see National Human Development Report, Lebanon 2001–2, *Globalization: towards a Lebanese Agenda*, Beirut, July 2002, pp. 98–103.

39. On a more general level, in-depth studies of the potential long-term comparative advantages of the Lebanese economy are needed.

40. Empirical investigations that measure the impact of governance on the rate and quality of Lebanon's development have yet to be carried out.

41. On this point see Makdisi and Sadaka, 'The Lebanese Civil War'.

Bibliography

Abî Farah, A., 'Les émigrés libanais, 1975–1996', in *Al-Chu'ûn al-'Iqtisâdîya* [Economic Affairs], Bulletin of the Chamber of Commerce, Industry and Agriculture for Saida and Southern Lebanon, November 1997.

—, 'Hawla al-Awda' al-Ma'îchîya al-Lubnânîya' [On the Living Conditions of Households], *Annahar*, 18 August 1999.

Abou Khalil, J., *Qissat al-Mawârina fi al-Harb, Sîra Khassa* [The Story of the Maronites in the War, a Personal Memoir], Beirut, 2000.

Abou Saleh, A., *Al-'Azma al-Lubnânîya 'âm 1958* [The Lebanese Crisis of 1958], Beirut, 1998.

Al Bouari, E., *Târîkh al-Haraka al-'ummâlîya wa al-Niqâbîya fi Lubnân* [History of the Labour and Union Movement in Lebanon], vols II and III, Dar al Farabi, 1987.

Alesina, A., and R. Perotti, 'The Political Economy of Budget Deficits', *IMF Staff Papers* 42, 1995.

Amin, A., A. Baydoun, A. Haddad, M. Shawool and K. Noureddine, *Qadâya al-jâmi'a al-Lubnânîya wa- Islâhuhâ* [Problems of the Lebanese University and Its Reform], Dar Annahar, Beirut, 1999.

Amoroso, B., *On Globalization: Capitalism in the Twenty-first Century*, Macmillan Press, 1998.

Atallah, S., *Âl-mu'assasât al-Hukûmîya wa 'Âlîyât Tahdîr al-muwâzana* [Governmental Institutions and the Budget Preparation Process], in *Al-Muwâzana wa al-Tanmîya al-'Ijtimâ'îya fi Lubnân* [The Budget and Social Development in Lebanon], Lebanese Centre for Policy Studies, 2000.

Attiyeh, A., *Makhâtr al-'Ajz wa al-Dayn al 'Âm 'ala al-'Istiqrâr wa al-Hurîyat fi Lubnân* [The Dangers of Deficits and Public Debt to Stability and Freedom in Lebanon], Dar Al Jadid, Beirut, 1998.

Ayyach, G., *Azmat al-Mâlîya al-'Âmma fi Lubnân: Qissat al-'Inhiyâr al-'Iqtisâdî, 1982–1992* [The Crisis of Public Finance in Lebanon, the Story of Monetary Collapse, 1982–1992], Dar Annahar, Beirut, 1997.

Bachir, I., *Al-Tanmiya fi Lubnân* [Development in Lebanon], Dar al 'Ilm Li-l-Malâyîn, Beirut, 1994.

Badre, A., 'Economic Development of Lebanon', in C. A. Cooper and S. A. Alexander (eds), *Economic Development and Population Growth in the Middle East*, American Elsevier, 1972.

Barakat, H., *Lebanon in Strife*, University of Texas Press, 1977.

Bates, R. H., 'Ethnicity, Capital Formation and Conflict', CID Working Paper no. 27, Harvard University, 1999.

Benhabib, T., and M. Spiegel, 'The Role of Human Capital in Economic Development: Evidence from Cross-country Data', *Journal of Monetary Economics* 34, 1994.

Berdal, M., and Malone D. M. (eds), *Greed and Grievance, Economic Agendas in Civil Wars*, Lynne Rienner, 2000.

Berg, A., and E. Bornsztein, 'The Dollarization Debate', *Finance and Development* 37(1), March 2000.

Boris, P., and J. Stiglitz (eds), *Annual Bank Conference on Development Economics, 1999*, World Bank, 2000.

Bsat, H., 'Malâat al-Jihâz al Maṣrafî, 1982–1989, Asbâb al-'Azma wa Dûrûs al-Tajruba' [Capital Adequacy of the Lebanese Banking System, 1982–1989: Causes of the Crisis and Lessons of Experience], in Association des Banques du Liban, *Rapport du Conseil, 1989–1990*.

Churchill, C., 'Village Life of the Central Beqa'', *Middle East Economic Papers 1959*, American University of Beirut.

Collier, P., 'On the Economic Causes of Civil War',*Oxford Economic Papers* 50, 1998.

—, 'On the Economic Consequences of Civil War', *Oxford Economic Papers* 51, 1999.

Collier, P., and A. Hoeffler, 'Greed and Grievance in Civil Wars', Working Paper Series, Centre for the Study of African Economies, Oxford, 2002.

Collier, P., A. Hoeffler and M. Soderbom, 'On the Duration of Civil War', Centre for the Study of African Economies, Oxford, 2003.

Collier, P., and N. Sambanis, 'Understanding Civil War: a New Agenda', *Journal of Conflict Resolution* 46(1), 2002.

Corm, G., 'The War System: Militia Hegemony and the Reestablishment of the State', in D. Collings (ed.), *Peace for Lebanon? From War to Reconstruction*, Lynne Rienner, 1994.

—, 'Sîyâsat 'I'âdat al-'I'mâr' [The Policy of Reconstruction], *Abaad*, Beirut, January 1994.

—, *Al- Furṣat al Dâi'at fi al-'Iṣlâh al Mâlî fi Lubnân* [The Missed Opportunity for Financial Reform in Lebanon], Beirut, 2001.

Crafts, N., 'Globalization and Growth in the Twentieth Century', IMF Working Paper (WP/00/44), March 2000.

Crow, R. E., and A. Iskandar, 'Administrative Reform in Lebanon, 1958–1959', *International Review of Administrative Sciences* 3, 1961.

Dagher, A., 'Siyâsat Si'r Ṣarf al-'Imla, al Tajriba al-Lubnânîya wa al-Dawr al-Maṭlûb min hâdhihi al-siyâsa' [Exchange Rate Policy: the Lebanese Experience], *National Defence Journal*, Beirut, October 2002.

—, 'Al Quuâ al-'Âmila fi Lubnân: al Waq'i wa al Afâk al Mustaqbalîya' [Manpower and Development in Lebanon: Reality and Future Prospects], *Linking Economic Growth and Social Development in Lebanon*, UNDP conference, Beirut, 11–13 January 2000.

—, *L'état et l'économie au Liban, action gouvernementale et finances publiques de l'indépendance à 1975*, Les Cahiers du CERMOC no. 12, Beirut, 1995.

Dah, A., G. Dibeh and W. Shahin, *The Distributional Impact of Taxes in Lebanon*, Lebanese Centre for Policy Studies, 1999.

Dasgupta, P., and I. Serageldin, *Social Capital, a Multifaceted Perspective*, World Bank, 1999.

De Soya, I., 'The Resource Curse: are Civil Wars Driven by Rapacity or Paucity', in M. Berdal and D. M. Malone (eds), *Greed and Grievance, Economic Agenda in Civil Wars*, Lynne Rienner, 2001.

Dessus, S., J. Devlin and R. Safadi (eds), *Towards Arab and Euro-Med Regional Integration*, Development Centre Seminars, OECD, ERF and the World Bank, 2001.

Dunning, J. H. (ed.), *Globalization, Trade and Foreign Direct Investment*, Elsevier, Amsterdam, 1998.

Dutt, A. K., *The Political Economy of Development*, Edward Elgar, 2002.

Economic Research Forum for the Arab Countries, Iran and Turkey, Indicators, *Economic Trends in the MENA Region* (various issues).

Economic Research Forum for the Arab Countries, Iran and Turkey, and Consultation and Research Institute (Beirut), *Preliminary Report on Micro and Small Enterprises*, 2000.

Edde, H., *Al Mâlu 'In Ḥakam* [Money, were It to Govern], Beirut, 1999.

Eken, S., P. Casin, S. Nuri Erbas, J. Martelino and A. Mazaaci, *Economic Dislocation and Recovery in Lebanon*, IMF Occasional Paper no. 120, February 1995.

Elbadawi, I., and N. Sambanis, 'How Much Civil War Will We See? Explaining the Prevalence of Civil War', *Journal of Conflict Resolution* 46(3), 2002.

El-Hojeiry, M., 'Siyâdatun fi 'uhdat al Ghayb' [Sovereignty in Absentia], *Annahar*, 22 September 2002.

El-Khazen, F., 'Tâ'if mâ ba'da al-Ḥarb, Chajara Judhûruhâ 'Aghṣânuhâ' [The Post-war Taif: a Tree Whose Roots Constitute Its Branches], *Annahar*, 31 December 1997.

—, 'Intikhâbât Lubnân mâ ba'da al-Ḥarb, 1992, 1996 wa 2000: Dîmuqrâtîya bila Khayâr [Post-war Lebanese Elections, 1992, 1996 and 2000: Democracy without a Choice], Dar Annahar, 2000.

—, *The Breakdown of the State in Lebanon, 1975–76*, I.B. Tauris, London, 2000.

ESCWA, *Applications of Sustainable Development Indicators in the ESCWA Member Countries*, United Nations, 2000.

—, *WTO Issues for Ascending Countries: the Cases of Lebanon and Saudi Arabia*, United Nations, 2001.

—, *World Summit on Sustainable Development, Assessment Report for the ESCWA Region*, United Nations, 2002.

Esfahani, H. S., 'Institutions and Government Controls', *Journal of Development Economics* 63, 2000.

—, 'A Reexamination of the Political Economy of Growth in MENA Countries', Institute of Financial Economics, American University of Beirut, Lecture and Working Paper Series no. 1, 2003.

Farhan, S., *Lubnân al-Junûbî, wâqi'uha wa Qadâyâhû* [Southern Lebanon, Its Reality and the Issues It Faces], Dar Al Talia, Beirut, 1973.

Gaspard, Toufic, 'The Gross Domestic Product of Lebanon in 1987', Banque du Liban, *Bulletin trimestriel*, fourth quarter, 1989.

Gendzier, I. L., *Notes from the Minefield. United States Intervention in Lebanon and the Middle East, 1945–1958*, Columbia University Press,1997.

Ghanage, E., 'La redistribution des revenues au Liban', in *Semaines sociales du Liban, l'économie libanaise et le progrès social, du 19 avril au mai 1955*, Editions Les Lettres Orientales, Beirut, 1955.

Gleditsch, N. P., P. Wallenstein, M. Erikson, M. Sollenberg and H. Strand, 'Armed Conflict: A New Dataset', *Journal of Peace Research* 39(5), September 2002.

Goria, W. R., *Sovereignty and Leadership in Lebanon 1943–1976*, Ithaca Press, London, 1985.

Gressani, D., and J. Page, 'Reconstruction in Lebanon, Challenges for Macroecnomic Management', MENA Working Paper Series no. 16, World Bank, April 1999.

Grundlach, E., and P. Nunnenkamp, 'Some Consequences of Globalization for Developing Countries', in J. H. Dunning (ed.), *Globalization, Trade and Foreign Direct Investment*, Elsevier, Amsterdam, 1998.

Haddad, A., *Al Faqr fi Lubnân* [Poverty in Lebanon], United Nations, ESCWA, 1996.

Hakim, S., and S. Andary, 'The Lebanese Central Bank and the Treasury Bills Market', *Middle East Journal* 5(2), 1997.

Hamdan, K., 'Emigration Policies, Trends and Mechanisms', ILO/UNDP Lebanon Project, Cairo, May 1992.

—, 'Siyâsat al-'Ujûr Wa al-Madâkhîl' [Policy on Wages and Remunerations], *Abaad* 2, November 1994.

—, *Al-'Azma al-Lubnânîya, al-Tawâ'if al-Dînîya, al-Tabaqât al-Ijtimâ'ya wa al-Huwîya al-Watanîya* [The Lebanese Crisis, Religious Communities, Social Classes and National Identity], Dar Al Farabi, Beirut, 1998.

Hanf, Theodor, *Co-existence in Wartime Lebanon: Decline of a State and Rise of a Nation*, Centre for Lebanese Policy Studies in association with I.B. Tauris, 1993.

Harik, I., 'The Economic and Social Factors in the Lebanese Crisis', in S. Ibrahim and N. Hopkins (eds), *Arab Society, Social Science Perspectives*, American University in Cairo Press, 1985.

Henry, C. M., and R. Springborg, *Globalization and the Politics of Development in the Middle East*, Cambridge University Press, 2001.

Hermes, N., and R. Lensink (eds), *Financial Development and Economic Growth*, Routledge, 1996.

Hoss, S., *Li-l-Haqîqa wa al-Târîkh; Tajârûb al-Hûkm ma baîna 1998 wa 2000* [For Truth and History, Experiences in Governing, 1998–2000], Beirut, 2001.

Hrawi, E. (as narrated to Camile Menassa), *Awdat al-Jumhûrîya, nim al Duwaylât ilâ al-Dawla* [The Return of the Republic from Mini-states to One State], Dar Annahar, 2002.

Hudson, M., *The Precarious Republic, Political Modernization in Lebanon*, Random House, 1968, reprinted by Westview Press, 1985.

Ibrahim, S., and N. Hopkins (eds), *Arab Society, Social Science Perspectives*, American University in Cairo Press, 1985.

'*I'mâr Bayrût wa al-Fûrsa al-Dâ'î'a, Wasat Bayrût al-Tijârî wa al-Sharika al-'Qârîya* [The Reconstruction of Beirut and the Missed Opportunity: the Beirut Central District and the Real Estate Company], Beirut, 1992 (various writers).

IMF, *Lebanon – Recent Economic Developments* (SM/79/3202), 27 July 1979.

—, *Lebanon – Economic Recovery, Stabilization and Macroeconomic Policies* (SM/91/207).

—, *Lebanon – Staff Report for the 1990 Article IV Consultation* (SM/91/21).

—, *Lebanon: Economic Recovery, Stabilization and Macroeconomic Stability* (background paper for the 1994 Article IV Consultation), 8 August 1994.

—, *Lebanon – Staff Report for the 1999 Article IV Consultation*, 9 August 1999.

—, *Lebanon – Staff Report for the 2001 Article IV Consultation*, 13 September 2001.

—, *Lebanon – Staff Report for the 2002 Article IV Consultation*, 6 December 2002.

IMF Staff Team, *Macroprudential Indicators of Financial System Soundness*, IMF, April 2000.

Institut International de Recherche et de Formation en Vue du Développement, *Besoins et possibilités du développement du Liban*, Mission IRFED, 1960/61.

Institute of Money and Banking, *Al-Damj al-Maṣrifî fi Lubnân* [Bank Mergers in Lebanon], American University of Beirut, 1990.

Issa, N., 'Unemployment and the Reconstruction of Lebanon', in ESCWA, *Unemployment in the ESCWA Countries*, Beirut, February 1994.

—, *Al-Quwâ al 'Âmila wa siyâsat al-'Âmâla fi Lubnân* [Manpower and the Policy of Employment in Lebanon], Lebanese Centre for Policy Studies, 1996.

Jain, A., *The Political Economy of Corruption*, Routledge, London, 2001.

Keen, D., 'Incentives and Disincentives for Violence', in M. Berdal and D. M. Malone (eds), *Greed and Grievance, Economic Agendas in Civil Wars*, Lynne Rienner, 2000.

Khalaf, S., 'The Lebanese Labour Unions: Some Comparative Structural Features', *Middle East Economic Papers, 1968*, American University of Beirut.

Khor, M., 'Effects of Globalization on Sustainable Development after UNCED', *Third World Resurgence* 81/82, May/June 1997.

Klat, P., 'Labour Legislation in Lebanon', *Middle East Economic Papers*, 1959, American University of Beirut.

Knack, S., and P. Keefer, 'Does Social Capital Have an Economic Payoff: a Cross-country Investigation', *Quarterly Journal of Economics*, November 1997.

—, 'Institutional and Economic Performance: Cross-country Tests Using Alternative Institutional Measures', *Politics and Economics* 7, November 1985.

Labaki, B., and K. Abou Rjeily, *Bilan des guerres du Liban, 1975–1990*, Editions L'Harmattan, 1993.

Lebanese Centre for Policy Studies, *Al-'Intikhâbât al-Niyâbîya fi Lubnân 2002: bayna al-'I'âda wa al-Taqhyîr* [Parliamentary Elections in Lebanon, 2000: between Repetition and Change], Beirut, 2002.

Lee, K., A. Holland and D. McNeill, *Global Sustainable Development in the Twenty-first Century*, Edinburgh University Press, 2000.

Mailat, J., *The Document of National Understanding, a Commentary*, Centre for Lebanese Studies, May 1992.

Makdisi, J. S., *Beirut Fragments, a War Memoir*, Persea Press, New York, 1990, reissued 1999.

Makdisi, S., 'Al-Jawânib al-'Iqtiṣâdîya li-l-'Azma al-Lubnânîya' [The Economic Aspects of the Lebanese Crisis], in *Al-'Azma al-Lubnânîya* [The Lebanese Crisis], Arab Organization for Education, Culture and Sciences, 1977.

—, 'Flexible Exchange Rate Policy in an Open Economy, the Lebanese Experience, 1950–74', *World Development* 6(7), July 1978.

—, *Financial Policy and Economic Growth: the Lebanese Experience*, Columbia University Press, 1979.

—, 'Political Conflict and Economic Performance in Lebanon, 1975–1987', Centre for Contemporary Arab Studies, Georgetown University, Occasional Paper series, September 1987; republished (with minor revisions) in Banque du Liban, *Bulletin trimestriel*, second and third quarters, 1987.

—, 'Al-Tawajûhat al-'Iqtiṣâdîya al Mustaqbalîya fi Lubnân, Muḥâdarât al Mawsem al-Saqâfî fi Jâmi'at Bayrût al-'Arabîya, 1992–1993' [Future Economic Trends in Lebanon], Annual Cultural Lecture Series, 1992–93, Arab University of Beirut.

—, 'Lubnân: al-Dayn al-'Âm wa al-Siyâsat al-'Iqtiṣâdîya ... Tasaûrât Mustaqbalîya' [Lebanon – Public Debt and Economic Policy ... Future Perspectives], *Annahar*, 21 November 1999.

Makdisi, U., *The Culture of Sectarianism, Community, History and Violence in Nineteenth-century Ottoman Lebanon*, University of California Press, 2000.

Mankiw, N. G., D. Romer and D. N. Weil, 'A Contribution to the Empirics of Economic Growth', *Quarterly Journal of Economics* 5(107), May 1992.

Manning, N., R. Mukherjee and O. Gokcekus, 'Public Officials and Their Institutional Environment, an Analytical Model for Assessing the Impact of Institutional Change on Public Sector Performance', World Bank Policy Research Working Paper 2427, August 2000.

Mansour, A., *Al-'Inquilâb 'ala al-Ṭâ'if* [The Turn against the Taif], Beirut, 1993.

Mueller, J., 'Dollarization in Lebanon', IMF Working Paper (WP/94/129), October 1994.

Nabli, M. K., and M.-A.Veganzones-Varoudakis, 'Exchange Rate Regime and Competitiveness of Manufactured Exports: the Case of MENA Countries', World Bank Discussion Paper, August 2002.

Nahhas, C., *Quel modèle de croissance économique pour la prochaine décennie?*, UNDP conference on 'Linking Economic Growth and Social Development in Lebanon', Beirut, 11–13 January 2000.

—, *Huzûz 'Ijtnâb Al-'Azma wa shurût Takhatîha: Sîrat Tajruba fi Al-'Islâh; Muqadimat Li Wasîkhat Barnâmj al 'Amal li-l Tashîh al Malî Ḥzairân 1999* [The Prospects for Averting the Crisis and the Conditions for Overcoming It: the Record of an Attempted Reform; an Introduction to the Work Programme for Financial Adjustment, June 1999], Dar Annahar, Beirut, 2003.

Nashashibi, K., C. Anders et al., 'Al Jawânib al'-Iqtisâdîya al-Kulîya li-l-Tadafuqât al Ra'smâliya fi al'-Âlam al 'Arabi' [Macroeconomic Aspects of Capital In-flows to the Arab World], in S. Makdisi (ed.), *Dawr al Qitâ al-Khâs fi al-'Iqtisâdât al-'Arabiya* [The Role of the Private Sector in the Arab Economies], Arab Fund for Economic and Social Development and the Arab Monetary Fund, 2000.

Nasr, S., 'The Crisis of Lebanese Capitalism', *MERIP Reports* 73.

Osseiran, F., 'Banking Performance in Lebanon, 1928–1987', Association des Banques du Liban, *Rapport du conseil, 1989–1990*.

Picard, Elizabeth, *Lebanon, a Shattered Country*, Holmes and Meier, 1996.

—, 'Liban: la matrice historique', in F. Jean and J. C. Ruffin (eds), *Economie des guerres civiles*, Hachette, Paris, 1996.

Przeworski, A., M. E. Alvarez, J. A. Cheibub and F. Limongi, *Democracy and Development, Political Institutions and Well-Being in the World, 1950–1990*, Cambridge University Press, 2000.

Reynal-Querol, M., 'Ethnicity, Political Systems and Civil Wars', *Journal of Conflict Resolution* 46(1), 2002.

Rizq, I., 'Al-Tanmiya al-'Ijtima'îya' [Social Development], in *Tanmiyat Muhâfazat al-Biqâ'* [Development of Muhafazat al Biqa'], Centre for Development Studies, Beirut, 1970.

Saba, E., *Hiwâr Hawla al-'Iqtisâd fi Jumhûrîyat al Tâi'f: Al Mashrû' al Badîl* [Dialogue about Economics in the Taif Republic: the Alternative Project], Beirut, September 1995.

—, 'Al-'Iqtisâd al-Lubnâni ... Min 'Ayn wa 'Ila 'Ayn' [The Lebanese Economy ... from Where to Where?], *Al Mustaqbal Al 'Arabi* 276, February 2002.

Saidi, N., 'The Effects of the War on Economic Activity in Lebanon: Quantitative Estimates', Bank of Lebanon *Quarterly Bulletin* 20, 1984.

Saidi, N., and S. Nasr, *The Development of Lebanon's Capital Markets*, Centre for Economic Policy Research and Analysis, Beirut, 1995.

Salameh, G., 'The Lebanese Crisis: Interpretations and Solutions', in N. Shehadi and B. Harney (eds), *Politics and the Economy in Lebanon*, Centre for Lebanese Policy Studies, Oxford, 1989.

Salem, E., *Violence and Diplomacy in Lebanon, the Troubled Years: 1982–1988*, I.B. Tauris, London, 1995.

Salibi, K., *Cross Road to Civil War, Lebanon 1958–1976*, Caravan Books, Beirut, 1976.

Schmeil, Y., *Sociologie du système politique libanais*, Editions Universitaires de Grenoble, 1976.

Scholte, J. A., *Globalization, a Critical Introduction*, St Martin's Press, New York, 2000.

Sena, S., and T. Helbing (eds), *Back to the Future, Postwar Reconstruction and Stabilization in Lebanon*, IMF Occasional Paper no. 176, Washington, DC, 1999.

Shehadi, N., and B. Harney (eds), *Politics and the Economy in Lebanon*, Centre for Lebanese Studies, Oxford, 1989.

Siemen, C. L. J., *Politics, Institutions and the Economic Performance of Nations*, Edward Elgar, 1998.

Sirriyeh, H., *Lebanon: Dimensions of Conflict*, International Institute for Strategic Studies, 1989.

Stewart, F., V. FitzGerald and associates, *War and Underdevelopment*, vol. 1, 'The Economic and Social Consequences of Conflict', and vol. 2, 'Country Experiences', Oxford University Press, 2001.

Stiglitz, Joseph, *Globalization and Its Discontents*, W. W. Norton, 2002.

Tabbarah, R., 'Population, Human Resources, and Development in the Arab World', *Population Bulletin of ESCWA*, 20 November 1981.

Teuni, G., *Une guerre pour les autres*, Jclattes, 1985.

UNDP, *Human Development Report for Lebanon*, 1997.

—, *Development Cooperation Report for Lebanon*, 1999.

—, National Human Development Report – Lebanon 2001–02, *Globalization: towards a Lebanese Agenda*, Beirut, July 2002.

Wakim, N., *Al-'Ayâdî al-Sawdâ'* [The Black Hands], Beirut, 1998.

World Bank, *Lebanon, Stabilization and Reconstruction*, March 1993.

—, *Expanding the Measure of Wealth, Indicators of Environmentally Sustainable Development*, Washington, DC, 1997.

World Development Report, 1997.

Yashoui, E., *'Iqtisâd Lubnân* [The Economy of Lebanon], Librarie du Liban, Beirut, 2002.

Unpublished papers/studies/theses/reports

Akkad, B., 'The Lebanese Banking System and the Effects of Globalization', project for a Masters degree in Money and Banking, Institute of Money and Banking, American University of Beirut, February 2000.

Andary, S., 'Tatwîr sûq Bayrût al-Naqdî' [Developing Beirut's Money Market], paper submitted to a seminar organized by the Institute of Money and Banking at the American University of Beirut, 22 February 1992.

Atallah, S., 'Reducing the Budget Deficit: a First Reading', paper prepared for the

Lebanese Centre for Policy Studies in collaboration with the Commission of the European Community, 1999.

—, 'Roadblocks to Recovery, Institutional Obstacles Facing the Private Sector in Lebanon', paper prepared for the Lebanese Centre for Policy Studies, 1999.

Atallah, T., 'Munzûmat al-Harb al Dakhilîya, 'Istrâtijîya Nzâ'îya Mu'âsirat fi Mujtama'n Mûtanawa', al-Hâlat al-Lubnânîya 1975–1990' [The Internal War System, a Contemporary Strategy of Conflict in a Diversified Society, the Lebanese Case, 1975–1990], doctoral dissertation, Lebanese University, March 2001.

Calvo, S. et al., 'Stabilizing Capital Flows, with Special Reference to the Debate on Capital Account Liberalization', World Bank, Managing Volatility, thematic group discussion notes, May 2000.

Castanheira, M., and H. S. Esfahani, 'Political Economy of Growth: Lessons Learned and Challenges Ahead', overview paper prepared for the Global Development Network, September 2001.

Chaaban, F., and G. Ayyoub, 'Database of Air and Noise Pollution in Lebanon', final report submitted to the Lebanese National Council for Scientific Research, 19 February 1999.

Collier, P., and A. Hoeffler, 'Economic Causes of Civil Conflicts and Their Implication for Peace', World Bank, 15 June 2001.

Consultation and Research Institute, 'Community Development Fund Project: Rapid Needs and Capacity Assessment Study, Phase I', report prepared for the High Relief Committee, April 1995.

—, 'Al Quuâ al-'Âmila fi Lubnân: al Fajwa Bâyna al 'Ârd wa al Talab' [The Lebanese Labour Market: the Gap between Supply and Demand], study prepared for the Ministry of Industry, 2002.

Dibeh, G., 'l-'Asar al-'Ijtimâ'î Li-L Siyâsât al-Mâlîya wa al-Naqdîya fi Lubnân ma Ba'da al-Harb' [The Social Effect of Financial and Monetary Policies in Post-war Lebanon], paper prepared for ESCWA, 2003.

Djoundourian, S., I. Nuwayhid and F. Chaaban, 'The Economic and Social Impacts of Mobile Source Pollution on Public Health in the Greater Beirut Area', country case study for METAP III, MedPolicies Initiative, submitted to the Harvard Institute for International Development, January 1999.

El Badawi, I., and N. Sambanis, 'External Interventions and the Duration of Civil Wars', paper presented at the World Bank conference on the 'Economics and Politics of Civil Conflicts', Princeton University, 18–19 March 2000.

El-Khalil, Y., 'Les facteurs de développement industriel dans une petite économie ouverte en voi de développement: les secteurs des biens capitaux au Liban', unpublished doctoral thesis, Université d'Auvergne, January 1996.

Fawwaz, M., 'Fâ'lîyat 'Idârat al-'ûmrân al-Tanzîmîya wa Hudûdiha' [Efficacy and Limits of Urban Regulatory Management], paper presented at a conference organized by the Ministry of Public Works and the Order of Engineers, 29–30 June and 1 July 2000.

Gleditsch, N. P., H. Strand, M. Eriksson, M. Sollenberg and P. Wallensteen, 'Armed Conflict 1946–99: a New Dataset', paper presented at a workshop on 'Identifying Wars: Systematic Conflict Research and Its Utility in Conflict Resolution and Prevention' held at Uppsala University, 8–9 June 2001.

Hamdan, K., and S. Makdisi, 'Lebanon: Labour Force', paper prepared for Dar Al Handassah Consultants, August 1991.

—, 'Lebanon: the Evolving Labour Market', paper prepared for the World Bank, 1995.

Hamdan, W., 'Policy Co-ordination with Reference to Lebanon', MMB thesis, Institute of Money and Banking, American University of Beirut, 1986.

Hantas, N., 'The Role of the Banking Control Commission in Controlling Bank Risks', MMB project, Institute of Money and Banking, American University of Beirut, 2000.

Hijazi, R., 'The Costs of Monetary Stabilization in Post-conflict Lebanon: a Political Economy Approach', MSc dissertation, School of Oriental and African Studies, London University, 16 September 2002.

Information International SAL Research Consultants, 'Lebanon – Anti-corruption Initiative Report 1999' and 'Benchmark Polls on Corruption in Lebanon 1999'.

Johnson, M., 'The New Patrimonial State before 1975', paper presented at a workshop on 'The Developmental State Model and the Challenges to Lebanon' organized by the Lebanese Centre for Policy Studies, Beirut, 15–16 February 2002.

Kaufmann, D., and A. Kraay, 'Growth without Governance', World Bank paper, 2002.

Khor, M., 'Globalization and the South: Some Critical Issues', UNCTAD/OSG/DP/147, April 2000.

Labaki, B., 'Lebanese Emigration after the Taif Agreement, 1990–2000', paper presented to a conference on 'The Lebanese Presence in the World' organized by the Lebanese–American University, 29 June 2001.

Makdisi, K., 'Trapped between Sovereignty and Globalization: Implementing International Environmental Treaties in Developing Countries', unpublished doctoral dissertation, Fletcher School of Law and Diplomacy, Tufts University, 2001.

Makdisi, S., I. Chatila, K. Hamda and M. Sader, 'Lebanon, the Gross Domestic Product and Gross National Product for 1988' (UNDP/LEB/89/001), Department of Technical Co-operation for Development, United Nations, 1991.

Makdisi, S., K. Hamdan and H. Bsat, 'Lebanon: the Structure and Evolution of the Financial Services Sector and Its Role in the Recovery Phase', paper prepared for Dar Al Handassah engineering group, October 1993.

Makdisi, S., and S. Neiame, 'Exchange Rate and Inflation under Conditions of Volatility and Relative Stability: the Experience of a Small Open Economy', Institute of Financial Economics, American University of Beirut, 2001.

Makdisi, S., and R. Sadaka, 'The Lebanese Civil War: Background, Causes, Duration and Post-conflict Trends', paper presented at a Yale/World Bank workshop on 'Case Studies of Civil War' held at Yale University, 13–14 April 2002.

Mueller, J., 'The Remnants of War: Thugs as Residual Combatants', 2001.

Nahhas, C., "Idârat al-'Umrân fi Lubnân Wâq'an wa-Hâjâtn, 'Adwâtn wa 'Islâhât' [The Management of Urban Urbanization in Lebanon: Reality, Needs, Instruments and Reforms], paper presented at a conference organized by the Ministry of Public Works and the Order of Engineers, 29–30 June and 1 July 2000.

Osseiran, F., 'Monetary Policy under Conditions of Currency Substitution: the Lebanese case, 1975–1986', doctoral dissertation, New York University, December 1987.

'Public Service Accountability in Lebanon', study prepared jointly by a team of American University of Beirut faculty members and senior government officials, in collaboration with the John Kennedy School of Government at Harvard (principal author Adnan Iskandar), 1996.

Regan, P., 'Data on Third Party Interventions in Intrastate Conflicts', paper presented at a workshop on 'Identifying Wars: Systematic Conflict Research and Its Utility in Conflict Resolution and Prevention' held at Uppsala University, 8–9 June 2001.

Ross, M., 'How Does Natural Resource Wealth Influence Civil War?', 6 December 2001.

Saghir, J., 'Urban Water and Sanitation in the Middle East and North Africa Region: the Way Forward', paper presented at the Third Mediterranean Development Forum, Cairo, 5–8 March 2000.

St Joseph University, 'L'entrée des jeunes libanais dans la vie active et l'émigration', preliminary results, June 2002.

Sambanis, N., 'Ethnic War: a Theoretical and Empirical Inquiry into Its Causes', DECRG World Bank paper, 2000.

Tarabulsi, F., 'Identités et solidarités croisées dans les conflits du Liban contemporaine', unpublished doctoral dissertation, University of Paris VIII, 1993.

—, 'The Role of War in State and Society Transformation: the Lebanese Case', November 1994.

Yale University–World Bank Workshop, 'Case Studies on the Economics and Politics of Civil War', Yale University, 13–14 April 2002.

National official documents / studies

Arab Fund for Economic and Social Development (in association with Team International and Coopers and Lybrand Deloitte), *Dirastun Hawl Majlis al'inma' wal 'I'mar* [Study of the Council for Reconstruction and Development], prepared at the request of the Lebanese government, July 1990.

Barnâmaj al-Hukûma al-Lubnânîya li-l-'Islah al-mâlî [Work Programme of the Lebanese Government for Financial Reform], 23 June 1999.

Central Directorate of Statistics, *Dirâsat al-Quwa al-'Âmila fi Lubnân, mash bi-l-'Ayyina* [The Workforce in Lebanon, a Statistical Sample Survey], vols 1 and 2, July 1972.

—, *L'enquête par sondage sur la population active au Liban, novembre 1970*, vol. 2, 1972.

—, *Recueil Statistiques Libanais*, no. 9, 1973.

—, *Takrîr Hawl Wad' al-Hisâbât al-'Iqtisâdîya, 1994–1995* [Report on National Income Accounts, 1994–1995], October 1997.

—, *Mîzânîyat al-'usra li-'Âm, 1997* [Household Survey for 1997], February 1998.

—, *La population active en 1997*, August 1998.

Central Statistical Office, Ministry of Planning, *Mîzânîyat al-'usra 1966* [Household Survey for 1966].

Council for Development and Reconstruction (CDR), *The Reconstruction Project*, April 1983.

—, *Progress Report on Reconstruction, 1983–87*.

—, *Progress Reports, 1994–2002*.

Republic of Lebanon, Ministry of Environment, *Lebanon's First National Communication under the United Nations Framework Convention on Climate Change: Final Report*, UNDP, Global Environment Facility, June 1999.

—, Ministry of Health, *Annual Reports*, 1959 and 1971.

—, Ministry of Social Affairs / UNDP, *Khâritat Ahwâl al-Ma'îcha fi Lubnân* [Map of Living Conditions in Lebanon], 1998.

—, *Global Medium Term Note Programme, Offering Circular*, 2 August 2001 and 23 December 2002.

Index

DATE DUE

GAYLORD			PRINTED IN U.S.A.